# THEOLOGICAL METAPHYSICS

**T&T Clark Systematic Pentecostal and Charismatic Theology**

*Series editors*
Wolfgang Vondey
Daniela C. Augustine

# THEOLOGICAL METAPHYSICS

# A Pentecostal Theology of Being

Ray C. Robles

LONDON • NEW YORK • OXFORD • NEW DELHI • SYDNEY

T&T CLARK

Bloomsbury Publishing Plc, 50 Bedford Square, London, WC1B 3DP, UK
Bloomsbury Publishing Inc, 1385 Broadway, New York, NY 10018, USA
Bloomsbury Publishing Ireland, 29 Earlsfort Terrace, Dublin 2, D02 AY28, Ireland

BLOOMSBURY, T&T CLARK and the T&T Clark logo are trademarks
of Bloomsbury Publishing Plc

First published in Great Britain 2024
Paperback edition published 2025

Copyright © Ray C. Robles, 2024

Ray C. Robles has asserted his right under the Copyright,
Designs and Patents Act, 1988, to be identified as Author of this work.

For legal purposes the Acknowledgments on pp. xi–xii constitute an
extension of this copyright page.

Cover design by Anna Berzovan
Cover image © naqiewei / GettyImages

All rights reserved. No part of this publication may be: i) reproduced or transmitted in any form, electronic or mechanical, including photocopying, recording or by means of any information storage or retrieval system without prior permission in writing from the publishers; or ii) used or reproduced in any way for the training, development or operation of artificial intelligence (AI) technologies, including generative AI technologies. The rights holders expressly reserve this publication from the text and data mining exception as per Article 4(3) of the Digital Single Market Directive (EU) 2019/790.

Bloomsbury Publishing Plc does not have any control over, or responsibility for, any third-party websites referred to or in this book. All internet addresses given in this book were correct at the time of going to press. The author and publisher regret any inconvenience caused if addresses have changed or sites have ceased to exist, but can accept no responsibility for any such changes.

A catalogue record for this book is available from the British Library.

Library of Congress Cataloging-in-Publication Data

Names: Robles, Ray, author.
Title: Theological metaphysics : a Pentecostal theology of being / Ray C. Robles.
Description: New York : T&T Clark, 2023. | Series: T&T Clark systematic Pentecostal and charismatic theology | Includes bibliographical references and index.
Identifiers: LCCN 2023022603 (print) | LCCN 2023022604 (ebook) | ISBN 9780567713780 (hardback) | ISBN 9780567713766 (paperback) | ISBN 9780567713759 (epub) | ISBN 9780567713797 (pdf)
Subjects: LCSH: Pentecostalism. | Theology, Doctrinal. | Metaphysics. | Philosophy and religion. | Christian philosophy. | Philosophical theology.
Classification: LCC BR1644 .R624 2023 (print) | LCC BR1644 (ebook) | DDC 270.8/2 –dc23/eng/20230825
LC record available at https://lccn.loc.gov/2023022603
LC ebook record available at https://lccn.loc.gov/2023022604

| ISBN: | HB: | 978-0-5677-1378-0 |
|---|---|---|
| | PB: | 978-0-5677-1376-6 |
| | ePDF: | 978-0-5677-1379-7 |
| | eBook: | 978-0-5677-1375-9 |

Series: T&T Clark Systematic Pentecostal and Charismatic Theology

Typeset by Integra Software Services Pvt. Ltd.

For product safety related questions contact productsafety@bloomsbury.com.

To find out more about our authors and books visit www.bloomsbury.com
and sign up for our newsletters.

*For Christina and Marlon Robles*

# CONTENTS

| | |
|---|---|
| Acknowledgments | xi |
| Abbreviations | xiii |

INTRODUCTION … 1
   The Task … 1
   Structure and Flow of the Study … 2

Chapter 1
CAN THERE BE A PENTECOSTAL ARTICULATION OF METAPHYSICS? … 5
   Introduction: Theological Metaphysics and
      North American Pentecostalism … 5
   Pentecostal Spirituality/Theology and the Nature of
      Christian Theological Discourse … 6
   Conclusion … 11

Chapter 2
COME, CREATOR SPIRIT: IMAGINING A PENTECOSTAL METAPHYSICS IN
DIALOGUE WITH THE WORK OF JAMES K. A. SMITH AND AMOS YONG … 13
   Introduction … 13
   Groundwork for Pentecostal Metaphysics: James K. A. Smith's Five
      Elements of a Pentecostal Worldview … 13
      "My Soon-Coming King": Eschatological Orientation … 15
      The Surprise of the Spirit: Radical Openness to God … 16
      Signs and Wonders: Enchanted Theology of Creation … 17
      The Hem of His Garment: Nondualistic Affirmation of
         Embodiment and Materiality … 18
      "This Is My Story, This Is My Song": Affective, Narrative
         Epistemology … 19
   Groundwork for Pentecostal Metaphysics: Amos Yong's
      Foundational Pneumatology … 21
      In the Beginning Was the Spirit: Foundational Pneumatology … 21
      The Spirit and Nature: Pneumatological Naturalism … 26
      The Spirit and Spirits: Cosmic Pneumatology … 28
         Personhood and Spirit … 30
         Plurality and Emergence … 30
      The Spirit and Being: Pneumatological Nondualism … 31
      The Spirit and Knowledge: Pneumatological Epistemology … 33
   Conclusion … 34

## Chapter 3
### THE SPIRIT, REALITY, AND RENEWAL: INFERRING METAPHYSICS FROM THE WORK OF JAMES K. A. SMITH AND AMOS YONG — 37
- Introduction — 37
- The Spirit of the Real: Tacit Metaphysics in the Work of James K. A. Smith — 37
  - Foundational Claims, Formational Influences, Fundamental Presuppositions, and Final Aims — 37
  - Overcoming (Super)Naturalisms — 39
  - Stifling the Spirit: Radical Openness to God and Hostile Scientisms — 43
  - Conclusion — 45
- The Spirit of Renewal: Tacit Metaphysics in the Work of Amos Yong — 46
  - Foundational Claims, Formational Influences, Fundamental Presuppositions, and Final Aims — 46
  - Relationality, Rationality, and Dynamism — 48
    - The Spirit as Bond of Love — 48
    - The Spirit as Revealer of Truth — 49
    - The Spirit as Liveliness of God — 51
  - Speaking with the Spirit: Yong's Pneumatology and Process Metaphysics — 51
- The Spirit and the Renewal of the Real: The Possibilities of a Smithian/Yongian Pentecostal Theological Metaphysics — 53
- Conclusion — 56

## Chapter 4
### WORSHIP, WISDOM, AND THE WAYS OF THE SPIRIT: INFERRING METAPHYSICS FROM PENTECOSTAL SPIRITUALITY — 59
- Introduction — 59
- "This Is Your Reasonable Service": Reading the Internal Logic of Pentecostal Worship — 60
  - First- and Second-Level Discourse in Pentecostal Praxis — 60
  - Spirituality and Theology: Affirming the "and" — 63
- Liturgical Studies: Analyzing an Ecclesial Expression of Pentecostal Spirituality — 68
- Conclusion — 71

## Chapter 5
### TOWARD A PENTECOSTAL THEOLOGY OF BEING-IN-THE-SPIRIT: THE KNOWLEDGE OF THE TRIUNE GOD AND THE TRUTH OF THEOLOGICAL METAPHYSICS — 73
- Introduction — 73
- "Come Quickly, Lord Jesus": Eschatological Reorientation — 75
  - Introduction — 75

| | |
|---|---|
| A Trinitarian Nondualist Eschatology | 76 |
|    Introduction | 76 |
|    Cosmic Salvation and the Fullness of the Full Gospel | 77 |
|    The Universality of Jesus' Particular History | 82 |
|    History's Transfiguration | 83 |
|    "For from Him and through Him and to Him Are All Things": | |
|       The Triune Determination(s) of Creation | 87 |
|       The Father as Source | 87 |
|       The Son as Goal | 90 |
|          Jesus as Uncreated | 90 |
|          Jesus as Creator | 91 |
|          Jesus as Creature | 92 |
|          Jesus as Creation | 92 |
|       The Spirit as Guide | 95 |
|          Introduction | 95 |
|          "We Believe in the Holy Spirit …" | 95 |
|          "The Testimony of Jesus Is the Spirit of Prophecy" | 97 |
|          Between Ascension and Pentecost | 99 |
|          Robert Jenson's Pneumatological Naturalism | 101 |
|             Introduction | 101 |
|             The Spirit of Jesus Is the Freedom of Universal | |
|                History | 102 |
|             The Spirit of Jesus Is the Spontaneity of Natural | |
|                Process | 103 |
| Conclusion | 104 |
|    A Foundational Ecclesiological Pneumatology | 105 |
|       Introduction | 105 |
|       Simon Chan's Ecclesial Metaphysics | 105 |
|          The Church as the People of God | 107 |
|          The Church as the Body of Christ | 108 |
|          The Church as the Temple of the Holy Spirit | 108 |
|       Conclusion | 109 |
|    Summary/Conclusion | 110 |
| I Am That You Are: The Radical Openness of God | 110 |
|    Introduction | 110 |
|    "I Am": The Being of the One God | 112 |
|    "The Holy One of Israel": God's Life as Being-in-the-Spirit | 117 |
|    "The Lord, Your God": Being-in-the-World as Ontological | |
|       Participation | 122 |
|       Participatory Ontology and Pentecostal Spirituality | 122 |
|       Being-in-the-World | 126 |
|       Being-in-the-Spirit | 129 |
|    Conclusion | 130 |

## Contents

| | |
|---|---|
| Deep Calls Out to Deep: Re-Enchanting Nature and Rediscovering Creation | 131 |
| Introduction | 131 |
| The Liveliness of God and Gaps in Scientific Explanation | 132 |
| Questioning Yong's Questioning of Classical Metaphysics | 138 |
|     Eschatology and/or Teleology | 143 |
|     Creation and/or Causation | 145 |
| The End(s) of Emergence Theory | 147 |
| God Beyond Being: Revising Yong's Theses for a Pluralistic Cosmos | 153 |
| Conclusion | 160 |
| "This Is My Body": How Matter Matters | 160 |
| Introduction | 160 |
| Likeness in Unlikeness: Christological Paradoxes and the (Im)Possibility of Naming Reality | 162 |
| The Means of Grace and the Hope of Glory: Nondualistic Participatory Ontology and Pentecostal Models of Healing | 164 |
| Conclusion | 165 |
| "Do This for My Remembrance": Relating (to) the Truth | 166 |
| Introduction | 166 |
| Life in the Spirit as Storied Existence | 166 |
| Conclusion: Knowing as Affective Participation in the Truth | 169 |
| Conclusion | 170 |

### Chapter 6
### THE WORK OF GOD IN THE WORK OF THE PEOPLE: BEING-IN-THE-SPIRIT AND LITURGICAL RENEWAL

| | |
|---|---|
| | 173 |
| Introduction | 173 |
| Pentecost and the Spirit of the Liturgy | 174 |
| Conclusion | 187 |

### CONCLUSION

| | |
|---|---|
| | 189 |
| Contributions of This Work and Suggestions for Further Study | 189 |
| Bibliography | 191 |
| Index | 205 |

# ACKNOWLEDGMENTS

This monograph is a revised version of my PhD thesis completed at Bangor University, Wales, UK. The echoes of the variety of voices that have contributed to my writing this monograph are innumerable, so I will begin with those who have been involved in the process more directly. First, a big thank you to my *Doktorvater,* Chris E.W. Green. The seeds for this work were planted in your "Trinity, Personhood, and Prayer" course, and the conversations and reading that ensued therein and thereafter nourished my thought life to finally blossom into this work. Thank you for your instruction, keen editorial eye, counsel, and theological insight both before and throughout this process. Most of all, thank you for your friendship for the better part of a decade.

I must also acknowledge and thank John Christopher Thomas for creating what for me has quickly become sacred ground at both the Pentecostal Theological Seminary and the Centre for Pentecostal Theology. That sacred CPT ground was filled with brilliant scholars who spoke into this monograph, people I deeply admire and respect, like Robby Waddell, Frank Macchia, and Lee Roy Martin. Moreover, the input of my dear colleagues there was also invaluable. I will forever be numbered among what I like to call the "Cleveland Squad." Also, I am very grateful for the close engagement, encouragement, and helpful suggestions given by Wolfgang Vondey and Daniela Augustine. I am honored to contribute to the SPCT series, and I have you both to thank for helping me to get it there. Other helpful and gracious commentors that I must also note here have been Simo Frestadius, William Kay, and Amos Yong. Lydia Neeley, thank you for your excellent proofreading work, all of which have made a massive difference to the finished monograph.

Finally, I close by thanking those to whom I owe everything, my family. Christina Robles, my wife of fifteen beautiful years. You have sacrificed far beyond your call to see to it that I labor in the work the Lord has called me to. Your love, radical support, prayers of intercession, and self-sacrifice for my sake have revealed the heart of Jesus to me. Words fail to express what you mean for my life, so I will simply say that I love you. To my son, Marlon Robles for sharing your hugs, kisses, toys, making me laugh, and reminding me to make time for play. I love you so much. Mom and Dad, your emphatic support, generosity, and extravagant love in all areas have been the constant in my life. I would not be here without it. You have shown me what it is to live with love and grace toward family and beyond. I love you both, dearly. My grandparents Martinez and Robles for pioneering and modeling what it means to be Christian, and further, ministers of the gospel. Our whole family owes our being first, Christian, and second, pentecostal, to all of you. I must also thank my in-laws for your love and support, and for providing a beautiful farm for respite and fun for our family. It has been a lifesaver. Finally, to my dear friends Joseph Baker, Bishop D. A. Sherron, and Cheena Kumar for your prayers, intercession, prophetic direction, and words of encouragement. You all are among the reasons as I count myself blessed.

# ABBREVIATIONS

| | |
|---|---|
| *AJPS* | *Asian Journal of Pentecostal Studies* |
| *ANF* | *A Select Library of Ante-Nicene Fathers* |
| *ATR* | *Anglican Theology Review* |
| BUP | Baylor University Press |
| CPT | Centre for Pentecostal Theology |
| CUA | The Catholic University of America |
| DPCM | Burgess, S. M. et al. (eds), *Dictionary of Pentecostal and Charismatic Movements* (Grand Rapids: Zondervan, 1988) |
| *IJST* | *International Journal of Systematic Theology* |
| IVP | InterVarsity Press |
| *JBL* | *Journal of Biblical Literature* |
| *JEPTA* | *Journal of European Pentecostal Theology Association* |
| *JETS* | *Journal of the Evangelical Theological Society* |
| *JPT* | *Journal of Pentecostal Theology* |
| *JPTSUP* | *Journal of Pentecostal Theology Supplement Series* |
| *JSNTS* | *Journal for the Study of New Testament Supplement Series* |
| NIDPCM | Burgess, S. M. and E. M. van der Maas (eds), *The New International Dictionary of Pentecostal and Charismatic Movements* (Grand Rapids: Zondervan, 2003) |
| *NPNF* | *A Select Library of Nicene and Post-Nicene Fathers* |
| NTT | New Testament Theology Commentary Series |
| OUP | Oxford University Press |
| PIMS | Pontifical Institute of Mediaeval Studies |
| *Pneuma* | *Pneuma: The Journal of the Society for Pentecostal Studies* |
| SBL | Society of Biblical Literature |
| SNTSMS | Studiorum Novi Testamenti Societas Monograph Series |
| SVS | St Vladimir's Seminary Press |
| *SVTQ* | *St. Vladimir's Theological Quarterly* |
| TPNTC | Pillar New Testament Commentary Series |
| WJKP | Westminster John Knox Press |

# INTRODUCTION

## *The Task*

The gospel, in its most basic form, is the message that the God of Israel has raised his Son Jesus from the dead by the power of the Holy Spirit. Throughout history, those who have been grasped by this message and have gathered around it with the aim of speaking and living said message faithfully constitute the church. Considering that the gospel enters into history and perdures in it, it is a message that both clashes with and receives the discourses of the world around it. Rarely does the latter happen without severe modification, including especially those discursive enterprises in history that claim to speak truthfully about reality. Thus, the gospel imposes a task upon the church gathering around its message: to *communicate the truth* about reality—both to each other in reminder and formation and to the world in proclamation. This act belongs to the church's first-level discourse—which will later in this work also be identified as "spirituality." Connected to this essential task is the *thinking* necessary to ensure the church is indeed speaking and acting the gospel and its import faithfully, in that her speech and acts have not compromised the message or its vision of reality according to the dominant discourses that surround it. This act belongs to the church's second-level discourse—which will later in this work be identified as "theology." Further along in this work, we will discover that theology as second-level discourse is not a discipline reserved merely for scholars and academics but is a discipline in which some ministers, lay leaders, and anyone within a church community who speaks or writes formationally and reflectively on the basis of church practice also participate. Both first- and second-level discourses are doxological and essential for the church's faithful existence across time.

Pentecostals, a community that identifies as a movement within Christianity, are not immune to the task described above. We are a community that aims to gather around the same Christian gospel and are thus called to participate in the discourses just mentioned, adjudicated according to the same standards of faithfulness despite our distinctives. This is precisely the purpose that undergirds my thesis, which will focus on doing theological metaphysics according to our worship of the triune God. Put directly, this work has to do with not only reflecting on the God we worship but also explicating the reality we tacitly inhabit and create by our worship of this God. Therefore, this work should matter not only for pentecostal theologians given to deep scholarly reflection but for pentecostal ministers and laity that aim to know God, themselves, and the world around them as they seek to faithfully worship in Spirit and in Truth. In this thesis, what I am offering is a constructive and critical engagement of pentecostal *spirituality,* and of pentecostal *theology* via the larger ecumenical, creedal, and dogmatic Christian metaphysical tradition. This effort is aimed at constructing a pentecostal metaphysics that, at once, does justice to what is best in the first-level pentecostal experience while confronting that which is problematic. By "best," I mean that it is ecumenically promising and does not run counter to what the classical Christian tradition has said about God and creatures; moreover, I mean "best" in that it is fitted to my forthcoming engagement with Smith's five elements of a pentecostal worldview. Thus, this work is explicitly and intentionally *limited* to understand metaphysics in conversation with the historical Christian tradition, and to understand a pentecostal vision of it according to Smith's categories. What a reader can expect, then, is that my constructive proposals will at some point follow critical engagement—so that any issues raised critically will be in service to the constructive thought that proceeds it.

## *Structure and Flow of the Study*

For the sake of constructing a pentecostal metaphysics, Chapter 1 of this volume begins by first setting the terms of what constitutes pentecostalism(s) in the first place and then strives to seek the most embracing definition possible. Here the work defines the enterprise of metaphysics as it will be used throughout. Next, categories of theological discourse are introduced, which will prove beneficial as the argument progresses. This chapter closes by displaying, first of all, the call for a distinctively pentecostal metaphysics by previous pentecostal thinkers and, second, the *lacuna* left within pentecostal theology of an exhaustive attempt to answer that call.

Chapter 2 lays out the strategy for beginning the task of constructing a pentecostal theological metaphysics. James K. A. Smith's categories, which are called the "five elements of a pentecostal worldview," are determined to be a helpful scaffolding for the sake of construction. Within those categories, we move on to briefly survey what pentecostal theologians have already constructed that touch on metaphysics within Smith's categories. From there, Amos Yong is identified as a pentecostal theologian who has done the most work toward constructing a pentecostal metaphysics (both tacitly and explicitly), and a brief look at what he has written in light of the five elements ensues.

In Chapter 3, we once again note that James K. A. Smith and Amos Yong have by far done the most tacit, explicit, and exhaustive work toward constructing a pentecostal metaphysics. As such, we take a very close look first at the presuppositions, aims, and work on ontology and metaphysics done by Smith, followed by the same for Yong. We then compare and contrast their visions and trace their interaction on pertinent metaphysical topics. While their visions vary, their aims of public discourse are similar. Here, we start to get more explicit about the fact that the forthcoming pentecostal metaphysical proposal will be emphatically concerned not with its reifiability with other discourses, but on the internal logic of Christian theology and pentecostal practice per my imposed methodological limits. This approach will indeed yield a more exhaustive metaphysics radically focused on pentecostal spirituality.

In Chapter 4 I look at the work of Daniel Albrecht and Mark Cartledge and others as they have done the research that shows the world-making and identity-orienting power of pentecostal practice. Their work also contains ethnographic and empirical studies on what is practiced in more contemporary pentecostal contexts. I must note here that their work is limited in its scope as they study pentecostal practice in its popular forms found in North America and the UK. Accounting for these limits, their studies begin to display the gap between what is said in pentecostal first-level discourse and what is said in the theology of pentecostal scholars. Using their work, I argue that if we are to adduce the metaphysical vision of pentecostals in these contexts, we must pay close attention to what is being practiced in local assemblies, and by inference, determine what is tacitly and explicitly being said (from the platform, in our songs, and in our sermons) about God, creatures, and a vision of all reality. I note here that explicit naming of the triune God is mostly missing in contemporary and popular forms of pentecostal worship in the UK and North America, which produces massive consequences for attempting to construct a Christian metaphysics—that is a Christian vision of the God–world relation. Of course, the churches they observe do not exhaustively represent all pentecostal practice in worship—identifying such churches would be impossible for a worldwide movement. However, their studies are indeed consonant with the practices widely observed in pentecostal assemblies.

In Chapter 5, we note that in light of the studies of Albrecht and Cartledge (and others), there is a need to critically reexamine pentecostal spirituality as the metaphysics constructed therefrom can tend to be neither trinitarian and, therefore, not in alignment with what the historical Christian tradition has bequeathed to us as it pertains to a metaphysical vision. Nor does it align with what pentecostal scholars have assumed takes place in pentecostal worship. Given this situation, I argue that pentecostals are better served to explicate an orthodox and ecumenically promising theological metaphysics that resonates with their self-understanding and, on that basis, to critique the forms of pentecostal spirituality and theology that have lost touch with historical Christian teaching. The rest of the chapter is an attempt at developing a thorough and cohesive pentecostal metaphysics—via Smith's categories—informed by Scripture, the dogmatic Christian tradition with its norms of theological judgment, and pentecostal distinctives. That effort is aimed at assisting pentecostal scholars and ministers in discerning the theological integrity and soundness of contemporary beliefs and practices in various ministerial contexts.

Chapter 6 labors in light of the gaps the previous sections have displayed between a dogmatically faithful theological vision of reality and certain forms of pentecostal practice. I thus argue that the best way to reform unfaithful beliefs and practices is through pentecostal liturgical renewal. I then propose a loosely scripted, ecumenically and pentecostal-informed liturgy, as a way to hopefully ensure the gospel and its metaphysical import get said and embodied in our weekly gatherings.

The volume concludes with contributions made by this thesis, then makes some suggestions for further research.

## Chapter 1

## CAN THERE BE A PENTECOSTAL ARTICULATION OF METAPHYSICS?

*Introduction: Theological Metaphysics and
North American Pentecostalism*

Given the diversity of the movement, it is difficult, if not impossible, to define Pentecostalism. Therefore, any use of the term "pentecostal" is fraught. In this volume the term "pentecostal" will be used in a way that encompasses the various streams within it, insofar as that is possible.[1] Following James K. A. Smith's lead, in this work the term "pentecostal" will "refer not to a classical or denominational definition, but rather to an understanding of Christian faith that is radically open to the continued operations of the Spirit."[2] As manifold as the movement is, there is a common tendency throughout to privilege the Holy Spirit in experience, and the doctrine of the Holy Spirit in theology.[3] While the Holy Spirit is primary in pentecostal imagination, Jesus remains central. Therefore, "pentecostal" will also

---

1. The most prominent streams being Classical Pentecostals, the Charismatic Renewal, and Third-Wave neopentecostals. This work will focus on English-speaking North American pentecostalism which emerges from the Azusa Street Revival of 1906–9. Some hold that North American pentecostalism's roots were first formed in Topeka Kansas under the leadership of Charles Parham, which is chronologically accurate; however, the dominant narrative for the origins of the pentecostal movement belongs to the Azusa Street Revival with William Seymour. For a summary of these competing narratives, see Cecil M. Robeck Jr., "The Origins of Modern Pentecostalism," in Cecil M. Robeck Jr. and Amos Yong (eds), *The Cambridge Companion to Pentecostalism* (New York: Cambridge University Press, 2014), pp. 18–23.

2. James K. A. Smith, *Thinking in Tongues: Pentecostal Contributions to Christian Philosophy*, Pentecostal Manifestos (Grand Rapids: Eerdmans, 2010), p. xvii.

3. Wolfgang Vondey, *Pentecostalism: A Guide for the Perplexed* (London: T&T Clark, 2012), pp. 29–30.

refer to those who find their identity and defining theological narrative in the life of Christ via the pattern of the full gospel.[4]

## Pentecostal Spirituality/Theology and the Nature of Christian Theological Discourse

In response to the continued activity of the Spirit, pentecostals have developed an embodied set of practices, affections, disciplines, and habits of speech which serve as the form of our spirituality. Such a spirituality implicitly posits a worldview. As Smith has rightly observed, "this interpretive stance is what marks pentecostal spirituality that functions as nothing short of a revolutionary interpretation of the world unapologetically proclaimed as a *counter*interpretation of the world—one that counters the regnant interpretations ... of our world and events that unfold within it."[5] Smith thus calls for pentecostals to unpack the ontological implications of our worldview.[6]

Given that the above is true, another question arises: what are the ontological and metaphysical implications of pentecostal spirituality and theology? A helpful way of extrapolating these implications is to fit pentecostal spirituality and pentecostal theology into two distinct levels of discourse.[7] Pentecostal *spirituality*—that which manifests as proclamation, prayer, and praise in response to lived experiences—belongs to what will be called first-level discourse. Pentecostal *theology* will thus function as second-level discourse—that is, a discipline which

---

4. By the "full gospel," I mean the four/fivefold gospel. See Steven J. Land, *Pentecostal Spirituality: A Passion for the Kingdom* (Cleveland: CPT Press, 2010). Thomas argues that the full gospel is the theological heart of pentecostalism. See John Christopher Thomas, "Pentecostal Theology in the Twenty-First Century," *Pneuma* 20.1 (1998), pp. 3–19. For the history of the full gospel narrative, see Donald Dayton, *Theological Roots of Pentecostalism* (Grand Rapids: Baker Academic, 1987). More recently, Wolfgang Vondey has written a monograph on pentecostal theology using Pentecost as the core theological symbol and the full gospel as its defining narrative. See Wolfgang Vondey, *Pentecostal Theology: Living the Full Gospel* (London: Bloomsbury T&T Clark, 2017).

5. Smith, *Thinking in Tongues*, p. 24.

6. Smith, *Thinking in Tongues*, p. 87. Smith is reiterating a call made twenty-six years prior by David R. Nichols: "pentecostal spirituality is now at a stage of maturity and depth so that it may discover and set forth its own ontology, epistemology, and hermeneutic" (David R. Nichols, "The Search for Pentecostal Structure in Systematic Theology," *Pneuma* 6.2 (Fall 1984), pp. 57–76).

7. Robert W. Jenson, *Systematic Theology, I* (New York: Oxford University Press, 1997–9), p. 18.

reflects on how to elucidate the message and worldview embedded in pentecostal spirituality.[8] I must hasten to add that while these discourses are helpfully distinguished, they are indeed mutually informing "so that, on some occasions, belief conforms to experience and, on other occasions, belief is primary and either informs the interpretation of experience or else shapes experience in some other fundamental way."[9] As will become clear later, theology is not merely derivative, but also exerts critical, corrective, and interpretive force on its spirituality. In this work, then, pentecostal theology functions as something similar to a "grammar" as defined by George A. Lindbeck.[10] For pentecostals, this "grammar" is more than descriptive, because our theology and spirituality *prescriptively* envisage a unique cosmic reality that is dynamic, enchanted, and open to God's surprises. Yet for some reason, despite the fact that pentecostal spirituality functions in this way, and despite the fact that there have been calls for a construction of pentecostal ontology and metaphysics, few serious attempts have been made to answer this call.

Before proceeding to suggest that pentecostals ought to participate in the discipline of metaphysics—and later, developing a vision for what that might look like—I must pause to define key terms as they will be used for the purposes of this work. Some writers have used the word "ontology" as a subdivision of metaphysics, while others have used both words interchangeably.[11] For some of the latter, the concurrence of ontology and metaphysics is simply taken for granted.[12] Considering that in this work the word "ontology" will appear most prevalently under Smith's notion of "participatory ontology" (via Radical Orthodoxy), I will

---

8. While giving voice to their discursive distinctions, I want to also affirm that for pentecostals, theology and spirituality are closely related. As Vondey suggests, these enterprises relate as a reciprocal back-and-forth movement; however, he also says they are not synonymous, thus creating space for distinctions to be made. See Vondey, *Pentecostal Theology*, pp. 17–18. I must also note here that second-level reflection is not solely reserved for academic theologians. Some pentecostal ministers and lay leaders participate in this enterprise despite not seeking to do so exhaustively or systematically. While most of this work will attend to academic pentecostal theology, there will be a section below—namely, Chapter 4—dedicated to adducing the second-level discourse of certain pentecostal ministers and lay leaders in conversation with their church practice.

9. William K. Kay, *Pentecostalism: A Very Short Introduction* (Oxford: Oxford University Press, 2011), p. 7.

10. See George A. Lindbeck, *The Nature of Doctrine: Religion and Theology in a Postliberal Age* (Philadelphia: Westminster Press, 1984), pp. 79–84.

11. Alasdair MacIntyre, "Ontology," in Paul Edwards (ed.), *The Encyclopedia of Philosophy: Volumes 5 and 6* (New York: Macmillan Publishing), pp. 542–3.

12. See Kelly James Clark, Richard Lints, and James K. A. Smith (eds), *101 Key Terms in Philosophy and Their Importance for Theology* (Louisville: Westminster John Knox Press, 2004), pp. 51–2.

use those words in similar fashion. That is, "ontology" and "metaphysics" will be coterminous.[13] In addition to Smith and RO, this tendency is contemporarily prevalent among those inclined toward *ressourcement*. That is, contemporary thinkers who are more sympathetic toward ancient and medieval visions of reality—seeking to retrieve them faithfully, and creatively—and suspicious of modernity's attempts to overcome them.[14]

Therefore, I will not be using "ontology" in the modernistic sense, which is linked to the development of a kind of "natural theology" that is based on efficient causality and grounded in the univocity of being, and equivocity of beings.[15] This modernistic notion of "ontology"—which is allied to the kind of natural theology that implies a necessary completion of natural scientific enquiries—tends to posit God as the supreme being among beings. God is thus reduced as merely "an objective item within reality, alongside other items, which will passively endure one's active search to isolate its nature."[16] It is within this theological framework that both the Kantian and twentieth-century charge of "ontotheology" holds.[17] Ontotheology is, generally speaking, a modern pejorative term critiquing visions of reality wherein "God" is merely admitted for the sake of filling explanatory gaps, so that God (univocally conceived) is reduced as "the *causa sui* of a metaphysical system, not the living God of biblical revelation."[18] To briefly foreshadow what I will lay out in more detail in Chapter 5: in this work, I will follow ancient and medieval traditions which assert that the triune God is not a being among beings,

---

13. E.g., "metaphysics of participation" coincides with "participatory ontology," and "sacramental ontology," etc.

14. These theologians and Christian philosophers share a similar mood as the twentieth-century French Catholic renewal movement, known as *Nouvelle Théologie*. They are as varied as Hans Boersma, Catherine Pickstock, John Milbank, Rowan Williams, Matthew Levering, Adrian Pabst, David Bentley Hart, W. Norris Clarke, *et al.*

15. See Étienne Gilson, *History of Christian Philosophy in the Middle Ages* (New York: Random House, 1955), pp. 505–11; Louis Dupre, *Passage to Modernity: An Essay in the Hermeneutics of Nature and Culture* (New Haven: Yale University Press, 1993); Catherine Pickstock, "Duns Scotus: His Historical and Contemporary Significance," in John Milbank, and Simon Oliver, *The Radical Orthodoxy Reader* (New York: Routledge, 2009), pp. 116–48; Adrian Pabst, *Metaphysics: The Creation of Hierarchy* (Grand Rapids: W.B. Eerdmans Publishing Company, 2012), pp. 272–303; W. Norris Clarke, "Causality and Time," in W. Norris Clarke (ed.), *The Creative Retrieval of St. Thomas Aquinas: Essays in Thomistic Philosophy, New and Old* (New York: Fordham University Press, 2009), pp. 27–38.

16. Catherine Pickstock, *Aspects of Truth: A New Religious Metaphysics* (Cambridge: Cambridge University Press, 2020), p. 85.

17. See Immanuel Kant, *Lectures on Philosophical Theology*, trans. Allen W. Wood and Gertrude M. Clark (Ithaca: Cornell University Press, 1986); Martin Heidegger, *Identity and Difference*, trans. Joan Stambaugh (Chicago: University of Chicago Press, 2002).

18. Clark and Smith, *Key Terms in Philosophy*, p. 64.

but is "beyond being" as the infinite act of existence, and the wellspring of being in which all creation lives and moves and has its being. Moreover, as I will note below, the life, death, and resurrection of Jesus serves as the vantage from which this metaphysics is constructed. Therefore, the charge of "ontotheology" will not here apply.

Positively, then, just what is metaphysics? Succinctly put, in this work, metaphysics will be understood as that "which focuses its inquiry explicitly on the *vision of the whole*, that is, what is common to all real beings and what constitutes their connectedness to the universe as a meaningful whole."[19] For the Christian, this involves a coherent account of the God–world relation in light of the gospel, so that the gospel message of Christ's resurrection and its concomitant metaphysical import make a profound difference in our revisionary counterinterpretation of reality. More on this to follow.

Because pentecostal spirituality is embedded in corporal practices and first-level discourse, thinking in the way second-level discourse requires does not come naturally and, therefore, is often judged unnecessary. Pentecostals—with some exceptions that I will note later—tend to prefer to remain in first-level discourse, appealing to second-level discourse mostly when forced into it for pragmatic and apologetic purposes.[20] For the time being then, pentecostals apparently feel little

---

19. W. Norris Clarke, *The One and the Many: A Contemporary Thomistic Metaphysics* (Notre Dame: University of Notre Dame Press, 2001), pp. 5–6. To be clear, this is how "metaphysics" will be engaged in this monograph. There are modern understandings of metaphysics that vary, as well as differing opinions as to whether Christians ought to be engaging in metaphysics at all. The literature is vast and diverse. For example, consider the following: Erich Przywara, *Analogia Entis: Metaphysics* (Grand Rapids: Eerdmans, 2014); Martin Heidegger, *Introduction to Metaphysics*, second ed., trans. Gregory Fried and Richard F. H. Polt (New Haven: Yale University Press, 2014); Jean-Luc Marion, *God without Being*, second ed., trans. Thomas A. Carlson and David Tracy (Chicago: The University of Chicago Press, 2012); and Kevin Hector, *Theology without Metaphysics: God, Language, and the Spirit of Recognition* (New York: Cambridge University Press, 2011); Pickstock, *Aspects of Truth*. From surveying the vast literature on the matter, the utter rejection of metaphysics—prevalent especially following the advent of modernity—seems self-contradictory. The question seems to be not *whether* one decides for or against metaphysics, but *which* metaphysics one is rejecting in favor of another. After sketching this history of the discipline of metaphysics, Joseph Owens puts it so: "Anyone who seriously undertakes a refutation of metaphysics soon finds himself buried under metaphysical principles of his own, principles that he has to adopt in order to come to grips with his subject." See Joseph Owens, *An Elementary Christian Metaphysics* (Notre Dame: University of Notre Dame Press, 1963), p. 13. This adoption of metaphysical principles is not always explicit in modern thought, hence the often regnant assumptions that we can simply do without it.

20. Vondey points out that pentecostal focus on salvation, sanctification, Spirit baptism, divine healing, and the coming kingdom tends to put the human being at the heart of doctrinal conversations. When this anthropocentric lens is accentuated by apocalyptic

pressure to construct a coherent metaphysical vision. However, Daniel Castelo has noted that pentecostal urgency has stymied our ability to practice patience;[21] and it is precisely this patience that is needed to participate in constructing a connected "vision of the whole" which metaphysical theology requires. Therefore, the first reason pentecostals ought to participate in second-level metaphysical discourse is because it develops the virtue of patience in us. As such, it is sanctifying work.

The second reason pentecostals should engage in theological metaphysics is that it affords us the opportunity to be reflective and self-aware about the implications of our spirituality. Only insofar as we are explicitly committed to second-level discourse can we be discerning about the faithfulness of what we are positing when we worship, speak, and practice as a community.

Third, pentecostal participation in metaphysics is catechetically beneficial: it will help us proactively tradition our spirituality for the sake of future generations.[22] Amos Yong rightly observes that the pentecostal "oral mode of communication and narrative framework are conducive to the task of traditioning precisely because such traditioning is pneumatologically accomplished."[23] As pentecostals, we therefore tradition ourselves by the Spirit and just so are freed for the future that the Spirit is drawing us toward.

Fourth and finally, participating in the metaphysical enterprise via second-level discourse gives us the opportunity to join our voices to the larger Christian tradition in its metaphysical vocation by offering our unique "counterinterpretation" of the world. In so doing, pentecostals become ecumenically conversant with the ancient "community which anchors itself in the action of God and which says that that action is a reconstruction of what it means to be human."[24]

---

urgency, the conversations tend to focus on mission and evangelization, rather than on the being of God, the being of creation, and the God–world relation. However, second-level discourse became necessary "during the second half of the twentieth century with the global expansion of Pentecostalism and the challenges posed by various indigenous cosmologies absorbed in diverse Pentecostal contexts." See Vondey, *Pentecostal Theology*, p. 156. Glossolalia is another example of this tendency. For recent work on the subject, see Jordan Daniel May, *Global Witnesses to Pentecost: The Testimony of "Other Tongues"* (Cleveland, TN: CPT Press, 2013); and Robert P. Menzies, *Speaking in Tongues: Jesus and the Apostolic Church as Models for the Church Today* (Cleveland, TN: CPT Press, 2016).

21. Daniel Castelo, *Revisioning Pentecostal Ethics—The Epicletic Community* (Cleveland: CPT Press, 2012).

22. Simon Chan, *Pentecostal Theology and the Christian Spiritual Tradition* (JPTSup21; Sheffield: Sheffield Academic Press, 2000).

23. Amos Yong, *The Spirit Poured Out on All Flesh: Pentecostalism and the Possibility of a Global Theology* (Grand Rapids: Baker Academic Publishing Group, 2005), p. 117.

24. Rowan Williams, "The Authority of the Church," *Modern Believing* 46.1 (2005), p. 17.

## Conclusion

In summation, pentecostals ought to shed their reluctance to engage in second-level discourse and participate in metaphysical theology because it (1) sanctifies us by producing patience; (2) enables us to discern the faithfulness of our spirituality; (3) allows us to better understand how to pass on our tradition, living faithfully in the present toward the future; and (4) is ecumenically promising.

## Chapter 2

## COME, CREATOR SPIRIT: IMAGINING A PENTECOSTAL METAPHYSICS IN DIALOGUE WITH THE WORK OF JAMES K. A. SMITH AND AMOS YONG

### Introduction

If constructing a metaphysical vision of the whole is beneficial and perhaps even tacitly inevitable to being Christian—as a people who make truth claims about reality—then pentecostals are not immune to that enterprise. Having noted that pentecostal theologians have called for our engagement in it, what follows will be a brief sketch of the current state of pentecostal metaphysics, and it will be discovered that it has thus far remained, for the most part, undeveloped. However, James K. A. Smith and Amos Yong will emerge as exceptions in that they are scholars within our tradition who have given metaphysical reflection the most serious and sustained attention. Moreover, Smith's five categories will be identified as a helpful way of constructing a vision of the whole from a pentecostal perspective.

### *Groundwork for Pentecostal Metaphysics: James K. A. Smith's Five Elements of a Pentecostal Worldview*

It is one thing to say *that* pentecostals ought to be engaging in metaphysics; it is another to say *how*. History shows that the culture within a given context will be inclined to speak in its own ways about reality, and "on the account of the gospel's contrariness to human proclivity ... the history of Christian theology can be read as a sustained effort to dislocate that culture's 'common sense.'"[1] The gospel thus critiques all of the world's metaphysical projections and "opens anew the questions of being that enabled us to construct our metaphysics in the first place. But the answer to the question (what is it to be?) is now provided by the revelation of Jesus; the content of a Christian metaphysics is populated in advance by the life

---

1. Robert W. Jenson, "A Reply," in Stephen John Wright (ed.), *Theology as Revisionary Metaphysics: Essays on God and Creation* (Eugene, OR: Cascade Books, 2014), p. 3.

and history of Jesus of Nazareth."[2] Therefore, the starting point of this theological metaphysics which reflects on creaturely, cosmic, and divine reality is "found in this one particular life and not in a generalized metaphysical concept of being."[3] My proposed metaphysical vision is *Christian*, and so it labors from the antecedent dogmatic conviction—and the norms of theological judgment utilized to explicate its import—that the Father has raised his Son Jesus of Nazareth from the dead, by the Spirit. Just so, my work is intentionally and explicitly limited. Moreover, this vision of reality will be distinctly *pentecostal* because it privileges the work of the Spirit in the life of Jesus.

If the dogmatic convictions—along with the historical arguments that have produced them—just described serve as the foundation for the ensuing theological metaphysics, a modified version of James K. A. Smith's "five elements of a pentecostal worldview" will serve as the scaffolding for the sake of its construction from a pentecostal perspective. Again, there is an intentional limitation here as it is impossible to name a pentecostal perspective as *the* pentecostal perspective. That said, Smith is a pentecostal theologian whose fivefold rubric proposes that the pentecostal worldview contains (1) A Radical Openness to God, (2) An "Enchanted" Theology of Creation and Culture, (3) A Nondualistic Affirmation of Embodiment and Materiality, (4) An Affective, Narrative Epistemology, and (5) An Eschatological Orientation to Mission and Justice.[4] I will make one modification

---

2. Stephen J. Wright, "Introduction," in Stephen J. Wright (ed.), *Theology as Revisionary Metaphysics* (Eugene, OR: Cascade Books, 2014), pp. xi–xii.

3. Stephen J. Wright, *Dogmatic Aesthetics: A Theology of Beauty in Dialogue with Robert W. Jenson* (Minneapolis: Fortress Press, 2014), p. 50. Yet, the reader will notice that in my constructive section I have sketched a doctrine of being in conversation with the Christian tradition through thinkers such as Gregory of Nyssa, Thomas Aquinas, and John the Damascene, and the contemporary theologians—such as Matthew Levering, Rowan Williams, and David Bentley Hart—who engage their thought in developing a distinctly Christian ontology. It is therefore not my interest to pit the life and history of Jesus *against* the doctrine of being *qua* being. Rather, as a methodological starting point, I deduce a metaphysical vision considering the life, death, and resurrection of Jesus precisely because this is an explicitly *Christian* theological metaphysics. I do this over against the kind of natural theology that posits "a God who *waits* to be discovered … this is a God who has to be thought of as essentially silent, passively there to be uncovered by our enquiries" (Rowan Williams, *The Edge of Words: God and the Habits of Language* [London: Bloomsbury Publishing, 2014], p. 1 [emphasis original]). Therefore, I am assuming that the triune God actively *revealed* through the life of Jesus: initiates, sustains, and fulfills the doctrine of being. Throughout history, the doctrine of being as adduced by thinkers within a given context has been engaged appreciatively and critically by Christian thinkers for the sake of faith seeking understanding. Just so, the doctrine of being and the life of Jesus are not at odds. "Jesus said to them, 'Very truly, I tell you, before Abraham was, I am'" (Jn 8:58).

4. Smith, *Thinking in Tongues*, pp. 10–47.

to Smith's scheme, and that is to consider "An Eschatological Orientation" first because pentecostals live as an eschatologically oriented community, and thus view *all* of reality through eschatological lenses.[5]

*"My Soon-Coming King": Eschatological Orientation*

The eschatologically oriented imagination of pentecostals[6] has commonly manifested in the form of apocalyptic urgency. As such, the worldview inspired by pentecostal eschatology tends to be mission oriented—thus drawing our attention to its implications on humanity both individually and collectively for the sake of ministry

---

5. See Land, *Pentecostal Spirituality*, p. 56 wherein he states: "eschatology (and especially the apocalyptic vision) is neither an introduction nor a postscript to theology but a constituent part of the whole ... Pentecostal practices and beliefs are all under the apocalyptic vision which gave them ... focus." Amos Yong shares this sentiment and indeed applies this logic as he *begins* his systematic theology with a discussion on eschatological hope so that it runs throughout the monograph. See Amos Yong, *Renewing Christian Theology: Systematics for a Global Christianity* (Waco: Baylor University Press, 2014), p. 15. Here, Yong argues "the renewal of Christian theology ought to allow the Christian hope to inform and perhaps reform Christian theological reflection as a whole." I will, therefore, apply this logic to my construction of a pentecostal metaphysical worldview.

6. Pentecostalism's eschatology is doctrinally far from monolithic. Althouse notes that "its earliest expressions were closer to the tripartite millennialism of Joachim of Fiore mediated through Wesleyan sources, and covenantal eschatologies, articulated as the theology of the latter rain." See Peter Althouse, "The Landscape of Pentecostal and Charismatic Eschatology," in Peter Althouse and Amos Yong (eds), *Perspectives in Pentecostal Eschatologies* (Eugene: Wipf and Stock, 2010), p. 15. Present within early pentecostalism was an eschatological vision which believed that "as the new age dawned ... the Spirit would pour out spiritual gifts to empower Christians to prepare for the kingdom." See Peter Althouse, "Pentecostal Eschatology in Context: The Eschatological Orientation of the Full Gospel," in Peter Althouse and Robby Waddell (eds), *Perspective in Pentecostal Eschatologies* (Eugene: Wipf and Stock, 2010), pp. 210–11. This understanding has opened the door for later pentecostal theologians to converse with theologians of eschatological hope (Moltmann and others), which labor from the belief that the hopeful future is profoundly influencing and "breaking-in" to the present. Pentecostal theologians like Althouse, Land, Macchia, and Yong converse with these German theologians of eschatological hope for the sake of constructing an eschatological vision that is faithful to the pentecostal ethos. Room is afforded for them to do this precisely because "Pentecostal eschatology is diverse, both in its current manifestations. Latter rain, threefold dispensationalism, historic millennialism, covenantal and inaugural eschatologies are just some of the options Pentecostals employed to understand their role in god's plan for the world and the kingdom-to-come." See Althouse, "Pentecostal Eschatology in Context," p. 211. See also Larry McQueen, *Toward a Pentecostal Eschatology: Discerning the Way Forward* (Sheffield: Deo Publishing, 2012).

and mission.[7] More recently, however, pentecostal theologians have also explicitly opened up the conversation to touch on the *cosmic* implications of understanding the world through eschatologically oriented lenses, thus widening our reflection toward metaphysics. For example, laboring from his conviction that Pentecost is the core theological symbol for pentecostals, Vondey points out that "the motif of the outpouring of the Spirit orients the full gospel toward a 'cosmic Pentecost' where Spirit baptism identifies the power to accomplish the transformation of the whole creation toward its goal in Jesus Christ."[8] Frank Macchia holds a corresponding view, stating rather strongly that "the apocalyptic theological context of the Spirit's work in the New Testament ... makes a restriction of our pneumatological categories to personal, existential, and even ecclesial contexts unthinkable (cf. Rom. 8.18-25)."[9] To live by the Spirit, then, is to live proleptically toward the future of all things. Therefore, our imaginations must not only begin and end with eschatology but be thoroughgoingly infused with it, while remaining attentive to its cosmic implications. For Althouse, this task begins with rearticulating pentecostal theology "within the context of eschatological hope, in a way that the future hope of the entire cosmos is accessible in the present. In other words, the world and creation together is the context for eschatology and therefore any holistic eschatological construction must be founded in a creational eschatology."[10] The following survey of a pentecostal metaphysical worldview, therefore, will begin with and be infused by an "eschatological orientation" as it helps us make sense of our "vision of the whole" in light of our pneumatological, and therefore, trinitarian convictions.

*The Surprise of the Spirit: Radical Openness to God*

Because pentecostals are eschatologically oriented toward a *telos* we can only know in part, our metaphysical disposition is one that is shaped by a radical openness to God. For pentecostals, to be open to God is to live with the expectation of being

---

7. Indeed, this is displayed by the fact that Smith uses the words "mission and justice" in this element of a pentecostal worldview. See Smith, *Thinking in Tongues,* p. 44. Of course, Smith includes "mission and justice" because he is drawing on the work of Land, Faupel, and Althouse, which all give voice to the mission-oriented character of pentecostal apocalyptic urgency. See Land, *Pentecostal Spirituality*, pp. 58–121; D. William Faupel, *The Everlasting Gospel: The Significance of Eschatology in the Development of Pentecostal Thought* (Sheffield: Sheffield Academic Press, 1996); and Peter Althouse, *Spirit of the Last Days: Pentecostal Eschatology in Conversation with Jurgen Moltmann* (London: T&T Clark, 2003). See also, Byron Klaus, "The Holy Spirit and Mission Is Eschatological Perspective: A Pentecostal Viewpoint," *Pneuma* 27.2 (2005), pp. 322–42; Julie Ma, "Eschatology and Mission: Living in the 'Last Days' Today," *Transformation* 26.3 (2009), pp. 186–98.

8. Vondey, *Pentecostal Theology*, p. 163.

9. Frank D. Macchia, *Baptized in the Spirit: A Global Pentecostal Theology* (Grand Rapids, MI: Zondervan, 2006), p. 102.

10. Peter Althouse, "Pentecostal Eschatology in Context," p. 206.

surprised by him—to understand that from our perspective he will act in ways that are different and new.[11] The radical pentecostal openness of being surprised by God is explicitly displayed in our defining theological narrative–identified above as the full gospel. The full gospel is based on interconnected and perennially new pentecostal experiences. It tells the story of a God who "breaks into" our world in unexpected ways to save, sanctify, transform, and heal us as foretastes of what is to come at the King's eschatological appearance. This openness need not be confined to our understanding of God's activity toward humanity alone; as Smith rightly observes, "If it is an essential feature of pentecostal belief and practice to be open to God's surprises, this presupposes a sense that the universe and natural world must also remain *open systems*."[12]

*Signs and Wonders: Enchanted Theology of Creation*

We have now arrived at Smith's third element of a pentecostal worldview, "an enchanted theology of creation." The central claim of this element is that "endemic to a pentecostal worldview is the implicit affirmation of the dynamic, active presence of the Spirit not only in the church, but also in creation. And not only the Spirit, but also other spirits."[13] At a second level of discourse, then, according to Kärkkäinen, "What is needed could be called a 'plural' pneumatology: it is mindful of the meaning, role, and effects of other spirits vis-à-vis, along with, and as opposed to the Spirit of God."[14] I would hasten to add that what is also needed is a metaphysical account of the kind of being and agency these spirits have; especially in light of Yong's desire to remain conversant with various religious contexts across the globe—such as Africa, Asia, and Latin America—where rapid "pentecostalization" happened in part because, like pentecostals, the spirits posited by the local religious worldview(s) permeate all aspects of life.[15]

---

11. See Chris E. W. Green, *Surprised by God: How and Why What We Think about the Divine Matters* (Eugene: Cascade Books, 2018).

12. Smith, *Thinking in Tongues*, p. 86 (emphases original).

13. Smith, *Thinking in Tongues*, p. 39.

14. Veli-Matti Kärkkäinen, "Spirit(s) in Contemporary Christian Theology: An Interim Report of Unbinding of Pneumatology," in Veli-Matti Kärkkäinen, Kirsteen Kim, and Amos Yong (eds), *Interdisciplinary and Religio-cultural Discourses on a Spirit-Filled World: Loosing the Spirits* (New York: Palgrave Macmillan US, 2013), p. 29.

15. Kärkkäinen, "Spirit(s) in Contemporary Christian Theology," p. 33. Yong has written extensively on this matter. For Yong's standard monograph-length theology of religions, see Yong, *Discerning the Spirit(s)*; *Beyond the Impasse*. For pentecostal accounts of the spirits in Africa, parts of Asia, and Latin America see the collection of essays in Veli-Matti Kärkkäinen, Kirsteen Kim, and Amos Yong (eds), *Interdisciplinary and Religio-cultural Discourses on a Spirit-Filled World: Loosing the Spirits* (New York: Palgrave Macmillan Publishers, 2013); Martin Lindhardt, *Pentecostalism in Africa: Presence and Impact of Pneumatic Christianity in Postcolonial Societies* (Leiden: Brill, 2015); and Cecil M. Robeck and Amos Yong (eds), *The Cambridge Companion to Pentecostalism* (New York: Cambridge University Press, 2014).

Pentecostals presume benevolent angelic intervention,[16] as well as malevolent demonic and satanic disruption which inevitably lead to incarnate beings interacting with disincarnate ones through means of warfare or cooperation.[17] Moreover, many pentecostals extend beyond this understanding and believe in intermediary disincarnate spirits, often believed to belong to the deceased.[18] When the above is considered, pentecostal spirituality once again calls for a counterinterpretation; this time it is for an imagination geared toward a pluralistic spirit-filled cosmos wherein corporeal and incorporeal agents actively engage with and exercise influence over each other.

*The Hem of His Garment: Nondualistic Affirmation of Embodiment and Materiality*

For pentecostals, the promises of God are not to be confined to spiritual matters. Indeed, these promises are understood to be pregnant with good news for physical bodies, communities, and all of material reality.[19] Nowhere is this more apparent in pentecostal spirituality than in the central first-level affirmation of divine healing.[20] The implication of this belief fundamentally deconstructs a Manichean dualism

---

16. Carolyn Denise Baker, "Created Spirit Beings: Angels," in Stanley Horton (ed.), *Systematic Theology* (Springfield, MO: Logion Press, 1995), pp. 179-94.

17. See appendices A and B in Craig Keener, *Miracles: The Credibility of the New Testament Accounts*, 2 vols (Grand Rapids, MI: Baker Academic, 2011), pp. 769-856; Charles Kraft, "Spiritual Warfare: A Neocharismatic Perspective," in Stanley M. Burgess and Eduard M. van der Mass (eds), *The New International Dictionary of Pentecostal Charismatic Movements* (Grand Rapids: Zondervan, 2002), pp. 1091-6. Pentecostals are sympathetic to the demonologies and warfare theologies posited below: Gregory A. Boyd, *God at War: The Bible and Spiritual Conflict* (Downers Grove, IL: InterVarsity 1997); *Satan and the Problem of Evil: Constructing a Trinitarian Warfare Theodicy* (Downers Grove, IL: InterVarsity 2001); Felicitas Goodman, *How about Demons? Possession and Exorcism in the Modern World* (Bloomington: Indiana University Press, 1988); Peter Kreeft, *Angels and Demons: What Do We Really Know about Them?* (San Francisco: Ignatius, 1995); Stephen F. Noll, *Angels of Light, Powers of Darkness: Thinking Biblically about Angels, Satan, and Principalities* (Downers Grove, IL: Intervarsity, 1998).

18. See, for example, Amos Yong, "Going Where the Spirit Goes: Engaging the Spirit(s) in J.C. Ma's Pneumatological Missiology," *JPT* 10.2 (2002), pp. 110-28.

19. The term "prosperity gospel" comes to mind here, and it is indeed a charged one. For a nuanced and responsible engagement with the phrase, see James K. A. Smith, "What's Right with the Prosperity Gospel"? *Calvin Theological Seminary Forum* (Fall 2009).

20. See Vernon L. Purdy, "Divine Healing," in Stanley Horton (ed.), *Systematic Theology* (Springfield, MO: Logion Press, 1995), pp. 489-523.

which "sees material reality—both bodies and material elements associated with bodies (sexuality, the arts)—as fundamentally bad or evil, and therefore, something to be avoided, suppressed, and ultimately escaped."[21] The full gospel contrastingly values the whole person and *all* of created reality as good—which includes real, mental, and spiritual beings. Indeed, Christ is creator, savior, and healer of all things.

### *"This Is My Story, This Is My Song": Affective, Narrative Epistemology*

Pentecostal theologians have argued that there cannot be a distinct pentecostal theology without a distinct pentecostal epistemology.[22] As such, there have been some attempts to construct one.[23] What has emerged are pentecostal epistemic visions that value experiences, narratives, and the "pneumatological imagination" in communal context as pentecostal means of knowing. Regarding experience, the pentecostal definition is a holistic one, so that experience is understood as "a complex conscious, affective, psychological phenomenon, involving both cognitive awareness of external events and internal physiological, affective, and conscious reactions to such events."[24]

Smith's vision of what constitutes a pentecostal epistemology is methodologically intent on keeping with the implications of pentecostal spirituality itself for the sake of developing a distinctly pentecostal epistemology.[25] He identifies narrative, affections, and embodiment as crucial components of the pentecostal means of knowledge. Let us first trace Smith's understanding of how narrative functions in pentecostal spirituality.

The day of Pentecost itself, which remains *the* central biblical narrative for the pentecostal imagination (Acts 2), displays Peter making sense of the unfolding

---

21. Smith, *Thinking in Tongues*, p. 42.

22. Land, *Pentecostal Spirituality*, p. 184; Kenneth J. Archer, *The Gospel Revisited* (Eugene, OR: Pickwick Publishing, 2011), p. 7; Veli-Matti Kärkkäinen, "Epistemology, Ethos and Environment: In Search of a Theology of Pentecostal Education," *Pneuma* 34.2 (2012), pp. 248–50.

23. Cheryl Bridges Johns, *Pentecostal Formation: A Pedagogy among the Oppressed* (Sheffield, UK: Sheffield Academic Press, 1993); Paul W. Lewis, "Towards a Pentecostal Epistemology," *The Spirit & Church* 2.1 (May 2000), pp. 95–125; Mark J. Cartledge, *Practical Theology: Charismatic and Empirical Theology* (London: Paternoster, 2003), pp. 41–68.

24. Stephen Parker, *Led by the Spirit* (Sheffield: Sheffield Academic Press, 1996), p. 15.

25. He describes his approach as a kind of "ethnography" which attempts to trace a community's means of knowing a God who never ceases to surprise. See James K. A. Smith, "Pentecostalism: Epistemic Fit and Pentecostal Experience," in William J. Abraham and Frederick D. Aquino (eds), *The Oxford Handbook of the Epistemology of Theology* (Oxford: Oxford University Press, 2017), pp. 606–18.

events by fitting them into a larger, received narrative.[26] The pentecostal identity is formed by means of story, and "this narrative understanding of God's action yielded a practice that was integral to pentecostal worship: testimony."[27] Smith argues that through testimony, pentecostals imply their own epistemic grammar; and "this incipient epistemology is not anti*rational*, but antirational*ist*; it is not a critique or rejection of reason as such but rather a commentary on a particularly reductionistic model of reason and rationality, a limited, stunted version of what counts as 'knowledge.'"[28] As such, a Cartesian divorce of the mind from the body does not hold in pentecostal spirituality; persons are not primarily "thinking things"; therefore, truth is not merely formed in mental propositions but in *embodied* experiences and received narratives that mutually inform each other.[29] There are epistemological implications in the affirmation of embodiment, narrative, and the rejection of dualism. "For the pentecostal practice of testimony, narrative is not just a decorative form, a creative medium … The truth *is* the story; the narrative *is* the knowledge."[30] We must not allow the tendency of modernity—that is, to immediately distill story into propositional truths—to devalue the primacy of narrative.

---

26. Ken Archer states that the pentecostal use of narrative highlights "the importance of understanding Scripture as a grand meta-narrative with the Gospels and Acts as the heart of the Christian story. Jesus Christ is the center and leader of Christianity; therefore, a narrative theology will emphasize the priority of the story of Jesus Christ and its significance for the Christian community and for the world." See Kenneth J. Archer, "Nourishment for Our Journey: The Pentecostal *via Salutis* and Sacramental Ordinances," in Chris E. W. Green (ed.), *Pentecostal Ecclesiology: A Reader* (Boston: Brill, 2016), p. 145.

27. Smith, *Thinking in Tongues*, p. 51. Testimony has been a crucial component of pentecostalism. Indeed, the first edition of the *Journal for Pentecostal Theology* describes testimony as "the poetry of the Pentecostal tradition"; see Rickie D. Moore, John Christopher Thomas, and Steven J. Land, "Editorial," *JPT* 1 (1992), pp. 3–5. Furthermore, Scott A. Ellington's work argues that the pentecostal use of narrative and experience as mutually informing is in continuity with that of Israel's relationship with narrative and experience. See Scott A. Ellington, "The Reciprocal Reshaping of History and Experience in the Psalms: Interactions with Pentecostal Testimony," *JPT* 16.1 (October 2007), pp. 18–31; and Scott A. Ellington, "'Can I Get a Witness?': The Myth of Pentecostal Orality and the Process of Traditioning in the Psalms," *JPT* 20 (2011), pp. 1–14.

28. Smith, *Thinking in Tongues*, 53.

29. See James K. A. Smith, *Desiring the Kingdom: Worship, Worldview, and Cultural Formation* (Grand Rapids: Baker Academic, 2009), ch. 2. In this sense, Smith argues that pentecostalism is postmodern because it critiques modern rationalism. See James K. A. Smith, *Who's Afraid of Postmodernism? Taking Derrida, Lyotard, and Foucault to Church* (Grand Rapids: Baker Academic, 2006), pp. 59–80.

30. Smith, *Thinking in Tongues*, p. 64.

Narrative knowledge is intricately tied to emotions. It "works on this affective register precisely because the emotions are themselves already 'construals' of the world. The emotions are already hermeneutic filters, 'noncognitive affective appraisals' doing the work of interpreting our world."[31] Put differently, our affective registers combined with our micronarratives (testimonies), and macronarrative (the biblical narrative), work together to make sense of the world. This implicit truth is embodied in the practice of testimony, and varied practices around the pentecostal altar. "In short, we *feel* our way around the world more than we *think* about it, *before* we think about it."[32]

Now that a brief review of what pentecostal theologians have said about metaphysics within Smith's categories has been sketched, the following section will primarily focus on the work of Amos Yong by fitting his vision within Smith's five categories, as well. Again, methodologically, Smith's categories will feature prominently as the scaffolding for constructing a pentecostal metaphysics throughout. Yong, as we will see in the following section and throughout this work, is a key figure in laying the groundwork for developing a more comprehensive metaphysical vision that is both philosophically sophisticated and attentive to pentecostal proclivities. I will begin, then, by sketching Yong's vision along with a brief display of his preeminence as one upon whom like-minded pentecostal theologians deeply depend—or at least, converse with—for their own metaphysical grounding.

### *Groundwork for Pentecostal Metaphysics: Amos Yong's Foundational Pneumatology*

#### *In the Beginning Was the Spirit: Foundational Pneumatology*

While some pentecostal theologians have recognized the aptness of beginning theological and metaphysical reflection from an eschatological perspective, few have labored to holistically apply it in their monographs, instead devoting sections of their work to cosmic reflection.[33] Amos Yong is the exception as he is the main

---

31. Smith, *Thinking in Tongues*, pp. 65–6.

32. Smith, *Thinking in Tongues*, p. 72.

33. For examples, see Daniel Castelo, *Pneumatology: A Guide for the Perplexed* (London: Bloomsbury T&T Clark, 2015), pp. 65–80; Vondey, *Pentecostal Theology*, pp. 155–74; Macchia, *Baptized in the Spirit*, pp. 38–48, pp. 101–7. It is also worth noting that some of the pentecostals who have labored to discuss this matter have done so in theological essays. As helpful as their work is, due to the brief nature of essays they cannot detail what a holistic and cosmic eschatologically oriented metaphysics might look like. See Veli-Matti Kärkkäinen, "Spirit(s) in Contemporary Christian Theology: An Interim Report of the Unbinding of Pneumatology," in Veli-Matti Kärkkäinen, Kirsteen Kim, and Amos Yong (eds), *Interdisciplinary and Religio-cultural Discourses on a Spirit-Filled World: Loosing the*

pentecostal theologian to detail a holistic metaphysical vision undergirded by his trinitarian theology. Yong will therefore serve as our chief interlocutor—with other pentecostal voices joining the conversation—within Smith's "five elements of a pentecostal worldview" for the sake of discerning the metaphysical vision(s) of pentecostals to date. Of course, Yong himself does not explicate that he aims to construct a pentecostal metaphysics. That few, if any, pentecostals have engaged in this explicit work demonstrates the purpose of this present work. That said, as I will note later, Yong's Christian formation took place within a pentecostal context and his work is deeply pneumatological: privileging the Holy Spirit in experience, and the doctrine of the Holy Spirit in theology. Moreover, his work touches on metaphysics at various points; thus, I explicate the metaphysics in his work as I read it.

Like many pentecostal theologians, Yong postulates a close relatedness between eschatology and the Spirit's work.[34] This stance, combined with his conviction that pentecostals ought to be involved in the science and religion dialogue,[35] and his interest in a global theology of religions,[36] all underlie the construction

*Spirits* (New York: Palgrave, 2013), pp. 29–40; Jeffrey Schloss, "Hovering over Waters: Spirit and the Ordering of Creation," in Michael Welker (ed.), *The Spirit in Creation and New Creation: Science and Theology in Western Orthodox Realms* (Grand Rapids, MI: Eerdmans, 2012), pp. 26–49; Matthew K. Thompson, *Kingdom Come: Revisioning Pentecostal Eschatology*, JPTS 37 (Blandford Forum, UK: Deo, 2010), pp. 137–40.

34. He states, for example, "Paul explicitly connects cosmic salvation of all creation in and the human redemption of the body with the work and groanings of the Spirit of God (Rom. 8.19-23). Meanwhile the Spirit not only heralds the day of the Lord through the Messiah (Luke 4.19) but also works to bring it about. Indeed, the arrival of the day of the Lord is a thoroughly pneumatological event that transforms all creation (Isa. 32.15-16)." See Yong, *The Spirit Poured Out on All Flesh*, p. 95.

35. See Amos Yong (ed.), *The Spirit Renews the Face of the Earth: Pentecostal Forays in Science and Theology of Creation* (Eugene, OR: Pickwick Publications, 2009); Wolfgang Vondey, "A Passion for the Spirit: Amos Yong and the Theology and Science Dialogue," in Wolfgang Vondey and Martin Mittelstadt (eds), *The Theology of Amos Yong and the New Face of Pentecostal Scholarship: Passion for the Spirit* (Leiden: Brill, 2013), pp. 179-97; James K. A. Smith and Amos Yong (eds), *Science and the Spirit: A Pentecostal Engagement with the Sciences* (Bloomington: Indiana University Press, 2010).

36. See Amos Yong, *The Spirit Poured Out on All Flesh*; Amos Yong, *Beyond the Impasse: Toward a Pneumatological Theology of Religions* (Eugene, OR: Wipf & Stock, 2014, 2003); Amos Yong, *The Cosmic Breath: Spirit and Nature in the Christianity-Buddhism-Science Trialogue* (Leiden: Brill, 2012); Amos Yong, *Discerning the Spirit(s): A Pentecostal-Charismatic Contribution to Christian Theology of Religions* (Sheffield: Sheffield Academic Press, 2000); Amos Yong, *Hospitality and the Other: Pentecost, Christian Practices, and the Neighbor* (Maryknoll, NY: Orbis Books, 2008).

of what he calls a "foundational pneumatology."³⁷ Fundamentally, foundational pneumatology is Yong's way of accounting for the God–world relationship from a decidedly pneumatological perspective, animated by a "hope to arrive at the rudiments of a universal rationality, albeit one that is consciously anti-totalitarian precisely because … it is pneumatological."³⁸ Its pneumatological character, says Yong, creates space for a "diversity of tongues"—read: traditions, cultures, discourses, and methods of inquiry—in the quest for truth about reality. It thus "proceeds from what Peirce called a 'contrite fallibilism' wherein all knowledge is provisional, relative to the questions posed by the community of inquirers, and subject to the ongoing process of conversation and discovery."³⁹

Pentecostal theologian, Nimi Wariboko, lands on strikingly similar metaphysical and epistemological convictions, he simply does so while privileging and emphasizing social ethics. For Wariboko, the "pentecostal principle" is pentecostalism's—albeit locally embodied, fragmentary, perspectival—universally significant *transformative* principle. He defines it as that which "expresses the fluid dynamics of spirit and the conditions of creative emergence in the infinite fabric of life."⁴⁰ The concept of "emergence" is his grounding metaphysics for positing a vision of reality that is "incomplete," and so ontologically open to endless creativity. I will unpack this notion of emergence in more detail later, but for now I will simply note that emergence is a key correspondent metaphysical concept for both Yong and Wariboko. Moreover, the ontological openness of creation, says Wariboko, is connected to a unique understanding of God's "being" via pentecostal practices. Pentecostal practices at the "grassroots level," along with the ontological openness just described tacitly posit a God more aligned with open theism or some forms of process theology, than with the God of "classical theism,"

---

37. See Amos Yong, "On Divine Presence and Divine Agency: Toward a Foundational Pneumatology," *AJPS* 3.2 (2000), pp. 167–88; Amos Yong, *Spirit-Word-Community: Theological Hermeneutics in Trinitarian Perspective* (Eugene, OR: Wipf & Stock, 2002), pp. 83–118.

38. Yong, *SWC*, p. 84. Yong predicates his foundational pneumatology—for the sake of constructing an "anti-totalitarian" metaphysics—on a trinitarian vision which integrates Irenaeus' notion of Spirit and Word as the "two hands of God," with Augustine's model of the Spirit as "the bond of love" between Father and Son. These models combine to posit a coinhering, nonhierarchical Godhead. Integrating these models into a theology which privileges pneumatology establishes for Yong a vision of being and reality that takes seriously (1) the relationality of the Spirit, (2) the rationality of the Spirit, and (3) the dynamism of the Spirit's activity in the world. See Yong, *SWC*, pp. 83–118.

39. Amos Yong, "On Divine Presence and Divine Agency," p. 168; cf. Amos Yong, "The Demise of Foundationalism and the Retention of Truth: What Evangelicals Can Learn from C.S. Peirce," *Christian Scholar's Review* 29.4 (2000).

40. Nimi Wariboko, *The Pentecostal Principle: Ethical Methodology in New Spirit* (Grand Rapids: Eerdmans, 2012), p. 4.

as he understands it.[41] I must note here that Yong himself engages at length with process theology via Alfred North Whitehead, which I will say more about in the following chapter. Another similarity between Yong and Wariboko is that they understand the "diversity of tongues" in Acts 2 to affirm a pluralistic openness to a variety of discourses, traditions, and disciplines in discerning truth about an "open" and "gappy" reality. As Wariboko engages the Acts 2 narrative, he says, "Their number and the diversity of the tongues point to the irreducibly pluralistic nature of the power of the new. No one individual, entity, or institution is capable of incarnating it alone."[42] The pentecostal principle thus functions as an ecstatic and synthesizing[43] "principle of existence." That is, a principle of excessive, creative restlessness, an *emergent* de-absolutizing creativity that deeply resonates with Yong's future-opening, and discourse-enabling, foundational pneumatology. And, as we will briefly discuss later, Wariboko's pentecostal principle also resonates with Yong's pneumatological imagination.

Back to Yong. Once again, because his perspective is both trinitarian and pneumatologically focused, it is also eschatological. This point is crucial when following Yong's interdisciplinary dialogues.[44] Thinking christologically, pneumatologically, and therefore eschatologically grounds the conversation in the life of Jesus, so that Jesus' resurrection is the down payment of the promise of the future resurrection of *all things*. Therefore, the Christian faith contains at once an anticipatory element that looks "back" at the life, death, and resurrection of Jesus, and also looks "forward" to the resurrection of all things.[45] Yong suggests that if these convictions take hold, "then divine action 'works' unlike material or efficient causes proceeding from the past toward the present, proleptically (or teleologically, to use Aristotelian terms) in anticipation of the future."[46] So if the question raised by some in the science and theology dialogue is, can the resurrection as a divine act of God in history be susceptible to historical investigation? The answer is

---

41. See Nimi Wariboko, *The Split God: Pentecostalism and Critical Theory* (Albany: SUNY Press, 2018), pp. 44. He says so explicitly in p. 203n.57.

42. Wariboko, *Pentecostal Principle*, p. 20. For a longer engagement of this text and how it ties into Wariboko's overall method, ethics, and ontology, see Wariboko, *The Split God*, pp. 21–44.

43. That is, the synthesizing pentecostal principle: synthesizing the Tillichian "Catholic substance," and "Protestant principle." See Wariboko, *Pentecostal Principle*, pp. 42–70.

44. Especially the science and theology dialogue via the Divine Action Project (DAP) of the 1980s which involved both theologians and scientists. The hope of this group was to give empirical objectivity for God's action in the world, and it was assumed that the "laws of nature" could point to the theological means by which God sustains the world. See Amos Yong, *The Spirit of Creation: Modern Science and Divine Action in the Pentecostal Imagination* (Grand Rapids: Eerdmans, 2011), pp. 72–102.

45. Yong, *The Spirit of Creation*, p. 87.

46. Yong, *The Spirit of Creation*, p. 87.

no. The resurrection is an eschatological reality which belongs to *new* creation, and therefore cannot be fully empirically measured in this one. Yong suggests that this eschatologically oriented worldview does not disable the science and theology dialogue, but rather shifts the venue of inquiry to pentecostal perspectives on God's action in and through the life of the church. Following Polkinghorne's liturgy-assisted logic,[47] Yong says that the pentecostal community's experiences of the Spirit "provide historical, liturgical, experiential, and eschatological frames of reference to rethink fundamental notions of God's actions in the world."[48] This shift further affirms the relatedness of first- and second-level discourse for the sake of constructing a metaphysical vision. Further solidifying this crucial conceptual move, Yong says, "the basic elements of pentecostal piety and spirituality are deeply shaped by the charismatic works of the Spirit that signal the impending arrival of the eschatological kingdom."[49]

Despite Yong's recognition that there are certain unascertainable realities for science in Christian discourse, he elsewhere insists that theology must "translate its convictions into public discourse accessible to those without the community of faith and to provide for some means to clarify the validity of these interconnections" because "all truth is God's truth and therefore communicable universally and verifiable in other tongues."[50] Yong goes on to insist that for the sake of public discourse, what is needed is "a mediating discourse that allows for translation between the language of science and that of theology," thus "what we are calling for is a mutual context, a context as wide as the creation itself and amenable to the languages of the natural world, of the sciences, and of theology."[51] To foreshadow once again, I will later note that unfortunately, I cannot follow Yong on this point—at least, in part, due to my imposed methodological limits. The particularity of the church, its message, its risen savior, and its practices bespeak a cosmic vision of the whole (including nature) that only makes sense in light of its *radically decisive* eschatological consummation. Moreover, Yong's understanding of the science and theology dialogue anticipates important questions that will later be raised in my constructive section below. To briefly anticipate, I will show that despite Yong's affirmation of the inability of science to discern eschatological realities, he elsewhere identifies eschatology and teleology as "modes of reasoning" about eschatological divine action in an ontologically "gappy" natural world. In Yong's liturgy-assisted logic above, there is seemingly more of a decisive difference between eschatology over against teleology, or final causality. Elsewhere in his work, there is a much stronger correlation between the realities just named, so that Yong sometimes understands eschatology (or perhaps some eschatological realities) as a theological

---

47. John Polkinghorne, *Science and the Trinity: The Christian Encounter with Reality* (New Haven: Yale University Press, 2002), pp. 118–42.
48. Yong, *The Spirit of Creation*, p. 92.
49. Yong, *The Spirit of Creation*, pp. 92–3.
50. Yong, *All Flesh*, p. 283.
51. Yong, *All Flesh*, p. 283.

rendition for what science (non-reductively conceived) might call teleology or final causality. Again, more on this in my constructive section.

### The Spirit and Nature: Pneumatological Naturalism

Amos Yong and James KA Smith are the primary pentecostal theologians who have attempted to construct a metaphysics which posits the "natural world" as an open system.[52] Their aims compel them to do so in conversation with modern science.[53] In constructing a worldview that is consistent to a vision of the world as an open system, they agree that regnant naturalisms contain antithetical presuppositions that make faithful speech about the God–world relation difficult for pentecostals.[54] Lay pentecostals who adopt naturalism as self-evident cannot help but posit dualistic and Deistic supernaturalisms and naturalisms of various types. God's acts in the world are thus understood as "interventions," "miracles," and "supernatural," in a cosmos that is made to function autonomously without the Spirit of God's *immediate, constant, and providential sustainment*. What is needed, then, is a reconstructed vision of the world in which "*Spirit-matters are the most natural things there are*," that is, "*(n)ature is Spirit-graced to its core so that what is fundamentally characteristic of nature is that it is Spirit-related. If these claims hold, then 'interventionism' is illogical in that the natural is itself miraculous*."[55] For Smith, this means that for pentecostals, nature ought to be redefined in light of pneumatology, so that God does not merely intervene in "the so-called order of nature; rather … the Spirit is always already at work in creation, animating (and reanimating) bodies, grabbing hold of vocal cords, taking up aspects of creation to manifest the glory of God."[56]

---

52. That is to say, the natural world and its functional laws may be "disrupted" (i.e., miracles), and these disruptions need not be understood as God intervening upon a closed system designed to function mechanistically without him. Rather, these surprising events are better understood as witnessing to nature's Spirit-infusedness so that the possibility of surprise is built into the natural system itself.

53. Smith and Yong respect that the modern world has benefited profoundly from the sciences and correct the pentecostal tendency to dismiss them. However, neither do Smith and Yong want pentecostals to succumb to a naturalistic worldview. Their work seeks to make helpful distinctions between science as a discipline, and naturalism as a worldview so that pentecostals called to engage the sciences can do so *as pentecostals* without contradiction. Smith and Yong, (eds), *Science and the Spirit*; Yong, (ed.), *The Spirit Renews the Face of the Earth*.

54. For Smith's understanding of naturalism(s), see James K. A. Smith, "Is There Room for Surprise in the Natural World?" in James K. A. Smith, Amos Yong (eds), *Science and the Spirit: A Pentecostal Engagement with the Sciences* (Bloomington: Indiana University Press, 2010), pp. 34–49; and Smith, *Thinking in Tongues*, pp. 86–99. For Amos Yong's understanding of naturalism(s), see *The Spirit of Creation*, pp. 102–18.

55. Castelo, *Pneumatology*, pp. 74–5 (emphases original).

56. Smith, *Thinking in Tongues*, p. 101.

Like Smith, Yong recognizes that a new account of "nature" and how it functions is necessary to avoid the pitfalls of an interventionist, God-of-the-gaps account of the God–world relation. When dialoguing with Smith, he provides a "pneumatological assist" to his initial proposal of "participatory ontology" for better understanding God's activity in the natural world.[57] Yong's own construct, however, begins with positing a universe that is not rigidly governed by immutable scientific "laws" as conceived in a mechanistic world devoid of "final causes"; and he does this in conversation with Charles Sanders Peirce's triadic metaphysics.[58] Pushing back on the notion that Darwinian natural selection could give a full account of evolutionary progress, according to Yong, Peirce argued that Darwin's vision lacked a sufficiently open-ended final cause to make room for the emergence of novelty.[59] "Natural laws," for Peirce, are not precise blueprints, but are evolving habits and general pathways constituted by adventitious events so that they exist as indeterminate possibilities. Therefore, "the laws of nature are habitual tendencies that function teleologically like final causes."[60] From Yong's reading of Peirce's insights, along with Yong's previous arguments raised from his dialogue with the DAP, "what emerges is a pneumatological and charismatic view of divine action that sees the Holy Spirit as working in and through nature and its laws, but also proleptically and continually transforming such in anticipation of the general shape of the coming kingdom."[61] Yong believes this vision allows for a theology of miraculous divine action "that is consistent with the laws of nature as understood by modern science on the one hand, but that also preserves fundamental Christian commitments about God's redemptive presence and activity in the world on the other."[62] I will lay this out in further detail in the next chapter.

---

57. I will treat each of their visions by themselves along with their dialogue in greater depth later. For Smith's participatory ontology, see James K. A. Smith, *Introducing Radical Orthodoxy: Mapping a Post-Secular Theology* (Grand Rapids, MI: Baker Academic, 2004); for Yong's "pneumatological assist," see Amos Yong, "Radically Orthodox, Reformed, and Pentecostal: Rethinking the Intersection of Post/modernity and the Religions in Conversation with James K.A. Smith," *JPT* 15 (2007), pp. 233–50; for Smith's appreciative response, see James K. A. Smith, "The Spirit, Religions, and the World as Sacrament: A Response to Amos Yong's Pneumatological Assist," *JPT* 15 (2007), pp. 251–61.

58. See Yong, *SWC*, pp. 91–6; Yong, *The Spirit of Creation*, pp. 118–32.

59. Yong, *The Spirit of Creation*, p. 120. Elsewhere, Yong provides a reading of Genesis 1 and 2 that is fitted to Clayton's theory of emergence for the sake of affirming the world's openness to its future. See Amos Yong, "*Ruach*, the Primordial Waters, and the Breath of Life: Emergence Theory and the Creation Narratives in Pneumatological Perspective," in Michael Welker (ed.), *The Work of the Spirit: Pneumatology and Pentecostalism* (Grand Rapids: Eerdmans, 2006), pp. 183–204; Yong, *The Spirit of Creation*, pp. 133–72.

60. Yong, *The Spirit of Creation*, p. 124.

61. Yong, *The Spirit of Creation*, p. 125.

62. Yong, *The Spirit of Creation*, pp. 131–2.

## The Spirit and Spirits: Cosmic Pneumatology

Yong will remain our primary interlocutor as he has developed a philosophical grounding designed to make metaphysical sense of a cosmos populated with interactive spirits.[63] To accomplish this, he relies heavily on an adapted version of Philip Clayton's philosophy of emergence[64] combined with Nancey Murphey's concept of supervenience—still, undergirded by Peirce's triadic metaphysics.[65] Yong's conversations with the aforementioned deserve to be unpacked in brief detail as his is the most exhaustive pentecostal attempt to provide a coherent second-level metaphysical account of an enchanted cosmos. According to Yong, emergence theory "helps us see how the higher and more complex levels of reality appear unpredictably from, and are constituted and self-organized by, lower-level parts yet activate novel properties and even behaviors that are not explicable in terms of the sum of those parts."[66] Going further, Yong draws from Nancey Murphy and gives an analogy of the relationship between the mind and brain to help clarify how emergent realities relate to their lower-level constituents: The mind and brain exist in a relationship of "supervenience"—wherein "higher-level properties (mind) supervene on lower-level properties (brain) if they are partially

---

63. As expected, his convictions lead him to do so in conversation with science which will influence his philosophical constructs. To build the empirical side of his argument, he utilizes the discipline of parapsychology and the research it provides of the "big five" psi phenomena. Yong notes that the kind of empirical investigation these phenomena call for is not laboratory evidence, but eyewitness and case study accounts, and therefore count as evidence of the "intersubjectively observable kind." See Yong, *Spirit of Creation*, pp. 175–96. Craig Keener's work follows a similar approach as he too puts much weight on eyewitness accounts. See Keener, *Miracles* vols 1 and 2.

64. See Philip Clayton, *Mind and Emergence: From Quantum to Consciousness* (Oxford: Oxford University Press, 2004); "The Emergence of Spirit," *CTNS Bulletin* 20.4 (2000), pp. 3–20; *In Quest of Freedom: The Emergence of Spirit in the Natural World*, Religion Theologie and Naturwissenschaft/Religion Theology and Natural Science 13 (Gottingen: Vandenhoeck & Ruprecht, 2009); *Adventures in the Spirit: God, World, Divine Action* (Minneapolis: Fortress, 2008); Philip Clayton and Paul Davies (eds), *The Re-emergence of Emergence: The Emergentist Hypothesis from Science to Religion* (Oxford: Oxford University Press, 2006).

65. Nancey Murphy, *Anglo-American Postmodernity: Philosophical Perspectives on Science, Religion, and Ethics* (Boulder, CO: Westview Press, 1997); "Supervenience and the Nonreduciblity of Ethics to Biology," in Robert John Russell, William R. Stoeger, S.J., and Francisco J. Ayala (eds), *Evolutionary and Molecular Biology: Scientific Perspectives on Divine Action* (Vatican City State: Vatican Observatory Publications; Berkeley: Center for Theology and the Natural Sciences, 1998), pp. 463–89; and "Nonreductive Physicalism: Philosophical Issues," in Warren S. Brown, Nancey Murphy and H. Newton Malony (ed.), *Whatever Happened to the Soul? Scientific and Theological Portraits of Human Nature* (Minneapolis: Fortress, 1998), pp. 127–48.

66. Yong, *Spirit of Creation*, pp. 58–9.

constituted by the lower-level properties but are not directly reducible to them."[67] Supervenience, then, gives language to what happens when an emergent—self-conscious, morally responsible, teleologically directed—reality freely exercises influence over the material realities from which it emerged.[68] This process indicates the emergence of the spirit of individual persons and communal collective groups. Yong uses this construct—along with insights from Walter Wink—to suggest that the spirits that emerge from these individuals, communities, and institutions are indeed what pentecostals know to be principalities, powers, angels, demons, and intermediary spirits.

I would be remiss if I did not here remind the reader of Wariboko's use of Yong's (irreducible) emergence as a grounding for his ethical methodology.[69] He briefly "adds" to Yong's metaphysical reflection on emergence, an exploration of the *teleological character* of the pentecostal principle. Wariboko, like Yong, redefines teleology to not be synonymous with "final cause" as it pertains to "fixed essence"; rather, in conversation with Peirce (Thirdness), teleology denotes realities like dynamism, possibility, unpredictability, and novelty. From here he argues that there is a "gap" between "facticity" and "intelligibility." "As finite human beings, our knowledge of this gap is ... only knowledge *of something* ... and thus in thinking of the telos of emergence we easily reach the limit of knowledge. We are confounded by the fact of emergence."[70] For Wariboko, the phenomenon of emergence provokes wonder. "Since it is not reducible to its earlier parts, emergence in a very crude sense has the ring of enigma of *creatio ex nihilo*. This wonder is related to the gap."[71] The notion of "gap" might ring familiar as I briefly mentioned Yong's notion of an ontologically "gappy" world above. Connecting the dots, we find that Wariboko appropriates a metaphysics which privileges potency over act, becoming over being, and novelty over "fixity." Therefore, "What emergence creates is relation, the groundless ground of being ex-posed, of being with others."[72] Furthermore, Wariboko here related emergence to a modified understanding of *creatio ex nihilo* posited by Yong, which he developed in conversation with his reading of the creation narratives in Genesis.[73] Once again, Yong's preeminence for some pentecostals as their "grounding" metaphysician is displayed.[74]

---

67. Nancey Murphy and George F. R. Ellis, *On the Moral Nature of the Universe: Theology, Cosmology, and Ethics* (Minneapolis: Fortress, 1996), p. 23. Via Yong, *The Spirit of Creation*, p. 61.

68. Yong, *The Spirit of Creation*, p. 63.

69. Wariboko, *Pentecostal Principle*, pp. 71–106.

70. Wariboko, *Pentecostal Principle*, p. 73 (emphases mine).

71. Wariboko, *Pentecostal Principle*, p. 73.

72. Wariboko, *Pentecostal Principle*, p. 73.

73. We will take a brief look at this in the subsection "The Spirit and Being: Pneumatological Nondualism," and a more extended one in Chapter 3.

74. For other extended treatments of Yong's emergence, see: David Bradnick, *Evil, Spirits, and Possession*; David Bradnick and Bradford McCall, "Making Sense of Emergence: A Critical Engagement with Leidenhag, Leidenhag, and Yong," *Zygon* 53.1 (2018), pp. 240–57.

## Personhood and Spirit

Thus far, I have traced Yong's proposed alternative account of spiritual realities as emergent from individuals, communities, and institutions—which subsequently influence them—rather than as mythological spiritual entities that precede them. What kind of personhood, then, do these benevolent, malevolent, and intermediary spirits possess? Yong's philosophical arguments thus far now lead him to engage Walter Wink for theological insight. Wink argues that angels, demons, authorities, and heavenly rulers are cosmic forces which represent the world domination system constituted by social, economic, and political structures.[75] Once emergent, these powers supervene upon embodied and historical structures, for good or for ill. Putting all of these pieces together, Yong suggests that the pentecostal imagination fitted to an emergentist framework accounts for at least these two levels of spiritual realities:

- personal spirit-beings constituted initially by physical bodies, but irreducible to them and capable of surviving the death of such bodies, at least for a period of time; and
- corporate spirit-beings constituted initially by corporate realities, but irreducible to them and capable of surviving the dissolution of such realities, at least for a period of time.[76]

## Plurality and Emergence

Finally, Yong closes his reflections with ten speculative theses for a pluralistic cosmos.[77] The theses most pertinent to answer the questions about the personhood of spirits posed in this section are theses one, five, six, nine, and ten.[78] The first thesis, serves as a reminder to the reader that regardless of how foreign the proceeding theses may sound to inherited pentecostal proclivities, its foundation is the orthodox conviction that God is triune, and the only necessary, transcendent reality. Thesis five explicitly works out the personhood of angels in conversation with the theory of emergence. Yong affirms that they are personal, ecclesial, institutional, terrestrial (emerging from geographic regions), and celestial. Therefore, angels work alongside God, and are personal realities which proceed from human beings, their relations to each other, and multiple environments. Their personhood is thus conceived as suprapersonal realities which supervene upon human relations from which

---

75. Particularly, Walter Wink, *Naming the Powers: The Language of Powers in the New Testament* (Philadelphia: Fortress, 1984); *Unmasking the Powers: The Invisible Forces That Determine Human Existence* (Philadelphia: Fortress, 1986); and *Engaging the Powers: Discernment and Resistance in a World of Domination* (Minneapolis: Fortress, 1992).

76. Yong, *The Spirit of Creation*, p. 107.

77. See Yong, *The Spirit of Creation*, pp. 207–25. For my engagement with Yong's theses, see Chapter 5 below.

78. Theses two through four are also pertinent, but for the most part restate the theory of emergence which has already been dealt with.

they emerge.⁷⁹ According to thesis six, then, demonic spirits emerge in similar fashion as do angels, but their aims and mode of existence are precisely the opposite. Therefore, as privations, they are not emergent personalities, but *divergent anti*personalities. As such, they are ontically parasitic and emerge (or diverge) through the dehumanizing intentions, behaviors, and actions of creatures.⁸⁰ Finally, both theses nine and ten point to the fact that our material bodies and communities, as well as the spirits that emerge from them, will be eschatologically judged, which will manifest as renewal or destruction. Tersely put, our temporal bodies and material actions ought to be eschatologically oriented as they will be eschatologically acted upon.

In sum, Yong's aim of being interdisciplinarily conversant lead him to develop a metaphysical grounding—utilized by Wariboko and colleagues—in conversation with an emergentist theory of the cosmos. He develops this in such a way that brings him to a novel conclusion—at least in pentecostal circles—that spiritual realities, except for the triune God, proceed from material realities.⁸¹

*The Spirit and Being: Pneumatological Nondualism*

Yong argues that the pentecostal pneumatological imagination overcomes the mistaken post-Enlightenment spirit-nature opposition.⁸² When the creation narratives of Scripture are read with a nondualistic pneumatological imagination, the Spirit of God comes to be understood as intricately involved in the orders of creation in such a way that the world is both generated by, and infused with, *ruach Elohim*. This same Spirit enlivens and gives responsibility to *ha adam* thus enabling creation to respond to the divine command.⁸³ Precisely because Yong's reading of the creation narrative is pneumatologically imagined, it also eschatologically oriented. Therefore, the Spirit of God "sweeping across the primordial waters infuses the orders of creation with a teleological dynamic, so that creation is best understood in terms of processes directed toward the eschatological intentions of God."⁸⁴

---

79. Yong, *The Spirit of Creation*, p. 216.

80. Yong, *The Spirit of Creation*, p. 219.

81. His conclusions have recently inspired lengthy engagement. See David Bradnick, *Evil, Spirits, and Possession: An Emergentist Theology of the Demonic* (Leiden: Brill, 2017).

82. For a brief history of, and pentecostal engagement with, the emergence of the three dominant post-Enlightenment metaphysical claims (supernaturalism, naturalism, and cessationism), see Vondey, *Pentecostal Theology*, pp. 122–30.

83. As Yong points out, this response-ability is not only breathed into a personal *ha adam*, but to nonpersonal entities. For example, "'Let the earth *put forth* vegetation; plants *yielding* seed, and fruit trees … that *bear* fruit" (1.11); "Let the waters *bring forth* swarms of living creatures" (1.20); and "Let the earth *bring forth* living creatures of every kind" (1.24)". See Yong, *All Flesh*, p. 282.

84. Yong, *All Flesh*, p. 282. Also, worth noting is that this reading leads Yong to suggest that Gen 1:2 may imply an evolutionary struggle because it is through the formlessness that the Spirit of God brings complexity and order out of chaos, thus reimagining *creatio ex nihilo*.

Now that Yong has set a biblical precedent for denying a spirit-nature dualism by demonstrating creation's Spirit-infusedness, he is committed to constructing a metaphysical grounding to that effect. Yet again, it is important to begin with a metaphysical construct because as Yong rightly states, "not to articulate a metaphysics leaves one working with unquestioned metaphysical assumptions at best or presuming faulty metaphysical ideas antithetical to one's experience at worst."[85] Therefore, he relies heavily on Donald L. Gelpi's "metaphysics of experience"[86] which posits a foundational *triadic* structure to all reality. Yong notes that Gelpi's triadic structure borrows from Peirce's nomenclature of quality, fact, and law. Furthermore, Peirce's threefold nomenclature is upheld by his argument that any datum of reality is understood *experientially* through categories of Firstness, Secondness, and Thirdness.[87] Peirce's construct, precisely because it is triadic, overcomes regnant dualisms and posits a realistic/experiential understanding of creation oriented toward its future. In this metaphysical system, experiences are ultimately real; therefore, objects of experience "lie within, not without, the semiotic triad—and subjects and objects are mutually ... in-existent. If this is the case, then mind is not opposed to nature, nor is spirit opposed to matter."[88]

We have now arrived, finally, to Yong's central hypothesis on this matter: in the same way that pneumatology overcomes binitarianism, a triadic metaphysical vision analogously overcomes dualism and moves us toward a dynamic, and interrelational view of creation. The central elements of a pneumatological theology of creation undergirded by an experiential triadic metaphysics are: (1) a reaffirmation of Scripture's creation narrative wherein the Spirit hovers over creation *and within it* as the Breath of Life; (2) this same Spirit orders creation toward its Goal in anticipation of the eschatological reign of God. "Insofar as the new Jerusalem comes down 'out of heaven from God' toward the earth (Rev 21:10), and insofar as our eschatological reality will include the resurrection of our

---

85. Yong, *All Flesh*, p. 290.

86. See Donald L. Gelpi, *The Turn to Experience in Contemporary Theology* (New York: Paulist, 1994); *The Gracing of Human Experience: Rethinking the Relationship between Nature and Grace* (Collegeville, MN: Liturgical Press, 2001); *The Varieties of Transcendental Experience: A Study in Constructive Postmodernism* (Collegeville, MN: Liturgical Press, 2000). For Yong's essay-length engagement with Gelpi, see Amos Yong, "In Search of Foundations: The Oeuvre of Donald L. Gelpi, SJ, and Its Significance for Pentecostal Theology and Philosophy," *JPT* 11, no.1 (2002), pp. 3–26.

87. Summed up, Firstness is the quality of a thing in its particularity and suchness, not dependent upon action and thought from another. It is sheer possibility. Secondness is a thing in its brute concreteness as its stands either in relation to, or over-and-against another. Thirdness mediates between Firstness and Secondness. Thirdness acts as the intelligibility, generality, and lawfulness of a thing in its habits and tendencies as it is oriented toward its future. See Yong, *SWC*, pp. 91–6; Yong, *All Flesh*, pp. 287–9.

88. Yong, *All Flesh*, p. 292.

bodies, we see that the goods God created will ultimately be redeemed as well."[89] (3) The Church, then, discerns this dynamic, nondualistic creation we inhabit and participates in caring for God's *good* Spirit-infused material reality in a way that is faithful to God's eschatological purposes.[90]

## *The Spirit and Knowledge: Pneumatological Epistemology*

The pneumatological imagination[91] serves as the central concept for Yong's epistemology. The "pneumatological" portion of the phrase comes from Yong's foundational pneumatology already discussed above. The "imagination" aspect of the phrase refers to the "world-making" that emerges from the observer as he or she forms images in his or her mind through experiencing the world and its relatedness to God.[92] The process of the observer forming images is not merely accomplished in the mind objectively, but it is also oriented by the observer's "heart"—that is, oriented by affections. Put succinctly, "The pneumatological imagination observes the phenomena of the world and ... attempts to discern reality. The Spirit, then, both instantiates the world as rational and makes its rationality accessible to human knowing."[93]

How then does the human observer acquire the knowledge to which the Spirit grants access according to Yong? Because the Spirit is present in and through all of creation, the world *in its fullness* provides the source for theological knowledge, thus removing the boundaries set by certain traditions and disciplines.[94] However, Yong asserts that not all experiences in the world ought to be taken as divine encounters. Therefore, guiding principles for discernment are required. Beliefs about God must pass through "pragmatic" and "coherence" criteria in order to be deemed appropriate.[95] To test a belief for its pragmatic truth, it ought to harmonize with the way reality is.[96] Regarding the coherence criteria, it "refers to a proposition's dependence on consistency with other statements within the same thought system."[97] Yong therefore posits a critical realism because as his metaphysics and ontology—via his foundational pneumatology—suggest, things

---

89. Yong, *All Flesh*, p. 301.

90. Yong, *All Flesh*, pp. 300–2.

91. Yong, *SWC*, pp. 119–220.

92. Yong, *SWC*, p. 144.

93. Christopher A. Stephenson, "Reality, Knowledge, and Life in Community: Metaphysics, Epistemology, and Hermeneutics in the Work of Amos Yong," in Wolfgang Vondey and Martin William Mittelstadt (eds), *The Theology of Amos Yong and the New Face of Pentecostal Scholarship* (Leiden: Brill, 2013), p. 67.

94. This is what drives Yong's passion for interdisciplinary dialogue with the sciences and religions.

95. Yong, *SWC*, pp. 165–74.

96. Yong, *SWC*, pp. 164–5.

97. Stephenson, "Reality, Knowledge, and Life in Community," p. 68.

do indeed exist whether or not a human mind knows them as existing. The gap between being and knowing "is spanned by the pneumatological imagination, which is an orientation to God and the world that the Pentecostal charismatic life in the Spirit continually nurtures and shapes."[98]

Yong's epistemology is appropriately experiential because pentecostal spirituality centralizes personal experiences and encounters of the Holy Spirit. However, Yong's critical realism acknowledges that all experience is semiotically mediated.[99] This leads to the important and conversation-enabling notion of epistemic fallibilism,[100] which argues that because human knowledge is finite, it is necessarily partial and perspectival. "The significance of Yong's epistemic fallibilism is that the process of justification of beliefs through pragmatic and coherence theories must be perennial because of the fallible nature of all human knowing."[101] As such, a pentecostal epistemology—precisely because it is pneumatological—must also be eschatologically oriented: that is, willing to engage in the incessant process of discernment toward, and until, the eschaton.

I must note once again, Yong's profound influence on pentecostal thinkers who engage metaphysics and epistemology at the "ground" level. Indeed, the resonance between Yong and Wariboko on this epistemological point is so palpable that Wariboko was compelled to explicitly comment on it in his monograph. I will let Wariboko's own words describe their similarities as he sees them: "My intuition about the triadic nature of the pentecostal principle parallels and complements the (Yongian) triadic hermeneutic." He goes on to say that "Even my suggestion about the ... 'excess' element is thematized pneumatologically in his book as the pneumatological imagination (*vis-à-vis* a trinitarian epistemology), as foundational pneumatology (*vis-à-vis* a trinitarian ontology) and as the pneumatological dynamic that undergirds this interpretive process."[102]

## Conclusion

The purpose of this chapter has been to argue that metaphysics is necessary work for pentecostals to be engaged in as it has been called for in the past, and is tacit in our spirituality. Although difficult, participating in the metaphysical enterprise as second-level discourse is sanctifying, faithfully traditioning, and ecumenical work. This chapter also sought to briefly sketch

---

98. Stephenson, "Reality, Knowledge, and Life in Community," p. 67.
99. Yong, *Beyond the Impasse*, p. 61; Yong, *SWC*, p. 200.
100. Yong, *SWC*, pp. 176–210.
101. Simo Frestadius, "In Search of A 'Pentecostal' Epistemology: Comparing the Contributions of Amos Yong and James K.A. Smith," *Pneuma* 38 (2016), p. 100.
102. Wariboko, *Pentecostal Principle*, p. 38.

the state of pentecostal metaphysics by looking at what pentecostals have said and done—within the framework of Smith's five elements of a pentecostal worldview—to implicitly and explicitly construct a metaphysical vision in light of the speech and practices embedded in our spirituality. Furthermore, what was also discovered is that, for the most part, a coherent and comprehensive pentecostal metaphysics has remained undeveloped. With that said, James K. A. Smith and Amos Yong have emerged as the pentecostal scholars who have given this serious and sustained attention. I offered a brief and general sketch of their overall projects and inserted the work of other pentecostal theologians where appropriate. Indeed, the preeminence of Smith and Yong remained constant and obvious. The following, then (Chapter 3), will be a deeper, more exhaustive, and more exclusive dive into the work of Smith and Yong. It will include a deep compare/contrast between their metaphysical visions after I have made them explicit. This will be followed by a suggested method for moving the conversation forward (Chapter 4), and an attempt to construct a pentecostal metaphysics considering the discoveries and methods of the previous chapters (Chapter 5).

## Chapter 3

## THE SPIRIT, REALITY, AND RENEWAL: INFERRING METAPHYSICS FROM THE WORK OF JAMES K. A. SMITH AND AMOS YONG

*Introduction*

Because Amos Yong and James K. A. Smith have come to the fore as leading voices in the metaphysical enterprise from a pentecostal perspective, their work to that end deserves in-depth treatment. The goal of the following section will be to explicate their metaphysical visions individually—taking note of the presuppositions and aims which undergird them—and then to compare them and locate precisely where (and why) their visions align or veer. The following study of the two most prominent voices in pentecostal metaphysics—combined with the previous study of the metaphysics derived from various pentecostal voices in conversation with the five elements of a pentecostal worldview—will bring even further clarity regarding the state of pentecostal metaphysics. Once again, neither Yong nor Smith explicate that they aim to construct an exhaustive pentecostal metaphysics. However, Yong explicitly works from a pentecostal perspective and privileges the Holy Spirit doctrinally and experientially. Moreover, a key Smith text that I engage in this work seeks to explicate a pentecostal worldview and an ontology suitable to pentecostal practice. Thus, much of their work which I engage is from a pentecostal perspective and touch on metaphysics at various points. My aim is to explicate the tacit pentecostal metaphysics in their work as I read it. The findings of the previous study and of the one to come will serve as the background of my own construction as I hope to advance the conversation beyond where we have landed thus far. We begin with the work of Smith.

### *The Spirit of the Real: Tacit Metaphysics in the Work of James K. A. Smith*

*Foundational Claims, Formational Influences, Fundamental Presuppositions, and Final Aims*

James K. A. Smith is currently Professor of Philosophy at Calvin College, where he is the Gary and Henrietta Byker Chair in Applied Reformed Theology and Worldview. He received his academic training in Philosophical Theology and Contemporary

French Philosophy from the Institute of Christian Studies in Toronto, and also at Villanova where he studied under John Caputo. Given his training, he works from a Dutch Reformed perspective and is thus highly influenced by the likes of Herman Dooyeweerd and Abraham Kuyper when it comes to theology, philosophy, and cultural engagement. His ecclesial formation took place as he worshiped within the pentecostal tradition, namely at what he considers to be his forever home church, Bethel Pentecostal Tabernacle in Stratford, Ontario. His involvement with the community at Bethel led him to stay abreast of what was unfolding within pentecostalism's early academic stages, which subsequently led him to engage the likes of John Christopher Thomas, Steve Land, and Rickie Moore, as well as having formative conversations with Donald Dayton, Frank Macchia, and others. Couple this with a close friendship with Amos Yong, and Smith's early presuppositions can be identified in his emergence as a Spirit-baptized, Dutch Reformed philosopher and cultural critic.

Early in his career, Smith carried the presuppositions mentioned above as he retained his focus on cultural engagement. These proclivities led him to a movement known as Radical Orthodoxy,[1] which was catalyzed by the seminal work of John Milbank.[2] Laboring from a "high church" Catholic and Anglican background, and sympathetic to Milbank's insights which fundamentally reject the hegemonic discourse of modernity, Radical Orthodoxy—as an ecumenical program[3]—gathered diverse theological voices to deconstruct secularism while constructing a fivefold post-secular offensive. RO's five key themes are: (1) a critique of modernity and liberalism, (2) post-secularity, (3) materiality, sacramentality, and liturgy, (4) aesthetics, and (5) cultural critique and transformation.[4] Smith's early work with RO's five themes[5]—informed by his Dutch Reformed Tradition—preceded his construction of the five elements of a pentecostal worldview. One need not

---

1. I will sometimes refer to Radical Orthodoxy as "RO."

2. Namely and primarily, John Milbank, *Theology and Social Theory: Beyond Secular Reason* (Oxford: Blackwell, 1990). For Milbank's further development of some of the themes put forth in this work, see John Milbank, *The Word Made Strange: Theology, Language, Culture* (Oxford: Blackwell, 1997).

3. As Smith makes clear, Radical Orthodoxy "is not a monolithic phenomenon; it is, rather … a symphony made up of different 'movements.'" See James K. A. Smith, "What Hath Cambridge to Do with Azusa Street? Radical Orthodoxy and Pentecostal Theology in Conversation," *Pneuma* 25.1 (Spring 2003), p. 99. There are enough similarities and shared convictions for RO to posit a "program" for self-identification. See John Milbank, "The Programme of Radical Orthodoxy," in Laurence Paul Hemming (ed.), *Radical Orthodoxy?: A Catholic Enquiry* (New York: Routledge, 2017), pp. 33–45.

4. For a concise treatment of these five themes, see Smith, "What Hath Cambridge to Do with Azusa Street?," pp. 102–9.

5. James K. A. Smith, *Introducing Radical Orthodoxy: Mapping a Post-Secular Theology* (Grand Rapids: Baker Academic, 2004).

probe too deeply to notice the similarities between Smith's Reformed engagement with RO's five themes, and his development of pentecostalism's five elements.⁶ We can now identify four seemingly unrelated discourses which Smith brings together and labors from: "the evangelical and Pentecostal theology nurtured by his ecclesial experiences; the Reformed theological tradition … the continental philosophy at the heart of his PhD program of study; and the … Radical Orthodoxy movement."⁷ It is worth noting here that for nearly the past decade, Smith's engagement with, and references to, pentecostalism has waned.⁸ On the other hand, his commitments remain steadfast and explicit to the Dutch Reformed tradition as he continues his work in cultural engagement.⁹

*Overcoming (Super)Naturalisms*

With Smith's presuppositions and early influences in view, we can labor to elucidate his metaphysical vision. To understand Smith's metaphysical proposals, we must first extrapolate the ontology that serves as the foundation of RO's project. RO has pointed out that modernity's domineering secularism is undergirded by ontological presuppositions which cannot be accepted by the Church. Modernity's dogmatic pre-commitments posit an ontology of immanence which produce metaphysical dualisms such as nature against spirit, material over against spiritual, and immanence over against transcendence. Smith shares RO's vehement denial of modernity's dualisms, but splits with them in their ontological vision insofar as RO is dependent on Platonism.¹⁰

---

6. In fact, he first proposes the five elements in conversation RO. Smith, "What Hath Cambridge to Do with Azusa Street?," pp. 97–114.

7. Amos Yong, "Radically Orthodox, Reformed, and Pentecostal: Rethinking the Intersection of Post/Modernity and the Religions in Conversation with James K.A. Smith," *JPT* 15.2 (2007), p. 235.

8. This is not an evaluative judgment. It is simply an observation of the traditions he consistently and explicitly turns to throughout his career as opposed to the traditions he intermittently engages and references.

9. See his three "Cultural Liturgies" volumes wherein he constructs his argument undergirded by Augustine's *City of God*, in conversation with Kuyper and Dooyeweerd: James K. A. Smith, *Desiring the Kingdom: Worship, Worldview, and Cultural Formation*, Volume 1 of Cultural Liturgies (Grand Rapids: Baker Academic, 2009); James K. A. Smith, *Imagining the Kingdom: How Worship Works*, Volume 2 of Cultural Liturgies (Grand Rapids: Baker Academic, 2013); James K. A. Smith, *Awaiting the King: Reforming Public Theology*, Volume 3 of Cultural Liturgies (Grand Rapids: Baker Academic, 2017).

10. In Smith's taxonomy of Platonisms, he identifies RO's vision as Deleuze's Involuntary Platonism, which, for Smith, is debatable as to whether or not this is the "real" vision of Plato in first place. Smith's critique—specifically of Pickstock's arguments (in Catherine Pickstock, *After Writing: On the Liturgical Consummation of Philosophy* [Maiden: Blackwell Publishers, 1998])—which are representative of RO—is based on the fact that RO's Platonism

In the face of modernity's attempts to sever the immanent world from transcendence, RO answers by producing a participatory ontology with the goal of positing a material reality that is wholly dependent on transcendence. For RO, material reality is "suspended" in that its being and worth are "held up" by transcendence; therefore, all things participate in the divine and can only be properly understood in light of that participation. Over against an ontology of sheer immanence, RO's vision is incarnational and nonreductive so that created matter exists only insofar as it is suspended from its Source; as such, there is a real sense in which transcendence resides in immanence and gifts material reality with its being and true value. Created order, then, does not "have any kind of sheer autonomous existence, as if possessing some kind of inalienable right to be. Rather, being is a gift from the transcendent Creator such that things exist only insofar as they participate in the being of the Creator—whose being is goodness."[11] Through participation, creation's goodness is affirmed as is the presence of the Creator. "Just as only transcendence can properly retain the depth of immanence, so also only transcendence can properly value embodiment."[12]

While Smith is sympathetic to what RO rejects—namely, nihilism and fundamentalist dualism—he offers a nuanced vision to that of RO, with a Reformed caveat which seeks to do away with Platonism.[13] It is worth noting here that Smith is *especially* averse to the dualism which "erects a hierarchical and oppositional bifurcation between the immaterial and material, the soul and the body, the visible and the invisible."[14] He rejects this so vehemently because this is precisely the kind of dualism that he witnessed in his early Christian formation in Protestant fundamentalism which resisted anything associated with creaturely embodiment.

---

fails to get Plato right and does not properly account for the tenets of his thought that are in direct opposition to a Christian vision, especially when it comes to Plato's denigration of the material world. What Pickstock seems to be arguing for, says Smith, is not a strictly Platonic vision, but a *theurgical* Neoplatonism of the Iamblichian tradition; however, she fails to name it as such, and therefore, RO directly attaches its vision to Plato himself. As such, their lack of accounting for—and confrontation with—Plato's bifurcation between the material and transcendent, and denigration of the former are major problems for Smith. See James K. A. Smith, "Will the Real Plato Please Stand Up?: Participation versus Incarnation," in James K. A. Smith and James H. Olthius (eds), *Radical Orthodoxy and the Reformed Tradition* (Grand Rapids: Baker Academic, 2005), pp. 61–72.

11. Smith, *IRO*, p. 191.
12. Smith, *IRO*, p. 192.
13. A more thorough engagement between RO and many in the Reformed tradition took place at the 2003 Calvin College conference; the fruit of which yielded a book, edited by Smith, which thoroughly traces their differences and similarities. See James K. A. Smith, and James H. Olthius (eds), *Radical Orthodoxy and the Reformed Tradition* (Grand Rapids: Baker Academic, 2005).
14. Smith, *IRO*, p. 198.

Smith identifies RO's ontology—per RO themselves[15]—as heavily reliant upon the Platonic doctrine of participation, and essentially challenges the notion that it can be baptized into a Christian understanding of material reality. Smith argues that the goodness of creation from RO's Platonic perspective becomes suspect when viewed eschatologically. Smith argues that Milbank and Pickstock (key figures of RO) 'seem to suggest that the beatific vision—and the *theosis* that is the *telos* of participation—is an event of nondiscursive immediacy; the need for material mediation, they conclude, is something we shall "outgrow."'[16] Outgrowing material mediation is *not* an *appropriated* Platonic vision made to fit the Christian perspective, says Smith, but a *traditional* Platonic vision which sees the goodness of the immanent as remedial at best. Materiality and time are good only insofar as we remain on this side of the Eschaton. Smith finds this unacceptable.

Aside from his eschatological critique, Smith also denies that RO's suspension model posits the goodness of creation *as such*. He argues that if nothing can be in itself, then reality is as occasionalism would view it: a reality wherein "God must continually and constantly reach into creation for it to *be* creation."[17] Creation under this model, critiques Smith, "requires the incessant activity of the Creator to uphold what would seem to be a deficient creation."[18] Smith is concerned that while RO seeks to critique modernity's presupposition that nature is autonomous, it overcorrects in that it does not grant any independence to creation whatsoever. In light of these objections, Smith's ontology seeks to answer the questions: "how can we affirm both the radical dependence of the creation on the Creator and also the goodness of creation as created?"[19] Moreover, "How will we understand the being of material reality? Is it something to be affirmed as positive, even glorified?"[20]

Constructively, Smith argues for a creational or incarnational ontology that utilizes Deleuze and Leibniz in such a way that glorifies the Creator precisely in positing a high view of the integrity of creation.[21] For Smith, Leibniz and Deleuze provide "the resources for countering a Platonic and modern disenchantment of the world via the reenchantment of nature, emphasizing the creational character of reality by an affirmation of the integrity of immanence."[22] In this view, the material world is where reality is actualized, so that "this world does not itself

---

15. See John Milbank, Graham Ward, and Catherine Pickstock, "Suspending the Material: The Turn of Radical Orthodoxy," in John Milbank, Graham Ward, and Catherine Pickstock (eds), *Radical Orthodoxy: A New Theology* (London: Routledge, 1999), pp. 1–20.
16. Smith, *IRO*, p. 200.
17. Smith, *IRO*, p. 204.
18. Smith, *IRO*, p. 204.
19. Smith, *IRO*, p. 204.
20. Smith, *IRO*, p. 204.
21. As indicated by the hyphenation below, there is a mutually informing—and therefore, difficult to distinguish—character to these voices as he utilizes them for his construct.
22. Smith, *IRO*, p. 207.

exist outside of its expressants."²³ Leibniz is interested in an understanding of materiality that is not deficient, and deficiency is precisely what he charges occasionalism's view of materiality to be because it demands constant intervention by God in order to be itself. Moreover, if creation is deficient, so is its Creator. And so, we arrive at Leibniz's theory of creation as a "preestablished harmony" wherein creation is front-loaded from the beginning to function self-sufficiently without God's constant tinkering. Smith, reading Leibniz, says that "creation is a collection of hypostatic unions, therefore, not only is the plane of immanence imprinted with a divine order from the beginning, but it is only in this materiality that the original fold of the command can be unfolded; matter, or the body, is the theater of unfolding *ad infinitum*."²⁴ Of course one could argue that Leibniz is positing an autonomous creation, but to push back on this notion Smith notes that in Leibniz "there is a sense in which self-sufficiency and independence are the results of a fundamental dependence on the Creator."²⁵ Put concisely, for Smith the real, immanent acts of creation happen "independently" in that creation has been front-loaded to function as such. It is in the original "enfolding" that creation finds its fundamental dependence on God.

In sum, Smith's critique of RO's ontology insofar as it is dependent on Platonism has yielded a Leibnizian-Deleuzian creational ontology, which can be identified by three thematic trajectories. The first theme of Smith's creational ontology is the affirmation of immanence. The primary purpose of this theme is utter rejection of dualism and Platonism. Creational ontology is characterized by a love for the material world so that "one does justice to the Creator by affirming the zone of immanence or region of materiality as the theater of his glory."²⁶ The second theme of Smith's creational ontology is the affirmation of transcendence. Smith's understanding of transcendence is key for the sake of maintaining the Creator/creature distinction while also affirming immanence as the locus for creation's integrity. Creation is marked with transcendence insofar as its referential structure points to an origin. It is worth noting that this model identifies *meaning* as the *being* of creation. "Thus, the zone of immanence is invested with transcendence, not as a kind of container for an ethereal substance but rather as a structure of phenomenological reference to an origin that is not itself subject to temporal conditions (or even being)."²⁷ Put differently, transcendence is that which "inheres in the structure of creation insofar as it points to a Creator."²⁸ The final theme of Smith's creational ontology is the notion of "folding." Again, this concept is meant to uphold the integrity of creation as

---

23. Smith, *IRO*, p. 211.
24. Smith, *IRO*, p. 217.
25. Smith, *IRO*, p. 217.
26. Smith, *IRO*, p. 220.
27. Smith, *IRO*, p. 220.
28. Smith, *IRO*, p. 221.

created. Embedded within creation is the reality of "unfolding that characterizes the differentiation and development of the material world."[29] Smith says that the concept of the fold works like the Dooyeweerdian *enkapsis*.[30] The term *enkapsis* names the relation of individuality structures which is essentially the idea that the whole is not merely the sum total of its parts, but something altogether new. Also, the parts themselves are somewhat independent individuals as their growth is both continuous self-division and self-propagation.[31] Smith argues that the Leibnizian-Deluzian concept of the fold is reminiscent of *enkapsis* in that wholes are enfolded into larger wholes, thus preserving the integrity of immanence. Therefore, "the appearance of something new is not the result of a power above and beyond nature bringing into it what was not there before. Rather, what is already there is disclosed through the subjective activity of individual creatures within created constant structures."[32]

Smith believes that the creational ontology model with its three thematic trajectories provides the means to resist both Platonism and nihilism. The main concern is to preserve the goodness of creation and the Creator without cost to either. As such, transcendence is located in that which was enfolded at the origin of creation, and as creation unfolds without the God's constant tinkering, both its integrity and God's integrity as Creator are maintained.

### *Stifling the Spirit: Radical Openness to God and Hostile Scientisms*

Smith's creational ontology—developed through his conversation with RO and nuanced by his Dutch Reformed convictions—is well established as he seeks to construct a pentecostal ontology. It is worth noting that as he works this out, he aims to do it "*as* a pentecostal scholar working unapologetically from a pentecostal worldview."[33] In his ontological construction *as* a pentecostal, the concept of creation as enfolded or front-loaded does not explicitly make an appearance. In fact, Smith seems more interested in placing ontological weight not on creation's integrous "independence" (in the sense described above), but

---

29. Smith, *IRO*, p. 221.

30. This word is meant to name the relation of individuality structures. Dooyeweerd borrowed this term from Theodor Haering, who borrowed it from the famous anatomist Heidenhain.

31. Think of the relationship of separate organs to the total organism that is the human body.

32. Johan Diemer, *Nature and Miracle* (Toronto, Canada: Wedge Pub., 1977), p. 5. Cited in Smith, *IRO*, p. 222.

33. Smith, *Thinking in Tongues*, p. 87.

on creation's Spirit-infused character.[34] Smith begins his construction by pointing out the inhospitable, if not hostile, character of modernity's regnant naturalisms wherein the universe is closed and "immune to any interventions or interruptions by any meddling deity. Sealed off as an autonomous and independent machine, the material universe is understood to be a self-sufficient system … without any interference from something (or someone) outside or beyond it."[35]

What prompts Smith to construct a pentecostal ontology is the hope of making room for pentecostal involvement in the science and theology dialogue. He does this by first identifying science as a product of *culture*, which therefore makes it function as a cultural institution replete with "material practices, constructed environments (including laboratories, instrumentation, etc.), traditions of apprenticeship, learned rituals, and so forth."[36] These practices constitute empirical observation designed to attend to the regularities of "nature" for the sake of predicting and understanding how it operates. Given that science is dependent on regularities (read: laws), does that not imply a world not open to a pentecostal ontology which requires that the cosmos remain open to surprise? Making matters more difficult for pentecostal engagement is the dogmatic assertion of naturalism, which Smith argues is a pre-commitment and not the result of scientific investigation.

Smith deals with the problems above by distinguishing between three types of naturalisms: reductionistic, nonreductionistic, and methodological.[37] While the nonreductionistic approach is preferable to the reductionistic one, they both err in that they are metaphysically *pre*-committed to the nonexistence of

---

34. I am not sure what to make of the fact that when speaking from the Reformed tradition, he critiques RO's participatory and "suspension" model of materiality as fundamentally opposed to the integrity of creation (see *IRO*, pp. 197–206; "Will the Real Plato Please Stand Up?" pp. 61–72), but then when speaking *as* a pentecostal, Smith recommends RO's vision without caveat or qualification (see *Thinking in Tongues*, pp. 99–103). I will foreshadow, however, that my forthcoming constructive ontology will indeed be more reminiscent of Smith's recommendations for a pentecostal ontology and will therefore not utilize Smith's Reformed caveats.

35. Smith, "Is There Room for Surprise?," p. 36.

36. Smith, "Is There Room for Surprise?," p. 38.

37. Reductionistic naturalism is simply the assertion that nothing exists beyond what can be empirically observed. Nonreductionistic naturalism shares reductionistic naturalism's rejection of supernatural phenomena but is open to the possibility of the existence of phenomena, like the mind and consciousness, which cannot be reduced to chemical or physical processes. Finally, methodological naturalism is metaphysically agnostic in that it does not hold to a particular assumption, but functions *as if* the universe is governed regularities. See Smith, "Is There Room for Surprise?," pp. 40–1. Elsewhere, Smith provides a fourfold continuum: (1) reductionistic naturalism; (2) Nonreductionistic naturalism; (3) enchanted naturalism or noninterventionist supernaturalism; (4) interventionist supernaturalism. Smith, *Thinking in Tongues*, pp. 97–9.

supernatural beings. Being that methodological naturalism does not require that one be metaphysically predisposed to shut out the supernatural, Smith finds an open door which allows a pentecostal to retain his or her own pre-commitments as a metaphysical supernaturalist—or enchanted naturalist—while laboring and conversing in the sciences *as if* the universe is a predictable and closed system. What a pentecostal ontology is incompatible with, then, is not science but metaphysical naturalism. Finally, for Smith, pentecostal ontology is also opposed to an interventionist supernaturalism which is essentially Deism.

Embedded in pentecostal spirituality is not only a radical openness to the Spirit, but a kind of materiality that recognizes the Spirit's sacramental immanence. As such, Smith argues that pentecostals ought to be sympathetic to the ontological vision posited by *nouvelle theologie* and RO's participatory ontology which say, "creation *is* (and 'nature' is) insofar as it participates in and is indwelled by God, in whom we live and move and have our being."[38] This participatory ontology affirms a sacramental existence so that the material world *as created* exists as a "suspended" participant from the Creator while also affirming the inherence of transcendence precisely *in* immanence. Being, then, is a sheer gift as creation is granted its being by (and only by) participation in the transcendent Creator. This ontological commitment provided by RO, says Smith, is foundational for rethinking the God-world relation in a way that is faithful to pentecostal practice so that "nature" is understood as "always already *primed* for the Spirit's manifestations."[39] Amos Yong comes along at this point and offers a "pneumatological assist"[40]—wherein he proposes that the agent in whom the immanent world is "suspended" is the Holy Spirit—to Smith's ontological construction. In response, Smith says yes, *all* of creation is suspended in transcendence, but creatures (and institutions thereof) participate in varying intensities. In such a construct, miracles "are not instances of God 'breaking into' the world, as if God were outside it prior to such events; rather, they are instances of a unique and special mode of participation that always already characterizes creation."[41]

*Conclusion*

In sum, for Smith, pentecostals see creation as infused with, and "suspended" in, the active and dynamic presence of the Spirit so that the material world sacramentally participates (in varying intensities) in transcendence. This vision "makes it possible to account for both the *regularity* of natural processes and the *special* action of the miraculous."[42] In the context of attempting to answer Smith's original problem

---

38. Smith, *Thinking in Tongues*, p. 100.

39. Smith, *Thinking in Tongues*, p. 101.

40. More on this later. See Yong, "Radically Orthodox, Reformed, and Pentecostal," pp. 233–50.

41. Smith, *Thinking in Tongues*, p. 102.

42. Smith, *Thinking in Tongues*, p. 103.

of pentecostal participation in the scientific discourse, this ontology proves to be viable solution. In addition, this ontology serves his other aims of identifying the church as the Spirit's (intense) locus of God's redemption while also affirming God's (less intense) work in the world through the arts, politics, public education, and other "fallen" structures. As the intense locus of God's activity, "the church engages the world not apologetically or dialogically but confessionally and kerygmatically" as it "attempts to outnarrate and offer an immanent critique of their plausibility conditions."[43] Smith's aims and propositions, then, are "held up" by his ontology. It is also worth pointing out here, that the weight of Smith's emphasis seems to shift depending on the tradition he finds himself speaking for. As a Dutch Reformed thinker, he is insistent on putting weight on the integrity of material reality *as such*. As a pentecostal thinker, Smith emphasizes the Spirit-infused and dependent character of creation on God.

### *The Spirit of Renewal: Tacit Metaphysics in the Work of Amos Yong*

*Foundational Claims, Formational Influences, Fundamental Presuppositions, and Final Aims*

Amos Yong is currently Dean of Theology and Mission at Fuller Theological Seminary, where he directs their Center for Missiological Research. He received his academic training from an Assemblies of God institution called Bethany University and went on to earn his MA at both Western Evangelical Seminary and Portland State University. He then went to Boston University to earn his PhD in Religion and Theology under the supervision of Robert Cummings Neville.[44] Born to Chinese Malaysian parents who converted to Christianity from Buddhism, Yong immigrated to the United States with his family where he was formed in the Pentecostal tradition.[45] Yong was so entrenched in pentecostalism that it was not until his seminary training at a non-pentecostal school that he learned that good virtues were also prevalent in people from other Christian traditions. This experience would lead Yong to ask more questions about the Spirit's ubiquity in unexpected spaces. A brief return visit to Malaysia further inspired these questions and he wondered if and how the Spirit might be at work in Buddhists, Jews, Hindus, and Muslims.[46] Yong kept these questions in mind as he continued to work *as*

---

43. Yong, "Radically Orthodox, Reformed and Pentecostal," p. 239.

44. https://www.fuller.edu/faculty/amos-yong/

45. Amos *Yong, Discerning of Spirit(s)*, pp. 9–11; For an autobiographical essay on the life of Yong, see Amos Yong, "The Spirit, Vocation, and the Life of the Mind: A Pentecostal Testimony," in Steven M. Fettke, and Robby Waddell (eds), *Pentecostals in the Academy: Testimonies of Call* (Cleveland: CPT Press, 2012), pp. 203–20.

46. Amos Yong, *Pneumatology and the Christian-Buddhist Dialogue: Does the Spirit Blow through the Middle Way?* (Leiden: Brill, 2012).

a deeply committed pentecostal. Indeed, he has served as the president of the Society for Pentecostal Studies (2008–9), went on to co-edit *Pneuma*, and served as the founding co-chair of the Pentecostal-Charismatic Movements Group for the American Academy of Hope and Religion from 2006 to 2011. Moreover, he has worked on projects such as Pentecostal Manifestos (Eerdmans) and continues to work as a licensed minister with the Assemblies of God. His quest as a pentecostal to discern the Spirit's work in unexpected spaces has also moved him to be heavily involved with *Charis: Christianity and Renewal—Interdisciplinary Studies* (Palgrave Macmillan), *Mission in Global community* (Baker Academic), and *Missiological Engagements* (IVP Academic). As such, his scholarly efforts since 2012 have been largely committed to constructing a global Pentecostal theology, interreligious dialogue, conversations between science and theology, and a theology of disability. We may now explicitly identify his presuppositions as a pentecostal, and his aims as constructing a global theology that would make mutually informing dialogue with other religions and ideologies in the public sector possible.

Yong has emerged as a key representative of the new face of pentecostal scholarship. His presuppositions give way to three major methodological emphases: (1) pneumatology, (2) pentecostalism, and (3) renewal. First, his emphasis is on Pneumatology in the sense that it functions as both a launching point and end to which his theological task is aimed. For Yong's purposes, more suitable than the question, "what is a faithful theology *of* the Spirit"? is the question "what theology derives *from* the Spirit"? With such an understanding of pneumatology "the repercussions are not exclusively bound to the doctrine of God but more broadly located across the spectrum of theological and beyond the confines of traditional doctrinal systems."[47] In Yong's understanding, pneumatology is not an end but a means of extending beyond itself.

Yong's second methodological emphasis is tied to his pentecostalism in the adjectival sense more so than the denominational sense (although he retains his commitments to the Assemblies of God). That is, he is committed to understanding God as thoroughly active in the church and the world through the continued operations of the Spirit. Finally, Yong's pneumatological foreground and pentecostal background are joined under the umbrella of Renewal. "Renewal is that counter-critical and prophetic element within a pentecostal and pneumatological framework that allows both sides to remain in ongoing critical conversation about both the subject and the object of theological interpretation, its epistemology and metaphysical trajectories."[48] It is precisely the "renewal" aspect of pentecostal and pneumatological trajectories that move their concerns beyond themselves while continuously opening themselves up for transformation.

---

47. Wolfgang Vondey, and Martin William Mittelstadt, "Introduction," in Wolfgang Vondey and Martin William Mittelstadt (eds), *The Theology of Amos Yong and the New Face of Pentecostal Scholarship* (Leiden: Brill, 2013), pp. 1–24.

48. Vondey and Mittelstadt, "Introduction," p. 18.

### Relationality, Rationality, and Dynamism

Now that Yong's (1) presuppositions as a pentecostal, (2) aims of constructing a global and public theology, and (3) methodological emphases of pneumatology and renewal have been briefly adduced, we may now attempt to discern his ontology and metaphysical vision. The principle holding all the aforementioned together and that which serves as the basis for Yong's metaphysics is his foundational pneumatology.[49] Foundational pneumatology functions as a pneumatological account of the God–world relationship and posits an ontology and metaphysics marked by God's (1) relationality, (2) rationality, and (3) dynamism.

### The Spirit as Bond of Love

Much of what follows is dependent on Yong's understanding and appropriation of the Doctrine of the Trinity. The first of the two particular trinitarian models he leans on is Irenaeus' "two-hands" model which promotes the co-inherent and interrelational nature of the divine persons while resisting ontological subordination. The second trinitarian model utilized by Yong is Augustine's vision of the Spirit as the "bond of love" between the Father and the Son. God's life immanently is one of perfect relatedness. The same Spirit that joins the Father and the Son in perfect love also economically joins God to the world and joins all things—insofar as they are truly themselves as God intends—to each other. It is important to note here that for Yong, relations in creation are neither accidental nor a category which helps elucidate what happens between substances in reality; rather, relations constitute the real identities of things. So that, "things in the world exist as such because they are products of the creative activities of the Spirit and Word and because their relationships to other things constitute them as such."[50]

To help elucidate just *how* the triune God might relate himself to the world, and us to each other so that distinct "things" can be held together without eradicating diversity, Yong evokes the work of C. S. Peirce and his concepts of Firstness, Secondness, and Thirdness while keeping the two Trinitarian models in mind.[51] Firstness is the sheer possibility which *enables* things to be experientially present, although it is not itself experienced. However, what *can* be vividly experienced by humans is the brute physical and competitive interactions that is the Secondness of things. Thirdness, mediates Firstness and Secondness while providing "the impulses that drive both the evolution of the world and the trajectories of lived-experience, thereby structuring our experience of the emergence of actualities (Secondness) from possibilities (Firstness)."[52] Like God, reality is structured triadically. To be clear, it is

---

49. See Yong, "On Divine Presence and Divine Agency," pp. 167–88; Amos Yong, *SWC*, pp. 83–118.
50. Stephenson, "Reality, Knowledge, and Life in Community," p. 66.
51. Yong, *SWC*, pp. 84–96.
52. Yong, *SWC*, p. 93.

not that we have three distinct realities which we experience, but that we experience one reality that is triadically structured. Firstness (the sheer possibility/qualities of things) "is abstracted from our experiences of Secondness (facts) and Thirdness (laws)."[53] Yong, now explicitly ties Peircean metaphysics to trinitarian theology with the help of Donald L. Gelpi: the "Father makes himself present to the world not directly but through two hands."[54] Pneumatically speaking, "Thirdness mediates Firstness and Secondness, and ... Thirdness is emergent from, and in that regard dependent upon, Firstness through Secondness."[55] And so, just as the life of the triune God *ad intra* via the "two-hands" and "bond of love" models display perfect relatedness without eliminating distinction by the Spirit's mediation, so reality as we experience it is triadically structured so that brute difference (Secondness, received through Firstness) is mediated (though not eradicated) by Thirdness.

Finally, a realistic and relational metaphysic emerges not only from a trinitarian logic but can also be posited via the complementarity of Spirit and Word. Both Spirit and Word witness to the particularity/universality of reality.[56] Therefore, "the logic of incarnation and Pentecost together defy the erasure of difference and the reduction of otherness to self-sameness. Rather, both establish difference and otherness, each in its own place within the context of the whole."[57] The logic of incarnation and Spirit Word in conversation with Peirce might be, "Secondness is not concreteness apart Thirdness, and Thirdness provides the legal shape for Secondness."[58]

*The Spirit as Revealer of Truth*
Just as the world's relational character is gifted by, and a reflection of the triune life, so is the world's rational makeup in a metaphysical sense.[59] At this point, it is worth noting that Yong has a unique definition of the doctrine of *creatio ex nihilo*.[60] He

---

53. Yong, *SWC*, p. 94.
54. Yong, *SWC*, p. 94.
55. Yong, *SWC*, p. 94.
56. The Word is universal as holds all things in being (Jn 1:9; Col. 1:15; Heb. 1:3) and particular as the life of Jesus of Nazareth. The Spirit is also universally particular in that he establishes and sustains the particular body of Christ in such a way that makes room for a diversity of tongues, gifts, nations, etc.
57. Yong, *SWC*, p. 103.
58. Yong, *SWC*, p. 103.
59. While epistemology cannot be wholly abstracted from rationality, Yong is here talking about a metaphysical rationality—that is, the quality or state of being reasonable, or, the notion of intelligibility itself. With that said, it should be further noted that Yong's conclusions here are key for his "pneumatological imagination" which will serve as the foundation for his epistemology.
60. Yong is attempting to bridge the Oneness and Trinitarian pentecostal divide by arguing that both understand the revelation of God as triune when looked at through the lens of the economy of salvation. Yong suggests we drop the speculation of the life of God *ad*

utilizes his modified definition of *nihil* in his argument for the rationality of the Spirit, which depends upon his reading of the Genesis narrative.[61] He states, "not only does the *ruach Elohim* restrain and reshape the primeval chaos, but this chaos is itself neither a messy something-or-other nor a literal void."[62] Rather, "the Priestly author indicates that the *ruach Elohim* hovered not over pure nothing, but over the waters (*mayim*)."[63] Yong proposes a connection between *tohu wabohu* and *mayim* and argues that the link between them "is suggestive of both the chaos of disorder and randomness (the vacuum) and also the primordial plentitude (*or plenum*), arguably consistent with the modern scientific notion of chaos and its unpredictable and nonlinear movement from simple perturbation of potentialities and possibilities to complex outcomes."[64] The Spirit, then is the spirit that lawfully, purposefully and rationally orders the primordially chaotic cosmic "stuff" into a coherent universe.

Besides the creation narrative account in Genesis, Yong argues that Scripture is replete with the Spirit serving functionally and ontologically as the divine mind, understanding, and wisdom of God.[65] The wisdom of God is also Scripturally associated with Christ (1 Cor. 1:24, 30; Luke 2:47, 52; 11:49; Mt. 11:19, *passim*). Yong ties this together in his reading of 1 Cor. 1-2 to argue that "while Jesus is clearly the content of the wisdom of God, Paul also goes on to clearly identify the Spirit as the one who mediates and communicates the message of the cross."[66] The Spirit, then, searches the deep things of God and reveals them. "Apart from the Spirit ... the divine wisdom remains incommunicable."[67] Put succinctly, "the Spirit will expand, illuminate, apply, and communicate the truth which is embodied in Jesus."[68] Therefore, Spirit and Word are inseparable.

*intra* "before" creation for the sake of unity and begin our reflection on his understanding of *creatio ex nihilo*. When we begin our reflection on God on his creative act, Yong argues: "Rather than there being nothing, creation *ex nihilo* says that there is something, the created order, and the fact that there is creation means that the Creator is conditionally determined with respect to the creation. While essentially indeterminate apart from creation, God has given Godself the characteristic of Creator in the very act of creation." See Amos Yong, "Oneness and the Trinity: The Theological and Ecumenical Implications of Creation *Ex Nihilo* for an Intra-Pentecostal Dispute," *Pneuma* 19.1 (1997), p. 92.

61. Yong's construct of a Pneumatological Theology of Emergence is also deeply dependent upon his definition of *ex nihilo*. See Yong "*Ruach*, the primordial Waters, and the Breath of Life," pp. 183–204; Yong, *Spirit of Creation*, pp. 151–62.

62. Yong, *Spirit of Creation*, p. 155.

63. Yong, *Spirit of Creation*, p. 155.

64. Yong, *SWC*, p. 95.

65. He points specifically to the Biblical wisdom literature. Yong, *SWC*, pp. 35–7.

66. Yong, *SWC*, p. 39.

67. Yong, *SWC*, p. 40.

68. Yong, *SWC*, p. 41.

Finally, in arguing for the rationality of the Spirit in creation, Yong argues that because human beings are created as intelligent creatures who are able to grasp the mind of God by the Spirit, it "presupposes some sort of point of contact between the divine and the human. The mediating key, it should now be clear, is pneumatological."[69] As such, human beings are rational creatures due to the fact that they are spiritually created in God's image. Creation in general and humanity in particular are what they are only insofar as they have been rationally ordered and soteriologically guided by the Spirit according to God's purposes.

*The Spirit as Liveliness of God*

Finally, foundational pneumatology posits an ontology and metaphysics that is marked by the Spirit's dynamism. At the heart of this idea is that *ruach/pneuma* is the dynamic presence of the Spirit within the life of God which also blows through humanity and the cosmos, enlivening and transforming the created order toward its intended End in surprising ways. "Creation can thereby be imaged as the product of the breath going forth and returning to the Godhead. History is the realm of this going forth and returning specifically vis-à-vis the affairs of humankind."[70] Creation and history, then, are essentially the stage on which God's drama is played out. Because this drama is infused with the presence of the Spirit, the developments within it cannot be predicted as they unfold. And so, says Yong, "breath bestowed on the cosmic order endows it with its own autonomy, a differentiated autonomy appropriately pertinent to the diversity of creatures which constitute the creation."[71] Yong goes on to give voice to the effects of sin and the fall, but maintains that it is the Spirit's dynamic transforming presence in history that is constantly reversing its effects and will finally triumph over death.

*Speaking with the Spirit: Yong's Pneumatology and Process Metaphysics*

For Yong, the dynamism of the Spirit is the transforming presence of God which keeps entities active rather than static. For the sake of developing an ontology with this in mind, Amos Yong utilizes the process metaphysics of Alfred North Whitehead (as developed by Charles Hartshorne) to posit an ontology of *becoming*. He begins by turning to Walter Wink's biblical exegesis regarding "the powers" and argues that Wink's findings provide a way for us to discern how things are immanently constituted. For Wink, immanent things are constituted in two modalities: spiritual and material. They are spiritually constituted as dynamic, subjective fields of force and power, and materially so as concrete objective manifestations. It is important to note here that Wink is not describing how two distinct entities are constituted, but rather the composition of single entities which are composed in such a way that "the outer reveals the inner even as the

---

69. Yong, *SWC*, p. 41.
70. Yong, *SWC*, p. 47.
71. Yong, *SWC*, p. 47.

inner directs, shapes, and informs the outer manifestations."[72] When applied to the condition of humanity, "the more appropriate categories would be history (meaning, interiority and transcendence) and nature (materiality, embodiment and environment)."[73]

Yong sees a similar "dipolarity" at work in Whitehead's process metaphysics in conversation with Hartshorne. If Wink's work is applied to a horizontal metaphysics of immanence, Yong sees in process thought an account of the vertical relationship between God–world and immanence–transcendence. As Yong reads process thought, in God there is an *abstract essence* which is his transcendence, immutability, and eternity on the one hand, as well as a *concrete actuality* that is his immanence, mutability, and temporality on the other. Set within the context of our temporal world, the abstract essence of God "survives the passage of time and provides ... an initial aim for each emerging occasion in the cosmic process";[74] conversely, the concrete actuality of God is "the totality of the creative process of becoming itself, conceiving the world therefore as, metaphorically, God's body."[75] To make this vision of reality a triadic one, Whitehead adds a notion of "prehension" which is supposed to mediate the abstract and the concrete. Because—according to process thought—reality is fundamentally constituted by fleeting temporal occasions, "prehension" is the name for the dynamic process which creatively connects these successive and fleeting occasions and entities. Prehension is essentially the principle of novelty and harmony which undergirds each successive moment in reality. "Each actual entity thus prehends all previous occasions ... and creatively negotiates and incorporates aspects of their influences in order to constitute itself as an at least partially novel reality."[76] For the sake of clarity, let us succinctly wade through the process construct again. Process metaphysics (via Whitehead and Hartshorne) is meant to posit a triadic structure of reality. There is, therefore (1) an abstract pole of reality because God is transcendent and pure *possibility*; (2) a concrete pole of reality because there is "a consequent nature of God consisting of the occasions or societies of such occasions which are reality's ultimate constitutive components";[77] (3) a mediating process which is, ontologically, creativity itself. This creativity is "the dynamic, ongoing emergence of harmonized actualities from the infinite number of possibilities and preceding occasions which structure the advance of reality."[78]

Yong supports the abstract and concrete poles of reality as put forth by process metaphysics. However, he takes issue with the notion of "prehension" in particular, and the general nominalism that undergirds process thought.

---

72. Yong, *SWC*, p. 88.
73. Yong, *SWC*, p. 88.
74. Yong, *SWC*, p. 89.
75. Yong, *SWC*, p. 88.
76. Yong, *SWC*, p. 89.
77. Yong, *SWC*, p. 89.
78. Yong, *SWC*, p. 89.

Because the ontological makeup of "prehension" is said to be "creativity," and because this creativity is conceived nominalistically, there is no enduring entity to advance, harmonize, mediate, or effect processive transformation. Reality remains as fleeting drops of actual occasions. Moreover, Yong argues that "process metaphysics ultimately reduces God to the world and defends the doctrine of creativity only rhetorically rather than actually. The triadic promise of process philosophy is ultimately lost either to the dipolarity of process theism or to the monopolarity of process naturalism."[79] Doing away with Whitehead's "prehension," as well as supporting Wink's dipolar construct of immanence, leaves reality with a dyadic structure that he wants to fill out pneumatologically. To do this, he begins by directing readers back to Wink's work on "the powers" as a means of moving toward reenvisioning the category of "spirit" as that of "field" or "energy" which can help overcome the dipolarity of process thought while more suitably conveying the idea of transcendence. Yong sets this in dialogue with his notion of *ruach/pneuma* as the enduring wind and breath of God that blows through all dualisms and provides once again a triadic structure to reality. Reality's triadic structure is then worked out by means of Firstness, Secondness, and Thirdness already described above.

In sum, Yong's (1) presuppositions as a pentecostal who is sympathetic to other traditions and ideologies, his (2) aims of contributing to a global and public theology, and his (3) renewalist methodology are what undergird his metaphysical construct. His metaphysical vision posits that (1) the Spirit *relationally* joins the triune God to himself, God to creation, and creation to each other; (2) the Spirit *rationally* and wisely orders the world to make it a coherent whole, orienting it toward God's eschatological intention; (3) the Spirit *dynamically* blows through and mediates a creation that is composed of sheer possibility and concrete occasions, both enlivening and surprising it. For Yong, then, creation is therefore not subjected to dualisms because *one* reality is triadically structured.

### *The Spirit and the Renewal of the Real: The Possibilities of a Smithian/Yongian Pentecostal Theological Metaphysics*

Now that the visions of Amos Yong and James K. A. Smith have been separately adduced, we may now proceed with a comparative analysis, beginning with their critical engagement of each other's work. Yong launches the first written interaction between the two by responding to Smith's metaphysics as put forth in *IRO*. Smith's approach to cultural engagement and the ontology that undergirds said approach is where Yong sees an irresolvable tension. Smith has a high ecclesiology in the sense that he puts a lot of weight on the distinction or discontinuity between the church and the world. Yet on the other hand, as a Kuyperian, Smith is not an

---

79. Yong, *SWC*, p. 90.

escapist. Rather, he strongly pushes for Christian engagement in the public political sector and calls for Christian appreciation and engagement in the arts. After all, for Smith, all things live, move, and have their being in Christ, and so participate in the divine life. If this is true, Yong wonders just how the church is called to "outnarrate" the competing *mythoi*—per Smith's suggestion—which spring forth from non-Christian communities? If all participate in God, does that not mean that these "competing narratives" derive from the same source? Moreover, how is the church to immanently critique the plausibility conditions of these narratives if worldviews emerge from engaging in communal practices that are set within the context of an identifying narrative? For Yong, Smith's understanding makes dialogue and immanent critiques impossible without full-fledged conversion into an opposing religion, ideology, or worldview.

While Yong's constructive metaphysical proposals are philosophically Peircean and Whiteheadian, and resourced theologically via Gelpi, Yong does not seek to do away with Smith's ontology, but to add a "pneumatological assist" (theologically resourced by the biblical phrase: "the Spirit poured out on all flesh") which he hopes will mend the otherwise irresolvable tension in Smith's epistemology, and ecclesiology. Ontologically, the Spirit poured out on all flesh overcomes the tension between transcendence and immanence, thus underwriting "the ontological participation of all creation in the divine presence and activity that sustains the world, thus providing a 'pneumatological assist' to a sacramental principle which re-values the material world."[80] For the purposes of Smith's theology of culture, Yong believes his assist "preserves a point-of-contact between God and the human realm and provides a theological explanation for a common humanity."[81]

Epistemologically, the Spirit leads us into all truth and provides the miracle of *understanding* in and through the diversity of tongues. Yong ties the diversity of tongues to the diversity of experiences as witnessed through testimony. "Testimony to the wondrous works of God can be received only through a multitude of voices, which all provide perspective (and must be discerned through the community of faith)."[82] As such, "the pneumatological epistemology of the Pentecost narrative turns out to be the flipside of the pneumatological ontology, one that features mutuality, reciprocity, and intersubjectivity."[83]

Finally, Yong applies his "pneumatological assist" ecclesiologically so that the church's unity is located in its diversity. As witnessed in her history, the Spirit is present in the tumult of the Church. Yong says that this fact means (contra Smith) that there cannot be hard and fast lines between the world and the church because "the historical Church is composed of communities and members within communities wherein identities are never pure but always already immersed in the historical world and therefore also overlapping with many other different

---

80. Yong, "Radically Orthodox," p. 247.
81. Yong, "Radically Orthodox," p. 247.
82. Yong, "Radically Orthodox," p. 248.
83. Yong, "Radically Orthodox," p. 248.

communities and identities."[84] This does not mean that all distinction is erased, but it does mean that adjudication cannot be properly rendered until the eschaton—that is, the event that will reveal the truth and de-absolutize human claims. Until then, the church is to remain a community radically open to dialogue with the world. As Yong notes, "the pneumatological assist I am commending opens up the possibility of our engaging in immanent critiques of other faith traditions, even as it also makes possible our being transformed by our encounter with those in other faiths."[85]

Smith begins his response to Yong by acknowledging that the tension pointed out in his vision—between his participatory or creational ontology on the one hand, and his emphasis on the antithesis between the church and the world on the other—is indeed present as a problem Smith has created for himself. As such, he gladly receives Yong's "pneumatological assist" with strong qualifications. Smith remains insistent on discontinuity and antithesis between the church and the world, pointing out that the New Testament witness is consistent on the matter. Moreover, Smith takes issue with how Yong uses the phrase "the Spirit poured out on all flesh"—a key component of Yong's pneumatological assist—noting that "the book of Acts does not conclude that the Spirit's outpouring is universal ... rather, it seems that the point is that the Spirit is outpoured without respect for persons, nations, or ethnicities—in other words, the people of God are detached from blood and land."[86] The church, then, remains God's called out and set apart community for Smith, whereas Yong wants to make the Spirit's impact the same for all communities.

Despite this radical discontinuity, Smith reaffirms his commitment to his creational ontology, and resolves the tension by arguing that the distinction does not necessitate an either/or choice, but rather locates the distinction along a continuum. While the Spirit upholds all of reality, distinctions emerge in the *intensities* which the world and the church participate in the life of God. As such, "it is structurally the case that all that exists participates in the divine, but not all that exists is properly ordered or directed *to* the divine."[87] For Smith, this model affirms both continuity and discontinuity between the church and the world.

With Smith's ontological clarity appropriated for his conversation with Yong, he finds new ground to further defend his approach to cultural critique and interreligious dialogue. He points out that Yong misunderstood him when it comes to what he means by "immanent critique" of the plausibility conditions of other communities. It does not require conversion but rather "points to the unsustainability of that perspective with only the resources of that perspective."[88] That is, "this mode of immanent critique respects the other by listening and taking

---

84. Yong, "Radically Orthodox," p. 249.
85. Yong, "Radically Orthodox," p. 250.
86. Smith, "The World as Sacrament," pp. 254–5 n.9.
87. Smith, "The World as Sacrament," p. 256.
88. Smith, "The World as Sacrament," p. 259.

seriously the confession articulated by the other, but then shows the way in which the resources of that perspective cannot sustain it."[89]

With Smith's revised ontological continuum, and his clarification regarding his immanent critique, he concludes that other religions and cultural institutions structurally participate in the divine, but in a less intense manner insofar as they are not properly ordered to the triune God as revealed in Jesus and witnessed to by the historical body that is the Church. While Smith concurs that there is much to learn from the wisdom of other traditions, and while he receives Yong's invitation to bring his work in conversation with other religions such as Buddhism and Islam, Smith invites Yong to bring his work into dialogue with "the *religions* of capitalism, militarism, and American patriotism."[90] Smith then asks the poignant question, "I wonder if this might temper his enthusiasm about the Spirit's presence in false religions."[91]

## Conclusion

Through this comparative study of Yong and Smith, it has become increasingly apparent that their systematic proposals are fundamentally shaped by the questions (read: aims) they bring into their constructions. Furthermore, their aims emerge from the presuppositions which are composed of their experiences and training. The tacit aims of Yong and Smith are strikingly similar: that is, to create an overall metaphysical system[92] that is both faithful to Christianity *and* can also allow for conversation in the public sector. The difference here is that Yong is more interested in a mutually informing dialogue with other religions, while Smith is more concerned with engaging and critiquing culture in the modern West. These differences are at least partially due to their varying presuppositions and experiences. Yong, as one who has encountered sincerity and fidelity in "otherness" through his parent's conversion, his subsequent experiences of being around others from outside of his pentecostal heritage in seminary, and a return trip to Malaysia. These events have sparked unrelenting questions about the Spirit's presence in unexpected places and have ultimately fueled his metaphysical construction. On other hand, Smith's foundation is more firmly placed in his Dutch Reformed training which provided a welcomed respite from the dualistic wasteland of his inherited fundamentalism which called for a separatist non-engagement with culture. Smith went on to

---

89. Smith, "The World as Sacrament," p. 259.
90. Smith, "The World as Sacrament," p. 261.
91. Smith, "The World as Sacrament," p. 261.
92. Consisting of: (1) accounts of the God–world relation; (2) accounts of finite creation's relatedness to itself/each other; (3) ontologies; and (4) epistemologies.

read Milbank's work and found his own voice within the Radical Orthodoxy movement. Finally, Smith states that much of his formation has come from worshiping at a pentecostal church, although as of late, his work has made little reference to it as he has been more explicitly writing from a Reformed perspective.

Aside from their distinct presuppositions and aims, the differences in Yong and Smith's metaphysical constructs are also symptomatic of their varying epistemic approaches. Because Yong wants to strongly push for a mutually transformative dialogue with those outside of the Christian tradition, he adopts a correlationist approach when it comes locating the sources of theological knowledge.[93] Heavily reliant on the Peter's Acts 2 proclamation that the Spirit has been poured out on all flesh, Yong understands the whole of creation and its varying communities as pneumatologically charged so that *all* of creation and its peoples are locales for divine encounters. Conversely, as a Reformed Christian, Smith favors an inner-logic, or "postliberal" approach so that he is primed to engage a culture *structurally* inhabited by the Spirit, but he does so coming from a particular community whose practices and identifying narrative (he argues) are upheld by the Spirit in such a way that it (the Church) is the best source for theological knowledge as it is more intensely and *properly* ordered to the one true and triune God.

With their aims and epistemic convictions adduced, it is now clear why their distinct ontological constructs are what they are. Yong is attempting to discern God's presence in unexpected places, and so develops a foundational pneumatology which posits a relational,[94] rational,[95] and dynamic[96] world wherein God is free to encounter us anywhere through anyone as he did for Yong when his world opened up through different experiences. Therefore, the locale of theological knowledge cannot be limited to the church, rather, the church ought to remain open to transformation by the Spirit precisely through engagement with "the other." Smith thinks culture ought to be engaged by Christians but puts more weight on critique than he does in mutual transformation. This is because Smith's training begins from a confessional theological stance which emphasizes the world's fallen nature. However, creation is not only fallen but is good as it is structurally characterized by its participation in God. While the world is fallen, creation still retains its integrity. As such, God is neither withdrawn as a deist would posit, nor is he constantly tinkering as an occasionalist would have it. Rather, God has "front-loaded" creation to be itself without constant intervention thus preserving its integrity as creation, and God's integrity as Creator. The

---

93. I am utilizing the definition of correlationism and postliberalism put forth by Simo Frestadius, "In Search of a Pentecostal Epistemology," pp. 93–114.

94. Via the "two-hands" model.

95. The *Ruach* of God is wise and orders chaos; The *pneuma* guides us into all truth.

96. Creation is charged by the Spirit, and so replaces "prehension" and gives a truly triadic structure to Whitehead's process metaphysics.

church, then, serves as a transformative counter-witness—informed by its narrative, affections, and practices—called out from a world that fails to properly order itself to its Creator.

This sketch of the two pentecostals who have most prominently contributed to the metaphysical enterprise will serve as the background for my own construction which will follow. As was demonstrated above, the aims undergirding a construct largely determine its structure and limitations. Furthermore, it was also shown that Yong and Smith had a similar aim (public engagement) but with nuanced approaches based on their presuppositions. I will be approaching my construct with an entirely different aim which will make use of their work where appropriate, but it will also call for serious critique and revision.

## Chapter 4

## WORSHIP, WISDOM, AND THE WAYS OF THE SPIRIT: INFERRING METAPHYSICS FROM PENTECOSTAL SPIRITUALITY

### *Introduction*

In the previous chapter, I explicated the presuppositions and aims of Yong and Smith in constructing their respective metaphysical visions. The foregoing demonstrated that their metaphysics do not seek to merely explicate what is implied in Christian and pentecostal thought and practice, but to do so insofar as it makes dialogue with other communities and institutions with different pre-commitments possible. While it is indeed a good and important aim, the aim of this work is to adduce a pentecostal metaphysics as grounded specifically in pentecostal spirituality. There is a wholly counterintuitive and radically audacious metaphysical vision inherent in church practice to which I wish to give more sustained attention precisely as a pentecostal conversing with the historical Christian tradition.

With that being said, the question that will drive this constructive work is: just how revisionary can a theological metaphysics be when it is constructed from the theology embedded in the practices found in both pentecostal spirituality and the Christian tradition? My aim is an ecumenical one. As such, attempting to make the Christian vision of reality tenable to "public" institutions—like modern science—or traditions which draw from different norms and pre-commitments is beyond the intentionally limited scope of this work. I will proceed with the conviction that the church does indeed have something unique to say about the God-creation relationship, personhood, spirit(s), knowledge, etc.—and it is said and enacted every week by the Christian community in their corporate worship services.

In light of the aims of my construct, a decisive move to favor a method very similar to Smith's "internal logic" approach must here be made.[1] There is much

---

1. This approach was antecedently named as a postliberal approach in this work. I would not shy away from this label insofar as it reflects a general ethos which hopes to free Christianity from playing by the rules set by modernity's hegemonic stipulations for what counts as true or rational. In turn, the church may be freed to rediscover her identity (and metaphysical commitments) in light of community, narrative, tradition, and intense

to be said that has not yet been said about the kind of world-making that takes place through the internal logic of the corporate church assembly and I will focus on that without being immediately concerned with how it might cohere with the vision(s) offered by the world, or succumbing to what they deem to be logical. As Cheryl Johns reminds us, "Worship ... results in an altered perception of reality."[2] This is the reason I favor Smith's approach over against Yong's. However, as noted earlier, Smith works out his metaphysics with an aim of cultural critique and mine will not have such an aim. While I remain greatly indebted to the groundwork laid out by Smith, this omission alone will likely yield some differences which will be noted when necessary. On the other hand, my appreciation for Yong's work will be located in his insistence on reality having a triadic structure precisely because it is grounded in the life of the triune God, as revealed in Christ. Again, there is much to appreciate in Yong but there will be some marked differences in what emerges for a variety of reasons that will become clear as this work progresses.

### *"This Is Your Reasonable Service": Reading the Internal Logic of Pentecostal Worship*

*First- and Second-Level Discourse in Pentecostal Praxis*

Theology's function as defined above—as reflection on how to elucidate the world created by our speech and practices—along with my ecumenical aims, foreshadows the liturgical and ecclesiocentric approach of this thesis.[3] Put differently, in this work, "theology" is not defined as a general quest or study of God but as

---

focus on Christian practices. For what is considered to be the manifesto which describes the "mood" of postliberal theology, see Stanley Hauerwas, William Willimon, "Embarrassed by God's Presence," *The Christian Century* (1985), pp. 98–100. The "fathers" of postliberalism are considered to be George Lindbeck and Hans Frei. Their key texts, respectively, are George Lindbeck, *The Nature of Doctrine*; and Hans Frei, *The Eclipse of Biblical Narrative* (New Haven: Yale University Press, 1980).

2. Johns, *Pentecostal Formation*, p. 89.

3. Here, ecclesiocentric does not mean a focus on the church *against* the world as such. If God sets a distinction (or antithesis) between the church and the world it is paradoxically for the sake of the world. As Peter Althouse notes, "The Church is the locale for the beginnings of the reign of Christ as the foremost sign and instrument of God's kingdom ... The Church is the place where God engages and brings people into redemptive participation for the sake of the world." See Peter Althouse, "Towards a Pentecostal Ecclesiology: Participation in the Missional Life of the Triune God," in Chris E. W. Green (ed.), *Pentecostal Ecclesiology: A Reader* (Leiden: Brill Academic Pub., 2016), p. 88. Congar puts it this way, "The Church is the world as believing in Christ, or, what comes to the same thing, it is Christ dwelling in and saving the world by our faith." See Yves Congar, "The Reasons for the Unbelief of Our Time: A Theological Conclusion," *Integr* (Dec. 1938), p. 21.

an enterprise wholly and specifically connected to the Christian church. This can indeed be considered a pentecostal approach to theology.[4] In fact, Wolfgang Vondey concludes that pentecostal theology "is at heart a liturgical theology,"[5] while Archer's work draws "attention to the importance of the worshipping community as the contextual arena for the discussion of theology including the sacraments (pneumatic ecclesiology)."[6]

In light of the way pentecostals have centered theological reflection on ecclesial practice, pentecostal theologians have argued that we are not so much anti-liturgical as we are against scripted practices because they can inhibit the "freedom" of the Holy Spirit, and the "freedom" of the worshipers.[7] However, even

---

The church then, is Christ's availability *to* the world as the body of Christ. That is, "it is a creature that through its ministries mediates the movement of the other creatures toward God." Chris E. W. Green, *The End Is Music: A Companion to Robert W. Jenson's Theology* (Eugene: Cascade Books, 2018), p. 83. The church is indeed responsible for the world and the Christian assembly is where we are properly shaped to think and live responsibly. Therefore, the church may be understood as distinct from the world, for the sake of the world.

4. Or better, by doing theology in this way, it can be argued that pentecostals are somewhat participating in and contributing to a tradition that long precedes them: "In the fourth century, we have four church fathers (Cyril of Jerusalem, Ambrose, Chrysostom, Theodore of Mopsuestia) who delivered 'mystagogies', or structured lectures on the theology of the sacraments ... This proliferation of mystagogies in the fourth century is without precedent in the early church. These 'mystagogical lectures' were delivered to those who had recently been baptized." Slightly differently, in Maximus the Confessor's mystagogy his "aim is to interpret the sacraments as framed by ultimate reality—a metaphysical or 'cosmological' reading of the sacraments" (Jonathan Armstrong, "Introduction," in Maximus the Confessor, *On the Ecclesiastical Mystagogy: A Theological Vision of the Liturgy* [Yonkers: SVS Press, 2019], pp. 21–3). That is, Maximus' mystagogy was a theological and so metaphysical reading of the liturgy. This is very reminiscent of what I aim to do in the following chapters.

5. Wolfgang Vondey, *Pentecostal Theology*, p. 281. Furthermore, because pentecostals value experience, there is a "practical" component to how doctrine is understood. "Doctrine is in this process a third-order moment of an implicit theological method that emerges from *and* aims at the experience of worship rather than systematization, abstraction, and formalization" (Vondey, *Pentecostal Theology*, p. 19). Before Vondey made these statements, Land had already observed, "The community of the Spirit and Word functions as a worshipping, forming, reflective whole; but at the heart of all this is the liturgical life of the community" (Land, *Pentecostal Spirituality*, p. 23).

6. Archer, "Nourishment for Our Journey," p. 81.

7. Telford Work, "Charismatic and Pentecostal Worship," in Geoffrey Wainwright and Karen B. Westerfield (eds), *The Oxford History of Christian Worship* (Oxford: Oxford University Press, 2006), pp. 574–85. Indeed, "free worship" is often also associated with lack of restraint or reservation during congregational singing as noted by Albrecht's conversation with the parishioners Ben, Sharon, and Carlos who identified "freedom" in this very way.

the services, camp meetings, and conferences that claim to create the most space for "freedom" of expression are ordered to serve a particular purpose.[8] Because it is not liturgy as such that pentecostals are suspicious of, the question is not whether pentecostal assemblies are liturgical, but whether our liturgical orders are faithful to the spiritual and theological tradition we have received, pentecostal and Christian. Once again, my proposed metaphysics aims to be both pentecostal and ecumenical. Smith and Yong have demonstrated that this kind of vision is possible, and I agree with them. However, as will be argued below, a metaphysics that is both pentecostal and faithful to the Christian tradition requires that we make serious revisions to our spirituality. Succinctly put, there is a wider gap between pentecostal spirituality and pentecostal scholarship than has been acknowledged. Therefore, later in this work, I will labor toward making suggestive liturgical revisions to pentecostal spirituality from which an ecumenically promising metaphysics can be constructed. I share Chris Green's concern here: "When we reject liturgical forms received from the historical Christian tradition, we end up inevitably replacing them, and what we craft as replacements often fail drastically (both aesthetically and theologically)."[9] Our liturgies must be crafted in light of what they are for. Green rightly suggests that liturgical worship: (1) gifts us with a narrative identity as participants in God's story with us, (2) orders our affections, and (3) "disciplines our imaginations and spiritual ambitions."[10]

---

"The Pentecostals at our churches enjoy and are attracted to the communities in part because of a perceived 'freer', 'uninhibited', *'expressive'* worship experience," see Daniel E. Albrecht, *Rites in the Spirit: A Ritual Approach to Pentecostal/Charismatic Spirituality* (JPTSup17; Sheffield: Sheffield Academic Press, 1999), p. 199.

8. That purpose can range anywhere from the salvation of souls, to creating the kind of space necessary for personal God encounters, or revival. Furthermore, Friesen states, "the gradual structuring and routinizing of certain worship practices in Pentecostal denominations cannot be assumed to hinder authentic Pentecostal experience." He goes on to note that "the basic elements of the classical Pentecostal worship service emerged from those corporate activities that were deemed to be most effective at passing on the Pentecostal experience to others while assuming unbiblical excesses or fanaticism." See Aaron Friesen, "Classical Pentecostal Liturgy: Between Formalism and Fanaticism," in Mark J. Cartledge and A. J. Swoboda (eds), *Scripting Pentecost: A Study of Pentecostals, Worship and Liturgy* (New York: Routledge, 2017), p. 53. Whatever the purpose may be, there is always an "order of service" aimed at serving that end.

9. Chris Green, "Saving Liturgy: (Re)imagining Pentecostal Liturgical Theology and Practice," in Mark J. Cartledge and A. J. Swoboda (eds), *Scripting Pentecost: A Study of Pentecostals, Worship and Liturgy* (New York: Routledge, 2017), p. 109. Green is quick to point out that there are exceptions to this rule so that there *can* be liturgical innovations in the Christian tradition that are actually improvements aesthetically and theologically. This opens up Christian liturgy to potential revisions on an ongoing basis because it is not innovation as such that he finds problematic.

10. Chris Green, "Saving Liturgy," p. 109 (emphasis mine).

In sum, I will remind readers of some previous arguments to be recalled as we turn our attention to the work of observing the internal logic and tacit metaphysics of pentecostal worship. First, I have drawn a distinction between first and second-level discourse. First-level discourse expresses that which belongs to pentecostal spirituality: proclamation, prayer, and praise in response to lived experience. Second-level discourse expresses that which belongs to pentecostal theology: a reflective—and sometimes, scholarly—discipline which labors to elucidate the tacit message, worldview—and in our case, metaphysics—embedded in pentecostal spirituality. While these two levels of discourses are distinct, they cannot be wholly separated as they ought to be mutually informing. This leads us to my second reminder: when these two distinct levels of discourse fail to be mutually informing, a chasm between the two develops so that what pentecostal academics are saying in their second-level discourse, and what the pentecostal church is practicing in the first, are at odds. Finally, what follows from these reminders in preparation for the forthcoming is that there is a difference between tacit and explicit metaphysics. Embedded in pentecostal spirituality is a presupposed, assumed and practically expressed metaphysical vision of the whole—this we name tacit metaphysics. Explicit metaphysics, then, is the act of explicating the tacit metaphysics so as to discern, name, and construct a coherent vision of the whole. Let us now turn our attention to the first-level discourse of pentecostal spirituality.

*Spirituality and Theology: Affirming the "and"*

Before I make my own suggestions for a revised metaphysics which will later move toward liturgical renewal, I want to—via the ethnographic and empirical work of Cartledge, Albrecht, and colleagues— first explore what is being said and practiced in pentecostal churches.[11] I must note here that the following studies were mostly done in North America, and the UK. Hence, they are mostly representative of a popular form of pentecostal church practice in those countries and far from representative of the full scope of global pentecostal worship. Those limitation being noted, I will specifically look for how God is being named and

---

11. Once again, this cannot be representative of what is happening everywhere as pentecostal practice is global and thus varied. Having said that, I must also note here that the reason for such a focus is that I share Simon Chan's concern about the widening gap that exists between contemporary pentecostal scholars and the leaders and pastors at the ground level. Chan laments that some pentecostal scholars "seem to be more familiar with the world of scholarship than with their own ecclesial tradition"; as such, "the result is that they are often unable to enter deeply into the life of the local Pentecostal church and theologize from the 'inside' and from 'below'. Good second-order theological reflection must come from the primary theology (*theologia prima*) implicit in the living faith of the church." See Simon Chan, *Pentecostal Ecclesiology: The Church as Worshipping Community* (Downers Grove: IVP Academic, 2006), p. 6. As I have just stated, part of the hope embedded in my approach is to labor toward minimizing that gap.

worshiped— which, as we have briefly discussed in previous chapters and will see more in depth later—makes a massive difference for a metaphysical vision of the whole, insofar as it aims to be a Christian theological metaphysics. Considering the significance this thesis is putting on the world-making character of pentecostal assemblies, we must endeavor to describe what actual practices and speech patterns seem to be taking place. To accomplish this, I will use Daniel Albrecht's categories to guide my analysis as they are broad enough to capture what generally takes place in pentecostal assemblies as they are rooted in his case studies of pentecostal worship.[12] Albrecht's work sets pentecostal worship in conversation with ritual studies.[13] What Albrecht's work identifies as ritual—that is, "acts, actions, dramas and performances that a community creates, continues, recognizes and sanctions as ways of behaving that expresses appropriate attitudes, sensibilities, values and beliefs"[14]—has a striking similarity to what has already been identified in this work as pentecostal spirituality.[15] I will retain the identification of pentecostal spirituality for the sake of consistency. Pentecostal spirituality, then, takes place in what Albrecht calls a "ritual field" which we will henceforth identify as the corporate worship service. Putting these ideas together, we may succinctly say that

---

12. Popular expressions of pentecostal worship in the countries just noted tend to fit within what Albrecht suggests is a fundamental structure—worship music, preaching, altar—for pentecostal and charismatic services, which he saw as normative in twenty different church settings he observed in the United States, two in Canada (see Albrecht, *Rites in the Spirit*, p. 152). While some pentecostal churches participate in the Lord's Supper, foot-washing, public reading of Scripture, and public speaking in tongues, etc., the structure proposed by Albrecht displays *necessary* and ubiquitous elements of worship service for pentecostals, as Josh P. S. Samuel has argued (see Josh P. S. Samuel, *Renewing Pentecostal Corporate Worship*, pp. 3–4). This fundamental structure is also displayed in the pentecostal churches studied by Stephen E. Parker, Mark J. Cartledge, (*et al.*). Parker performs an ethnographic study of a local congregation in North Carolina (see Parker, *Led by the Spirit*, pp. 62–116). Also, Cartledge, in order to investigate "the contribution that ordinary discourse makes in the construction of Pentecostal identity," observes a church in the UK, Hockley Pentecostal Church (see Cartledge, *Testimony in the Spirit*).

13. Daniel Albrecht, *Rites in the Spirit*. See also, Cartledge's reading and use of his work in Mark Cartledge, *Testimony in the Spirit: Rescripting Ordinary Pentecostal Theology* (New York: Routledge, 2016), pp. 29–54.

14. Daniel Albrecht, *Rites in the Spirit*, p. 22.

15. Indeed, Albrecht himself states that "authentic rituals vitalize Pentecostal spirituality ... the ritual helps to express and create, to sustain as well as transform, the community and its spirituality" (Albrecht, *Rites*, p. 196). Albrecht later goes on to explicitly identify pentecostal spirituality "as a particular configuration of beliefs, practices and sensibilities that put the believer in an on-going relationship to the Spirit of God" (Albrecht, *Rites*, p. 218).

pentecostal spirituality is embodied and expressed in the weekly corporate worship service.[16] We have thus arrived at the precise location of our present concern.

According to Albrecht, there are three ritual elements of time, space, and identity that emerge in a corporate pentecostal service.[17] First, ritual time is instantiated mostly through the weekly cycle of worship services which consist of three major movements: praise and worship, the sermon, and the altar call. These three movements are foundational to pentecostal services.[18] Second, the ritual space is the micro-world in which these events take place, also known as the sanctuary, which consists of the platform for the leaders, the pews or chairs for the congregation, and the altar as the climactic mediatory location wherein leaders and worshipers most prominently and expressively encounter God. Third, the final element is the ritual identity that participants take up within a worship service. According to Albrecht, some of the roles or identities available to participants are that of worshiper, prophet, learner, and doer. Unique to pentecostals in a corporate setting is the idea that the Spirit can inspire any lay member to step into a role where she or he essentially "has the floor" through testimony, prayer, prophecy, and tongues.[19] Despite this openness to the democratizing charismata, there is still facilitation that takes place through the anointed leader(s) who are typically the ordained pastors and the person(s) charged with leading transitions and the worship band. Finally, in addition to the temporal, spatial, and identifying elements in a corporate worship service, there are, according to Albrecht, three sensory domains: sounds, sights, and positional/bodily (kinesthetic) awareness. The sounds are the hearing of other worshipers and the voices of the leaders; the sights are the band, the large screen behind the platform, and the pulpit; and the

---

16. That is, pentecostal spirituality is *expressed* in the worship service, but it is not exhausted there. In other words, it is possible to be pentecostal as a way of life. "Private devotions, personal witness, individual experiences with God and a plethora of pietistic practices flourish apart from the Sunday services. Nonetheless, the fact remains that at the heart of Pent/Char spirituality, both corporate and individual, lies the liturgy" (Albrecht, *Rites in the Spirit*, p. 151).

17. Albrecht, *Rites in the Spirit*, pp. 121-50.

18. Albrecht names these three movements, "foundational rites." See Daniel E. Albrecht, *Rites in the Spirit*, pp. 150—76; Josh P. S. Samuel agrees as he says, "These three expressions—worship music, preaching, and the altar—are *necessary* and dominant elements of a Pentecostal worship service. Elements of Pentecostal corporate worship, like the reading of Scripture, testimonies, the Lord's Supper, the announcements, financial giving, foot-washing, dance, and benediction are found within Pentecostal corporate worship services, but are less dominant." Josh P. S. Samuel, *The Holy Spirit in Worship Music, Preaching, and the Altar: Renewing Pentecostal Corporate Worship* (Cleveland: CPT Press, 2018), pp. 3-4 (emphasis mine).

19. I must qualify this statement to say that there are other traditions where this is true (i.e., Quakers), and that contemporarily speaking, this is not as common for pentecostals as it once was—especially not in a corporate worship service, on a Sunday morning.

kinaesthetic dimension is the dancing, swaying, clapping, raised hands, kneeling, and falling of the worshipers. Albrecht has thus provided a helpful framework for generically yet accurately describing what takes place in pentecostal worship services. Furthermore, his observations display the immersive and deeply identity-orienting, meaning-creating, and world-making realities at work when pentecostals gather to worship in their corporate setting.

As deeply formative as pentecostal corporate services are, this point can go unnoticed at the first level of discourse by the worshipers themselves. Simon Chan notes that practices do not interpret themselves because they do not convey an unequivocal meaning as such. "Teaching the meaning of the practice is an important part of church practice itself. Ecclesial practice cannot be considered apart from the larger web of meaning … and the attitude and intention in which they are to be carried out."[20] Therefore, the role of the facilitating leaders and pastors is quite crucial to the overall flow and structure of the service. Furthermore, their words shape and effect the attitudes of the worshipers in how they ought to be immediately engaging or interpreting their surroundings and what God is either doing, or about to do.[21] As we will soon see, it is in these discursive moments that worshipers are given language for how to talk about the meaning of their practices which has implications for their understanding of God and how he engages his people, and his creation. Put more technically, the hermeneutical lens and language for interpreting God's acts are taught to the congregation by these leaders via their discursive content.[22]

---

20. Chan, *Liturgical Theology*, p. 89 (emphasis mine). At an even more basic level, the experiences themselves do not come upon a people *tabula rasa*, but on a people who have already been given a particular experience to hope for. Elsewhere, Simon Chan points out that the first Pentecostal experience of Spirit baptism was previously hoped for through a reading of the book Acts (specifically, with Charles Parham) which was subsequently formalized. Prior still, was the hope derived from their holiness heritage which longed for Spirit baptism as understood from their reading of the Acts narrative. See Chan, *Pentecostal Ecclesiology*, pp. 93–4; see also James R. Goff, *Fields White unto Harvest: Charles F. Parham and the Missionary Origins of Pentecostalism* (Fayetteville, AK: University of Arkansas Press, 1988), pp. 66–75.

21. The role of the worship leader is uniquely important in pentecostal circles. You will notice below the formational weightiness placed on Pastor Angela's words for the HPC community (Cartledge, *Testimony in the Spirit*, p. 35). The same importance can be seen for the "minister of music" at King's Avenue Church, the church of Stephen Parker's study. See Stephen Parker, *Led by the Spirit*, pp. 68–9. Josh P. S. Samuel laments just how much importance is placed on these leaders which inevitably leads to an inappropriate elevation of congregational singing and those who lead it, over other forms of worship. See Josh P. S. Samuel, *The Holy Spirit in Worship Music, Preaching, and the Altar: Renewing Pentecostal Corporate Worship* (Cleveland, CPT Press, 2018), p. 131.

22. The three foundational rites of a pentecostal service—described above as praise and worship, the sermon, and the altar call—are held together by transitions. These transitional moments in the service which are led by the appointed facilitators, Cartledge calls "minor

It is at this very point that I must draw attention to the power of the discursive content put forth by the facilitators in moments that might otherwise be overlooked as inconsequential. We get an explicit peek of the formative nature of the discursive content which takes place in both the "foundational rites" and transitions of pentecostal services in Cartledge's conversation with a focus group from members of Hockley Pentecostal Church (HPC),[23] who basically follow the service structure put forth by Albrecht above. Cartledge asked this focus group what practices they felt most connected them with God during the services when Brian, a member of the focus group from HPC, made explicit just how formative the discursive content about the practices from the facilitator during the service actually is:

> When you've got a good worship leader, like Pastor Angela, then they encourage you with certain practices. So very often at the start of the service it will be, you know, "Look, are you ready to worship? Have you got the correct mindset"? … when I've heard a sermon on praise and worship they've shown me Scriptures which talk about dancing, which talk about lifting your hands [agreement], which talk about clapping, which talk about a joyful noise and raising a shout and they said this is what God wants and because we're taught these things, you feel, well, that's a good thing to do [agreement] … there'll come times when they say, "look, let's give a clap offering to the Lord". So we'll clap and go for it and we're clapping for God … it connects in your spirit that this is something that we should do [agreement]. And at a time of quiet when we'll sometimes say "Well, seek God, seek God for what he is speaking to you about now". And sometimes when there's tongues and interpretation and prophecy and things like that then we'll stop and respond and say, "Look, God is speaking to us now in worship [agreement], as we're worshipping God is speaking. We must respond".[24]

As we have just seen through the comments of a worshiper, an interpretative grid about what is taking place in the liturgical practices can be received from the facilitators who orient the worshipers through their discursive content during the three foundational movements (praise/worship, sermon, altar), and during the transitional minor links.[25] Brian made reference to what Pastor Angela said which encouraged a correct mindset heading into congregational singing which led to the practices of the lifting and clapping of hands, as well as the act of shouting. Moreover, this mindset combined with these practices was undergirded by an attitude already given through the foundational rite of a previous sermon, which

---

links" (see Cartledge, *Testimony in the Spirit*, p. 32). The worshipers participate in these minor links by shouting praise, clapping, or orienting their hearts according to what has been said by the facilitator.

23. While this is a study of a British pentecostal church, it is very much in alignment with what happens in a North American context and is therefore relevant to this study.

24. Cartledge, *Testimony in the Spirit*, p. 35 (emphases mine).

25. Which Brian identified as "start of service," and "time of quiet," etc.

according to Brian, utilized Scripture for teaching. Therefore, in this example, the speech of the facilitator (Pastor Angela) heading into congregational singing along with the remembered speech of the pastor during his sermon oriented the attitudes, mindsets, and worldview of the worshipers.

We have observed, then, that pentecostal services are about engaging in identity-orienting, meaning-creating, and world-making practices which we participate in as we endeavor toward encountering or experiencing God. These are not silent affairs. On the contrary, I have argued that the discursive content from the facilitators is quite weighty for the vision and understanding of the worshipers and thus shapes their theological thinking precisely because these facilitators invoke God and make implicit claims on how he acts in creation, and how creation through worshipers are to respond.

That the discourse of ritual leaders orients worshipers to engage and understand their practices—and further, the world—in particular ways has been demonstrated above.[26] The theological discourse which will be given priority in this work is the first-level discourse which we have already identified as pentecostal spirituality with an emphasis on what is commonly practiced in ecclesial contexts. Put succinctly, pentecostal spirituality is embodied, thought, and spoken in the corporate worship service under the guidance of the discursive content that emerges from the leaders.

Cartledge's case study and the interviews contained therein are helpful for this work specifically because they demonstrate that the speech-acts from church leaders during the service orient the worshipers to engage and understand the communal practices in particular ways. As such, I will simply assume that fact to not be unique to HPC and so assume that words—spoken from the platform—carry deeply formative weight, making further focus groups or personal interviews unnecessary for this work.

### *Liturgical Studies: Analyzing an Ecclesial Expression of Pentecostal Spirituality*

I have suggested above that pentecostal spirituality and theology are liturgically informed. That is, pentecostal theology is wholly and intricately connected to its spirituality which is embodied in the context of the corporate worship service.

---

26. It has been demonstrated by looking at Cartledge's data gathered from his focus group in Cartledge, *Testimony in the Spirit*, pp. 32–6. Further hints of this are shown in Parker's ethnographic study of a local congregation in Stephen Parker, *Led by the Spirit*, pp. 62–116. Regarding the formative nature of the discourse from preachers, Lee Roy Martin writes "The orality of Pentecostalism has led, in part, to a celebration of preaching as a mode of divine revelation. In the Pentecostal tradition, therefore, preachers have served as authoritative interpreters of Scripture and formulators of ground level theology." See Lee Roy Martin, "Introduction," in Lee Roy Martin (ed.), *Toward a Pentecostal Theology of Preaching* (Cleveland, CPT Press, 2015), pp. 1–2.

The corporate worship service is structured—and worshipers, oriented—in such a way that world-making takes place. Pentecostal worshipers are formed through their liturgical structures, practices, and habits of speech embedded in them to understand themselves, God, and the world around them. Tersely put, church matters for the pentecostal in forming a metaphysical vision of the whole.

That said, insofar as the services of the churches and movements studied by Cartledge, Parker, and Samuel (and others) are representative of contemporary pentecostal spirituality, an inversion in the relationship between pentecostal first-level discourse and that of pentecostal scholarship is exposed. For example, we cannot—as some pentecostal scholars have tended to—assume that the trinitarian discourse that has shaped the metaphysics of the historic Christian church is faithfully present in pentecostal worship. When Cartledge looked and listened closely at Hockley Pentecostal Church in the UK, he noticed through their songs, prayers, prophecies, and testimonies, that "the theological discourse is either generally theistic, with occasional 'Father' language, or strongly Christocentric."[27] The trinity was hardly suggested, if at all. Furthermore, in a close look at their sung worship, he noticed that the full gospel—essential for pentecostal theology according to scholars—was missing: "Jesus as sanctifier, baptizer in the Spirit and as coming king do not appear to be represented in the hymnody."[28] Similar tendencies and omissions at Hockley described above are also apparent when observing the testimonies at "King's Avenue," in North Carolina via Parker's ethnographic study of a local congregation,[29] and in the popular music in the sung worship of contemporary pentecostalism according to Samuel.[30]

Taken together, these empirical studies indicate that there is an absence of a coherent doctrine of God in first-level discourse. Indeed, even when God is spoken of in pentecostal worship, it is often done in ad hoc fashion so that a developed grammar is missing. The absence of explicitly bespeaking God as triune in pentecostal spirituality is not without massive theological and metaphysical consequences. I will show just how essential the doctrine of the Trinity is to a faithful understanding of the Christian view of the God–world relation below as I briefly trace its historical and metaphysical development.[31] It will become increasingly apparent that one cannot work from a monadic, binitary, or tritheistic understanding of God toward a faithful Christian metaphysics. Considering the importance of pentecostal spirituality as a source for pentecostal theology and considering the emphasis many pentecostal scholars have placed on the doctrine

---

27. Cartledge, *Testimony in the Spirit*, p. 48.
28. Cartledge, *Testimony in the Spirit*, p. 47.
29. Parker, *Led by the Spirit*, pp. 62-112.
30. See Samuel, *Renewing Pentecostal Corporate Worship*.
31. See especially the section entitled "The Holy One of Israel: God's Life as Being-in-the-Spirit."

of the Trinity for gifting us with a triadic structure of creation as demonstrated above, we must seek to move trinitarian discourse at the center of our worship so that we might participate in the Christian metaphysical enterprise in a faithful and ecumenically promising way. More on this below.

The assumption in pentecostal scholarship has largely been that our spirituality outpaces our theology as the locus of pentecostalism's most faithful and robust expression. The calls of Steven Land (and others) for "a comprehensive theological analysis and constructive explication of Pentecostal spirituality,"[32] assumes that our communal praxis is mature and faithful, while our second-level theological discourse "is in a period of theological adolescence."[33] Of course, at the time it was written, Land and those who soon followed him were correct.[34] However, contemporarily speaking, when considering the case studies of the particular forms of pentecostal assemblies that have noted, we discover that it is no longer tenable to assume that what is said and practiced in our corporate worship services is necessarily the most faithful and robust expression of pentecostalism.

It seems, therefore, that today, pentecostal scholarship has, in many ways, at least in some fronts, outpaced our spirituality. Especially when considering the metaphysical and theological implications of the absence of explicit trinitarian discourse. As such, I suggest that James K. A. Smith and Amos Yong—and other pentecostal theologians such as Ken Archer—are theologizing or philosophizing from a revised spirituality; that is, they are working from a prescriptive interpretation of pentecostal spirituality, rather than a descriptive one. Through the ethnographic and empirical work of Cartledge, Albrecht, Samuel, and others, it seems as though contemporary pentecostal churches in North America and the UK—and those they influence around the world—have largely gone one of three ways. They are either: (1) the remnant who closely adhere to the spirituality and governance of their pentecostal denominations; (2) those who participate in the church-growth movement and the practices and techniques contained therein; or (3) those who have gone the neocharismatic route.[35]

---

32. Land, *Pentecostal Spirituality*, p. 12.

33. Land, *Pentecostal Spirituality*, p. 18.

34. Indeed, at the time, pentecostal theology was either in a state of either apologetic defense, or overly dependent on the traditional outlines of evangelical fundamentals with pneumatological caveats. See Land, *Pentecostal Spirituality*, pp. 15–17.

35. Neocharismatics and their "postdenominationalism" are currently the overwhelming majority in the pentecostal and charismatic movement(s). "Since 1945 thousands of schismatic or other independent charismatic churches have come out of the Charismatic Movement; these independents have throughout the 20th century ... numbered more than the first two waves combined," see D. B. Barrett, and T. M. Johnson, "Global Statistics," in S. M. Burgess and E. M. van der Mass (eds), *NIDPCM* (Grand Rapids: Zondervan, 2002), p. 291.

## Conclusion

It appears that we can no longer assume that pentecostal scholars are theologizing from a descriptive pentecostal spirituality. Rather, we must take seriously the possibility that they may very well be theologizing from a prescriptive one. As such, we may now be at a point where our theology has outpaced our spirituality in terms of the locale of our most faithful and robust expression. What this work has exposed, then, is that insofar as the case studies of contemporary pentecostal churches are generally representative of pentecostal spirituality in specific contexts, our worship and speech habits ought to be open to modification. For the sake of moving toward that revision, the concern of my next chapter will be to construct a comprehensive pentecostal and thus Christian metaphysics, and from there, work out a spirituality which embodies, bespeaks, and mutually informs it in an effort to reduce the gap between what our churches and theologians are saying.

## Chapter 5

## TOWARD A PENTECOSTAL THEOLOGY OF BEING-IN-THE-SPIRIT: THE KNOWLEDGE OF THE TRIUNE GOD AND THE TRUTH OF THEOLOGICAL METAPHYSICS

*Introduction*

As a reminder to the reader, the overall purpose of this project is to offer a constructive and critical engagement of pentecostal spirituality and academic pentecostal theology through conversation with the greater ecumenical, dogmatic, and Christian metaphysical tradition; this effort is aimed at constructing a pentecostal metaphysics that, at once, does justice to what is "best" in the first-level pentecostal experience while confronting that which can be problematic. By "best" in the previous sentence, I simply mean that it is ecumenically promising and does not run counter to what the classical Christian tradition has said about God and creatures; furthermore, I mean "best" inasmuch as it is fitted to my forthcoming engagement with Smith's five elements of a pentecostal worldview. Thus, this work is explicitly and intentionally *limited* to understand metaphysics in conversation with the historical Christian tradition, and to understand a pentecostal vision of it according to Smith's categories. To that ultimate end, thus far, this work has sought to demonstrate, first, that pentecostal spirituality, whatever form it takes, implies a metaphysics, a panoramic encompassing vision of reality, and, second, that this metaphysics, embedded in the first-level discourse of prayers, sermons, songs, testimonies, and similar practices, can be explicated through second-level discourse of philosophical and theological reflection. Third, this work has also shown that only a few pentecostal scholars have made even a passing attempt at articulating a full-fledged metaphysics. Even when some part of this work has been done, scholars either have assumed an idealized pentecostal spirituality, one which threatens to obscure, rather than reveal, the shape of contemporary pentecostal practice and belief or they have not engaged pentecostal spirituality at all, seeking to construct a metaphysics in conversation with other spiritual/theological traditions and scientific disciplines instead.

As already said, there is much in the work of some pentecostal scholars, including, especially, James K. A. Smith and Amos Yong, that is fruitful for ecumenical conversation and the development of a pentecostal metaphysics.

Nonetheless, I argue that because they are working with what seems to be an idealized form of Land's pentecostal spirituality—one which does not represent what many pentecostals are in fact practicing today—there are unnecessary and unfortunate limits to their constructive proposals, limits which are made explicit when one begins with a different understanding of pentecostal spirituality and praxis.[1] Once other versions of pentecostal practice are considered, we discover that in many ways, and in various contexts, academic pentecostal theology is out of step with ecclesial pentecostal practice and spirituality.[2] For the most part, pentecostal spirituality, at least in its popular expressions, no longer holds the status of the Landian *gestalt* it perhaps once did.[3] This is not to say that Smith and Yong were entirely wrong in their approach, but simply to say that their approach limited to a certain extent their ability to critique pentecostal spirituality by essentializing and idealizing the Landian form of it. This work, then, is not necessarily set in opposition to theirs, but is intended as a continuation and expansion of their projects. I attempt to do that by avoiding, insofar as it is possible, an idealized expression of pentecostal spirituality. Rather than idealizing

---

1. As made evident by the difficulty of defining pentecostalism itself, the diversity of the movement is too great for any particular version of pentecostal spirituality to be essentialized. Yong, Smith, and others are, for the most part, working from a version of pentecostal spirituality as defined by Land. Land's version of pentecostal spirituality, however,—as helpful as it has been for pentecostal scholarship—can no longer be assumed. Indeed, in the idealized reception of Land's account, there is an assumption that that ideal is the truest possible expression of what pentecostalism is, per se. To assume Land's version as *the* ideal form of pentecostal spirituality is to limit the ability of pentecostal scholarship to critique our spirituality with second-level discourse, when and where our first-level discourse is malforming us. As has been mentioned throughout this work, I am attempting to overcome the tacit assumption in pentecostalism that second-level discourse is mostly superfluous—or indeed, unnecessary—save for pragmatic and apologetic purposes. There is a fundamental contradiction here as it is only when reflecting on our spirituality (read: practicing second-level discourse) that such assertions are made. Therefore, I have argued that first and second-level discourse are two connatural and mutually informing "poles" that are necessary for a more complete participation in the theological enterprise. Put succinctly, in my view, second-level discourse is no less doxological and no less spirit-led than first-level discourse.

2. The particular churches and their practices as observed by Albrecht, Cartledge, and Parker are some examples of churches that illustrate forms of contemporary and popular pentecostal spirituality broadly conceived.

3. A few points regarding this "Landian *gestalt*" ought to be summarized at this point: first, it was not a straightforward historical description, but an idealization of what this form of pentecostal spirituality could be; second, insofar as it is descriptive, it is limited in that it is not representative of what is being practiced throughout the whole pentecostal tradition; third, because it was used in those ways, it kept pentecostal theologians from being able to critique the forms of our spirituality that needed it.

or assuming that pentecostal spirituality, on its own, can give the best and most mature expression of our faith, I argue that pentecostals would be better served to explicate an orthodox and ecumenically promising theological metaphysics that resonates with their own self-understanding, and on that basis to critique forms of pentecostal spirituality and theology that have lost touch with historical Christian teaching.

What follows, then, is an attempt at developing a more thorough and cohesive pentecostal metaphysics, one which is informed both by Scripture and the Christian dogmatic tradition, as well as pentecostal distinctives, and one which therefore promises to help pentecostal scholars and ministers discern the theological integrity and soundness of contemporary beliefs and practices in various ministerial contexts. Finally, I will later argue that the best way to reform unfaithful beliefs and practices is through liturgical renewal.

## *"Come Quickly, Lord Jesus": Eschatological Reorientation*

### Introduction

As indicated earlier in this project, the eschatological orientation of pentecostals in the past has been concerned mostly with apocalyptic urgency for the sake of mission. However, as of late, pentecostal scholars have shown a new openness to cosmic and metaphysical reflection, in part by identifying the eschatological character of the person of the Holy Spirit.[4] According to this line of thinking, and precisely because they distinctively privilege the Holy Spirit both doctrinally and experientially, pentecostals are necessarily eschatologically oriented. One of the hermeneutical consequences of that orientation means that pentecostals understand the Spirit to be actively at work in all things, drawing them toward their final cause that is their eschatological End. Following this line of thought, I would argue that in particular the church, as the people of God, the body of

---

4. By this—as mentioned in the beginning of this work—I mean that pentecostal scholars have argued that to live by the Spirit is to live proleptically toward the future of all things. That is to say, it is the character of the Spirit to draw all things toward their eschatological End, and as people who privilege the Holy Spirit, we are thus a people who are eschatologically oriented. As people of the Spirit, we live as a people of eschatological hope, believing that the future hope of the entire cosmos is accessible in the present. Therefore, as people of the Spirit, our imaginations must not only begin and end with eschatology, but be thoroughgoingly infused with it. One example of a pentecostal scholar who postulates the close relatedness between eschatology and the Spirit's work is Yong who states explicitly that "The Spirit not only heralds the day of the Lord through the Messiah … but also works to bring it about. Indeed, the arrival of the day of the Lord is a thoroughly pneumatological event that transforms all creation" (Yong, *The Spirit Poured Out on all Flesh*, p. 95).

Christ, and the temple of the Holy Spirit, is the primary sacrament through which creation is drawn toward its promised fullness in the Spirit.[5]

## A Trinitarian Nondualist Eschatology

### Introduction

As partially noted above, many pentecostal scholars privilege narrative—with a particular vision of an eschatological End—as a vital means to ontological self-understanding. Wolfgang Vondey, Kenneth Archer, and Chris Green are some examples of those who participate in this kind of work, but they do so with nuanced differences that ought to be teased apart for the purposes of this work.

---

5. While pneumatology is obviously privileged among pentecostals, the pneumatological lens through which pentecostals view reality is given and received in ecclesial contexts. See Daniel E. Albrecht, "Pentecostal Spirituality: Looking through the Lens of Ritual," *Pneuma* 14.2 (1996), pp. 107–25. Furthermore, Smith begins his reflections on the five elements of a pentecostal worldview by drawing from what pentecostals experience and expect in a pentecostal worship service. For example, under the category of "a radical openness to God" he states explicitly that "One of the reasons pentecostal spirituality is so often linked to spontaneity is that pentecostal *worship* makes room for the unexpected" (Smith, *Thinking*, p. 33 [emphasis mine]). He goes on to say that "It is because pentecostal faith constitutes a community characterized by a radical openness to God that pentecostal communities emphasize the continued ministry of the Spirit ... this translates into a dynamic ecclesiology *in practice*" (Smith, *Thinking in Tongues*, pp. 38–9). For Smith, then, it is in ecclesial contexts that a radical openness to God is embodied, expressed, and grasped. Additionally, when constructing a pentecostal epistemology, he begins by telling a story of a woman who gave a testimony in a pentecostal worship service (Smith, *Thinking in Tongues*, pp. 48–50). Upon becoming pregnant following prayer regarding that specific request, she proclaimed, "I know that I know that I know," that it was a miracle from God. God may have acted in her personal life outside the context of the church service, but a hermeneutical lens for how God acts in the world and language for how we know that God is acting were both illustrated and given to the hearers, and to her previously, within the context of the church service. This is explicit in the work of Wolfgang Vondey who says, "Pentecostal theology as liturgical theology is a hermeneutical exercise that aims to make explicit theologically the image of God in the worship of the people" (Vondey, *Pentecostal Theology*, p. 282). While for Vondey, the event of Pentecost itself is a theological symbol that emphasizes the pentecostal encounter with God, those encounters are ecclesiologically focused as they happen and are experienced in the church's shared life around the altar. Even Yong, who is known for emphatically privileging pneumatology, and for distinctly having a "passion for the Spirit" in his interreligious and interdisciplinary dialogues, has stated that theology emerges, at least in part, through ecclesial liturgy (Yong, *SWC*, p. 291). Therefore, for pentecostals, ecclesiology is tacitly privileged as the precise location from which we encounter God pneumatologically, and thus understand ourselves and the world theologically and metaphysically. The church's shared life is where hermeneutical, pneumatological, missiological, and sacramental (etc.) categories meet.

## Cosmic Salvation and the Fullness of the Full Gospel

In Vondey's theology, when he uses the word "narrative," he specifically means the narrative of the full gospel which structures the testimonies of pentecostals and how they come to experience Jesus as savior—namely, in first-level discourse at the pentecostal altar.[6] Salvation is the thoroughgoing theme that runs all the way through the full gospel. The full gospel is thus purported to be the soteriological story of Jesus as told and understood by pentecostals in such a way that Jesus' life is determinative for pentecostal worship and self-understanding—it, therefore, dramatically narrates the grounds by which pentecostals worship, and so understand themselves and all of reality.[7] The full gospel narrative thus gives pentecostals a pattern from which to understand the story of Jesus as the grounds

---

6. Chan, on the other hand, argues that the two major categories for the church's self-understanding—that is, (1) the church as instrumental to God's purpose or (2) the church as the visible expression of what God intends—entail their own readings the overall biblical narrative. Like Vondey, Chan understands practice and narrative as connatural and mutually determining; however, the question Chan begins with is how the church ought to be understood in relation to creation. Whether one presupposes option one or option two will shape, and is shaped by, the overall biblical narrative from creation to consummation. Therefore, Chan does not explicitly privilege the story of Pentecost nor the full gospel as a necessary means of self-understanding as do Vondey and Archer (see the next footnote). It is important to note here that, despite their distinct emphases, Chan, Vondey, and Archer understand the function of narrative as deeply formative for communal and personal self-understanding.

7. Vondey explicitly says:

> The full gospel is in the first place a theological narrative oriented towards doxology; its purpose is to direct to the worship of God. Hence, Pentecostal theology embraces the conviction that without a full narrative of the gospel, Christian worship of God is incomplete. The soteriological direction of the full gospel emphasizes that for Pentecostals participation in worship is not a consequence of but presupposition for participation in the fullness of salvation. The central concern of the full gospel is to direct our soteriological vision and activities to all possibilities of participating in the redemption of the world created with the outpouring of the Spirit at Pentecost.
>
> <div align="right">(Vondey, <i>Pentecostal Theology</i>, p. 290)</div>

Ken Archer shares a very similar vision to that of Vondey as he argues that "The Pentecostal narrative tradition is an eschatological Christian story of God's involvement in the restoration of the Christian community and God's dramatic involvement both in reality and the pentecostal community." Archer ascribes the same formative force to the particular story of Pentecost while aiming to keep Jesus central, as does Vondey. For example, Archer says, "The Pentecostal community's identity is forged from its reading of the biblical narrative of Acts and then the Gospels. Pentecostals desire to live as the eschatological people of God. They are caught up in the final drama of God's redemptive activity, which is channeled through Jesus and manifested in the community by the

in which their own stories participate, often expressed through their testimonies in communal context. Furthermore, Vondey argues that pentecostals place the story of the full gospel under the symbol of Pentecost, which shifts the theological emphasis from the story of Jesus "to the continuing eschatological and sanctifying work of the Spirit."[8] The soteriological full gospel story "ends" with eschatology under the motif of "Jesus the soon-coming King." For Vondey, "The primary eschatological question from the perspective of the full gospel is how an apocalyptic imagination serves the understanding of the first creation and its continuity and discontinuity with the new creation."[9] To answer this question, he points out that contemporary pentecostal scholars—prominently, Yong—have suggested engagement with science as a fruitful way forward. Those who suggest this are the pentecostal theologians who have (rightly) abandoned the dispensational paradigm in favor of "eschatologies of hope" championed by twentieth-century German theologians, and others. Moreover, combined with "apocalyptic urgency" and this-worldly missional fervor, these contemporary pentecostal theologians posit an eschatology with emphasis on continuity. That is, they apparently posit that their missional work in this world directly matters for the world to come in

---

Holy Spirit, and they enthusiastically embrace and proclaim the Full Gospel," see Ken Archer, "Pentecostal Story: The Hermeneutical Filter for the Making of Meaning," in Ken Archer (ed.), *The Gospel Revisited: Towards a Pentecostal Theology of Worship and Witness* (Eugene: Pickwick Pub., 2011), p. 25. The story of Pentecost and the pentecostal community who embodies it at the altar, both shapes, and is shaped by, the overall metanarrative of Scripture. In terms of how this narrative connects to an eschatological vision, Archer sees the "latter rain motif" as essential to pentecostal identity in that it provided "a persuasive theological apologetic account for the existence of their community," as such pentecostals "understood themselves as the prophetically promised eschatological community who would bring about the unity of Christianity and usher in the Second Coming of Christ" (Archer, "Pentecostal Story," p. 27). By connecting the pentecostal eschatological orientation with the "latter rain motif," Archer seems to be pointing to a very "realized" eschatological vision with the pentecostal community itself is that eschatological fulfillment (in part) and further inaugurates the fullness of God's eschatological act. When discussing the same movement, Vondey also says "Pentecostalism is the eschatological fulfillment of the outpouring of the Holy Spirit on all flesh. The latter rain teaching culminates in the idea of a revival, return to, or final completion of the day of Pentecost in the present age of the church, manifested by the Pentecostal movement" (Vondey, *Pentecostal Theology*, pp. 134–5). Narratively speaking, then, both Vondey and Archer argue that pentecostal self-identity is oriented around Acts 2 and the life of Jesus via the Full Gospel; eschatologically speaking, this narrative is culminated and reinterpreted by eschatological promises being at least partially fulfilled under the conditions of our present reality. While pentecostals—insofar as they follow the latter rain's lead—can be catalytic agents for the final eschatological appearing of Christ.

8. Vondey, *Beyond Pentecostalism*, p. 30.
9. Vondey, *Pentecostal Theology*, p. 172.

a somewhat straightforward way. This desire seems necessarily to spill over into their understanding of the ontological continuity of this world with the world to come. Hence, those who hold to a strong continuity like Vondey and Yong, argue that science can provide fruitful insights, or at least be a beneficial enterprise with which theology should dialogue. And so, says Vondey, "God acts in the world teleologically or eschatologically through the Holy Spirit in ways that can be explained by both theologically and scientific accounts."[10]

Such pentecostalism and its self-understanding in relation to narrative may be seen as "participation in the ongoing story of Pentecost … in the unfolding of the story of God in the world through Christ and the Spirit."[11] Pentecostals not only narrate themselves through the story of Pentecost and the fivefold gospel, but also "narrate the world through participation, celebration, and practices that tell of the possibilities of redemption opened with Pentecost. The full gospel is in this sense a form of living the Christian life that demands our confrontation with the fullness of the revelation of God."[12] As such, pentecostal theology "insists that the only way to participate in the fullness of the gospel is by living it. In practice, the full gospel is not merely story but liturgy."[13]

Vondey's second-level "shift in theological emphasis" from the story of Jesus to the events of Pentecost is manifested in the first-level liturgical shift of practice around the pentecostal altar as the locale wherein the story of Pentecost is privileged and expressed. While Vondey insists that the full gospel demands a confrontation with "the fullness of God," it is not always clear that the story of Pentecost is embodied in first-level pentecostal spirituality as the work of the *particular* Spirit of Jesus at the altar.[14] The work of Cartledge and Parker in their respective studies

10. Vondey, *Pentecostal Theology*, p. 172.
11. Vondey, *Beyond Pentecostalism*, p. 30.
12. Vondey, *Pentecostal Theology*, p. 291.
13. Vondey, *Pentecostal Theology*, p. 291.
14. Vondey argues that pentecostal spirituality has favored an unstructured, improvised, and "playful" approach to its liturgy, centered around the altar and embodying the events of Pentecost (see: Vondey, *Beyond Pentecostalism*, pp 109–40; Wolfgang Vondey, "The Theology of the Altar and Pentecostal Sacramentality," in Mark J. Cartledge and A. J. Swoboda (eds), *Scripting Pentecost: A Study of Pentecostals, Worship and Liturgy* [Aldershot, UK: Ashgate, 2016], pp. 94–107). My concern here is that Vondey's notion of "openness" necessitates an entire spirituality which resists structure for the sake of hospitality, so that there is no given discourse or practice to ground our worship to ensure that we are indeed acting *freely*, rather than in accordance with our inherited or local precommitments. It seems that structure in the pentecostal imagination, at least in Vondey's mind, is understood as inherently inhospitable and restraining (and therefore, *not* the work of the Spirit), while the public bewilderment of the day of Pentecost is necessarily the work of the Spirit so that said bewilderment functions as a *rule* for the events that happen in and around the altar on a regular basis. I, however, want to resist the notion of restricting the work of the Spirit

of particular pentecostal churches[15] illustrates a lack of trinitarian and full gospel focus in our first-level discourse, at least in its contemporary popular expressions. First-level discourse which privileges experiences of the Spirit at Pentecost apart from the *explicit* telling of Jesus' story and devoid of trinitarian discourse—which traditional church practices and confessions emphatically keep us rooted in—may result in privileging our stories while moving the story of Jesus to the periphery.

as evident primarily in the extraordinary, lest the Spirit be understood as rarely active in a church service. Moreover, it is not entirely clear that the altar in today's pentecostalism is approached free of expectations so that proper space is afforded for bewilderment. That is to say, if we are going to shift our theological emphasis from the story of Jesus to the events of Pentecost, as Vondey suggests, we must not assume that connecting the Spirit's activity to the life of Jesus will happen organically in our spirituality. If we do, then we risk repeating the errors of the respective churches observed by Parker and Cartledge in their monographs—that is, the errors of not naming or worshipping God trinitarianly, so that the triune God does not shape our worship (Cartledge, *Testimony*, p. 47; Parker, *Led by the Spirit*, pp. 62-116). In other words, I want to resist the fact that "Time and again, we see Pentecostalism professing a traditional doctrine of God, yet its very practices continually set the stage for the unraveling, liquidation, or reconstruction of that doctrine" (Wariboko, *The Split God*, p. xiii). I must hasten to add that Wariboko does not share my inclination to resist this. I think we ought to insist that the connection between the Spirit at Pentecost and the life of the Son as sent by the Father remains explicit in our first-level discourse, and that is what connecting our altar to the practices and discourse of the Christian tradition is aimed at accomplishing. Vondey's insistence about the necessity of the triune God's evocation in our second-level discourse ought to be reflected as he discusses our first-level discourse. The former is evident when critiquing Yong—"the Spirit poured out on all flesh"—for putting an article where the pronoun "my" belongs in Yong's paraphrase of Acts 2:17 and Jl 2:28-29. Vondey insists that "from God's perspective it is not *the* Spirit who is poured out but *my* Spirit ... the pneumatology Yong describes asks primarily what it means *that* the Spirit is poured out; it does not ask the question *who* pours out the Spirit." He continues, "A Pentecostal theology that finds its roots in the witness of Pentecost must take care to preserve the integrity of the operation of the Father and the Son, respectively, in the outpouring of the Holy Spirit" so that "Pentecostal theology must from beginning to end be constructed as an *explicitly* trinitarian pneumatology." (Vondey, "Pentecostalism and the Possibility of Global Theology: Implications of the Theology of Amos Yong" [*Pneuma* 28.2 Fall 2006], pp. 297-8). I share Vondey's concerns, and I fear that he simply might be overlooking that a pentecostal first-level discourse which lacks any structure or explicit connection to traditional or trinitarian practices will likely lead to the errors he is resisting in Yong's second-level discourse. Let us insist, then, that all bewilderment to take place at the pentecostal altar must be fitted to the mystery of the presence of Jesus in the offensively ordinary bread and wine. Indeed, what is more hospitable—in that it transcends cultural, ethnic, national, and even temperamental bounds—than eating and drinking in communion with one another as we share in the life of the triune God?

15. Parker, *Led by the Spirit*, pp. 62-116; Cartledge, *Testimony*, pp. 29-54, esp. 47.

I want to place more explicit weight on the story of Jesus, as does Hauerwas, who reminds us that we must not forget to subsume our stories and testimonies to the *particular* life of Jesus.[16] He says, soberingly, that "the emphasis on narrative is not an invitation to use whatever we take to be our 'experience' to test or determine the meaning of the language of the faith."[17] More provocatively, he goes on to say, "being Christian means that I must try to make sense of my life in light of the gospel, and so I do not get to determine the truthfulness of my story."[18] The particular narrative of Jesus, therefore, must be told and *privileged* in our *first-level* discourse, while the story of Pentecost as our participation and testimony may be fitted to it as the continuation of the story of Jesus with his people.[19] With those slight caveats regarding first-level discourse, I thoroughly affirm Vondey's second-level discourse on narrative, trinity, and the life of Jesus.

In light of what we have just adduced in Vondey's vision of narrative, participation, and liturgy, let us now look at his cosmic and metaphysical reflection. When Vondey looks at creation from a cosmic perspective while

16. While Hauerwas does not locate his narrative self-understanding primarily in Acts 2 as pentecostals do, he does, like pentecostals, understand narrative as deeply formative for Christian ontological self-understanding. I quote Hauerwas here because I think he serves as a helpful reminder for pentecostals to reflect on the truthfulness of our self-understanding by beginning with the life of God as explicitly revealed in Jesus. It is a mistake to take the Holy Spirit as the Spirit of Jesus for granted in our first-level discourse. If we do not explicitly connect the story of Pentecost with the work of Jesus in our first-level discourse, crucial errors about the being of God and so our own being can ensue. Hauerwas thus shows the importance of beginning with Jesus in order to make sense of ourselves, which will subsequently demand that we explicitly tell and live the story of the triune God in our first-level discourse.

17. Stanley Hauerwas, *Hannah's Child: A Theologian's Memoir* (Cambridge: Eerdmans, 2010), pp. 156-7.

18. Hauerwas, *Hannah's Child*, p. 159.

19. Vondey, in terms of second-level discourse, would likely agree and argue that this is precisely what the full gospel narrative is meant for. However, there seems to be nothing in place in his understanding of the first-level discourse of altar practices to ensure that the story of Jesus is told, or the triune God evoked. His primary concerns for altar *practices* seem to be space for bewilderment and hospitality toward different cultures and milieus as reminiscent in the story of Pentecost. With that said, I affirm Vondey's second-level discourse regarding the function of Jesus' narrative as determinative for pentecostal identity, and I also affirm his insistence on the particularity of the Holy Spirit as the Spirit of the triune God. My point of contention is on his first-level discourse and its resistance to a scripted liturgy as received from the historical Christian tradition. What enables this resistance, it seems, is that he overstates the explicit connection of the story of Jesus via the fivefold gospel and the—*prescriptive,* more so than descriptive—practices at the altar. If the studies of Cartledge, Parker, and Samuel are representative in any way, there is little to no explicit connection made, nor is the story of Jesus and the triune God explicitly bespoken.

focusing on the pentecostal eschatological orientation through the soteriological narrative of the full gospel, "Jesus is savior" is expanded to mean that creation itself is the "cosmic altar" of his saving acts.[20] Eschatology is a way of naming the final cause of soteriology so that soteriology determines the *character* of creation. Thus, Vondey says that creation "does not exist apart from but solely for the purpose of salvation. The doctrine of creation is subsumed under soteriology"; therefore, Jesus is savior means that "the notion of 'creation' is inexplicably defined by the expectation of a 'new creation' brought about by the work of God. In other words, creation and redemption, although temporally distinguished, are logically the same act."[21] Creation, then, is a storied journey, moving toward its eschatological end.[22] That is to say, rather than thinking of God's act of creating the world as merely a past event, it is perhaps better to think of creation as a standing and continuing relationship between the world as dependent upon God, so that creation is not "complete" until the relationship is consummated. Put poetically, creation and consummation as one dramatically narrated act may be described so: "God goes forth in all beings and in all beings returns to himself."[23] I want to hold fast to Vondey's vision of the narrative relationship between creation, salvation, and consummation while rejecting the idea that science reveals anything about *eschatological* realities. Moreover, I want to insist that it is the narrative of Jesus that must remain central and not peripheral in both first and second-level discourse. As far as I am concerned, Chris Green is the pentecostal theologian who does this best for the purposes of this work. More on this below.

*The Universality of Jesus' Particular History*
If the "cosmic altar" displays creation and redemption as the same act through the life of Jesus, then pentecostal metaphysics must come to grips with creation not as a mere thing that is constituted by aggregate parts which somehow come together to provide a stage for history to unfold; rather, creation is what it is

---

20. I am not necessarily concerned with following the logic of the full gospel completely—especially because from all of the studies from particular pentecostal churches presented here, it is not imperative for pentecostal spirituality in ecclesial contexts. I am simply pointing to it as an example of the fact that pentecostals understand the life of Jesus as that which orients their self-identity and vision of reality. As such, elements of the full gospel will appear here and there, but it will not be followed stringently as Vondey does for his work.

21. Vondey, *Pentecostal Theology*, p. 157.

22. W. Norris Clarke, "Fifty Years of Metaphysical Reflection: The Universe as Journey," in Gerald A. McCool, S.J. (ed.), *The Universe as Journey: Conversations with W. Norris Clarke, S. J.* (New York: Fordham University Press, 1988), pp. 49–91.

23. David Bentley Hart, *That All Shall Be Saved: Heaven, Hell, and Universal Salvation* (New Haven: Yale University Press, 2019), p. 71.

precisely *as* a history—a history that begins and ends with God.[24] That is to say that the universe is a meaningful storied journey from, toward, and within the life of God, and the church is called to embody, prefigure, and foretaste this reality for the sake of the world.

Creation so understood—and ecclesiologically embodied—as the soteriological history of all things in which Christians participate, categorically moves narrative beyond mere "illustrations of some deeper truth that we can and should learn to articulate in a non-narrative mode,"[25] and instead ascribes ontological status to it, so that propositions about reality are in service of the narrative, not vice versa. Once again, Hauerwas meets us with his insistence on our stories being connected to a particular story:

> My contention is that ... narrative ... is neither incidental nor accidental to Christian belief. There is no more fundamental way to talk of God than in a story. The fact that we come to know God through the recounting of the story of Israel and the life of Jesus is decisive for our truthful understanding of the kind of God we worship as well as the world in which we exist. Put directly, the narrative character of our knowledge of God, the self, and the world is a reality-making claim that the world and our existence in it are God's creations; our lives, and indeed, the existence of the universe are but contingent realities.[26]

Notice the particularity of the story to which Hauerwas grants ontological and reality-making status: it is the story of Israel and the life of Jesus with his creation. Narrative, as Hauerwas understands it, is as all-encompassing as the full gospel narrative, but it properly situates the testimonies and stories of God's people as contingent realities.

*History's Transfiguration*
Finally, the implications of granting one narrative—that is the soteriologically and so eschatologically directed story of God with his people and all things—ontological *primacy* is that creation itself *follows from* God's life as revealed in history. It is

---

24. Althouse appropriately quotes Newbiggin when making this exact point: "The Bible claims to show us the shape, the structure, the origin, and the goal not merely of human history, but of cosmic history. It does not accept a view of nature as simply the arena upon which the drama of human history is played out ... Rather it sees the history of the nations and the history of nature within the large framework of God's history—carrying forward to its completion of the gracious purpose that has its source in the love of the Father for the Son in the unity of the Spirit" (Lesslie Newbigin, *The Open Secret: An Introduction to the Theology of Mission*, rev. ed. (Grand Rapids: Eerdmans, 1995), pp. 30-1 via Peter Althouse, "Ascension—Pentecost—Eschaton: A Theological Framework for Pentecostal Ecclesiology," in John Christopher Thomas (ed.), *Toward a Pentecostal Ecclesiology: The Church and the Fivefold Gospel* (Cleveland: CPT Press, 2010), p. 234.
25. Hauerwas, *The Peaceable Kingdom*, p. 25.
26. Hauerwas, *The Peaceable Kingdom*, p. 25.

here where I must explicate what I have thus far been foreshadowing and identify Chris Green's understanding of eschatology and narrative as that which is most beneficial than that of other pentecostal scholars for the purposes of this work.[27] Chris Green grants the story of Jesus ontological primacy without concern for what sciences might reveal to us about the nature of the world to come. Indeed, it is his vision of the End and its relation to history that most resonates with this thesis.

Chris Green is among the pentecostal theologians who deny dispensational eschatology in favor of something more reminiscent of an eschatology of hope. However, unlike the constructive visions of some of the contemporary pentecostal eschatologies adduced above, for Green, the End that God brings is more radically decisive. That is, Jesus' "appearing in glory" "necessarily alters the very structures of reality. The apocalyptic moment at time's end is no less decisive than the primordial moment at time's beginning. The Last Judgment, therefore, takes place as a transfiguring moment in which time and space 'pass over into eternity' and all things are drawn into the new order of being."[28] The appearing of Jesus in glory, then, is "not an event within time, or even *after* time: it happens *to* time."[29] This is what it means for reality to be "taken up into Christ" in such a way that Jesus is unstintingly present to the world, and the world to him. This "unstinting" presence marks the difference between Christ's incarnate presence—under the metaphysical conditions of this reality—and his presence when he appears in glory, which will fundamentally alter this reality. Jesus' incarnate presence indeed affected everything and everyone around him. How much more, then, will the

---

27. Green's eschatology of hope is very much influenced by his reading of Robert W. Jenson. When Green wrote his *Lord's Supper* text earlier in his career, he was primarily engaging Jenson's later writings which emphasize Christ's fulfillment of nature over against his disruption of it. Throughout the scope of his career, however, Green engaged Jenson's earlier work more thoroughly, which has a more prophetic edge in that it emphasizes discontinuity (e.g., *Story and Promise*). We see Green's emphasis more clearly in his latest monograph, which is the second edition of *Sanctifying Interpretation*. This same trend is displayed when one looks at his earlier essay on eschatology, "Reimagining Parousia" in comparison with his latest chapter on the matter entitled "The End of all Endings" and later still, a sermon he wrote entitled "Transfiguring Death." In "Transfiguring Death", Green argues that the life of Jesus confronts our optimism that being Christian somehow guarantees good endings for us. Rather, what Scripture and the life of Jesus teach us is that to experience the wilderness, and to experience death, is to experience Christ. See https://macrinamagazine.com/sermon/guest/2021/03/07/transfiguring-death/ (Accessed 04/01/21). What follows is my reading of Green's eschatology and how it relates to our current reality in his later work wherein he emphasizes disruption and discontinuity.

28. Chris Green, "'In My Flesh I Shall See God': (Re)Imagining Parousia, Last Judgment, and Visio Dei," *JEPTA* 33.2 (2013), p. 178.

29. Green, "In My Flesh," p. 178.

eschatological appearance of *this one*—who simultaneously is the firstborn of all creation and holds all things together—creatively effect the reality to which he makes himself fully present? Green insists, therefore, that the appearance of Jesus is a *generative* event; that is, an event that alters time, space, and all of the material world in such a way that it is beyond the ability of science to access or predict.

As the appearing of Christ in glory alters biological reality into something radically new, so also does it transfigure history itself and its constituent narratives with their *penultimate* endings. For Green, narratives of Scripture do *not* give us satisfying penultimate endings that we can look to and hope that the penultimate ending(s) of our own stories in history will make equally satisfying sense; neither do said endings in the text straightforwardly prefigure the End that Jesus' appearing in glory effects. Upon a careful reading of the endings of each of the Gospel narratives along with the narrative ending of the Acts of the Apostles, Green argues that the narratives of Scripture point to the truth that there is *no* ultimate satisfaction in how our contingent stories end, until the fact that Jesus is all in all becomes sight both for history itself, and its constituent narratives.[30] Once again, then, resurrection happens *to* a history filled with narratives that tell of penultimate deaths, and simultaneously, history itself tends in the same direction. This is what it means to say that Jesus' appearing is every bit as decisive as God's act of *creatio ex nihilo*. We come from nothingness and tend toward nothingness, but for God—who doesn't save us from dying, but saves us by resurrecting us from death, just as he did to his Son. What then happens to history and its constitutive narratives which is the content of our lives? What can be said about continuity and discontinuity? Green turns to poetics, "God will turn the water of history into the wine of eternity; the loaves and fishes of our worldly experience will be taken up and multiplied infinitely in the banquet that is our knowing as we are known."[31]

For Green, the passing from the old world into the new at Christ's appearance is nothing less than creation's full share in Christ's resurrection. Thus, once again, this event effects the decisive creation of a *new* material world. He would thus reject Vondey and Yong's contention (*et al.*) that science—as good and necessary as it is—is in anyway revelatory for what God means for creation and eschatology. Much like science could not predict Jesus' resurrection by empirical method even if it had access to his living incarnate body, neither can it faintly discern the new reality that God means for all things. Whatever we might say cataphatically about the material reality that is promised to us, we can only faintly point to a fog, in hope, and say that it "is the kind of materiality that is fitted to the knowing of God as he knows himself."[32] This new embodiment is

---

30. See Chris Green, *All Things Beautiful: An Aesthetic Christology* (Waco: BUP, 2022), pp. 105–22.
31. Green, "In My Flesh," pp. 194–5.
32. Green, *The End Is Music*, p. 97.

possible only within a reality that is constituted by a new temporality. Time is currently experienced as it passes from present to past, thus *dying* to us. When Jesus is fully present to our realty, however, nothing is given to death. Indeed, "our bodies much like the time/space they inhabit, shall be of such a nature that *nothing* is lost. And all that had been lost shall be restored."[33] The "End of all endings" is good news, but it only *appears* so—much like Jesus' fear-inducing post-resurrection appearances—to those who have faith. Still, to those with faith, we can't know it by looking at penultimate death-bringing ends throughout history, but only through revelation and hope.

Narrative, ecclesiology, and eschatology thus converge in a particular way for Green. Ecclesial ordinances are indeed "nourishment for our (narrated) journey" still toward death. But these ordinances (primarily the Lord's Supper) are foretastes of the world to come as we faithfully embody Christ in this history as the gateway and mediators for the transformation of all things. As we nourish ourselves with what Christ has given us, his post-resurrection presence appears to us by faith. That is the only way we "see" him under the conditions of this world.[34] His post-resurrection appearances to and through the Body gathered around the bread and wine by the power of the Holy Spirit are every bit as confounding as his appearing through a locked door to the disciples without having opened it. Just this is what it means to be the church which is the community that is eschatologically ahead of creation in that we "see" and "experience" the eschatological reality of the world to come by faith; this happens in our gatherings where we offer up the water of our collective narrative acts—culminating at the Table of the Lord—believing it to be the wine of his real presence by faith and in hope that his unstinting presence will be made fully available *to* history. While we are still subjected to the death wrought by living in "adamic history," the Spirit frees God's people from mere historical contingency and into "Christic history," "and so allows them to participate in that history in a new, creative way."[35] That is, "The Spirit frees an actual human community from merely historical determinations, to be apt to be united with the Son and thus *to be the gateway of creation's translation into God.*"[36] For Green, the Lord's Supper (and the constitutive acts surrounding it) is the first-level embodiment of the church's narrative, eschatological, and so ontological self-understanding.

---

33. Green, *The End Is Music*, p. 98.

34. That is to say, we cannot see eschatological realities in an empirically verifiable way. In terms of the presence of the resurrected Jesus in the Lord's Supper, all that can be verified by that method is that we're drinking wine and eating bread, not that Jesus is *actually* present. By faith, however, that is precisely what is happening.

35. Chris Green, "'Then Their Eyes Were Opened': Pentecostal Reflections on the Church's Scripture and the Lord's Supper," in Chris Green (ed.), *Pentecostal Ecclesiology: A Reader* (Leiden: Brill, 2016), pp. 205–6.

36. Green, "'Then Their Eyes Were Opened,'" p. 206.

## "For from Him and through Him and to Him Are All Things": The Triune Determination(s) of Creation

### The Father as Source

A reminder to the reader: *ultimately*, what I am offering in this monograph is a constructive and critical engagement with pentecostal spirituality and academic pentecostal theology in conversation with the larger ecumenical, creedal, liturgical, and dogmatic Christian metaphysical tradition. The purpose of this effort is to construct a pentecostal metaphysics that simultaneously does justice to what is best in first-level pentecostal experience while confronting that which is unfaithful. In the previous section, I demonstrated that pentecostal theology can show that pentecostals have a storied identity which is aimed at the Consummation of New Creation and are thus a narratival and eschatologically oriented people. The next step is to develop an explicit doctrine of a lively and triune God, and to show how this God relates to a creation journeying toward becoming one with him. In the forthcoming subsections, I will lay out an eschatologically oriented vision of creation as narratable and triadically structured along the three poles of time, connected to the triune God. Let us begin our triadically structured, eschatological metaphysical vision beginning with the Father as *arche* of all that is, visible and invisible.

In light of what has thus far been argued and constructed, I will now turn to theological formulations—both within and without of the pentecostal tradition—and the Scriptures which the church privileges as norms for theological judgment for the sake of constructing the forthcoming metaphysics. I have argued that the story of Jesus and the End toward which it finds its fulfillment is prior to creation. Thus, the narrative of Jesus ought to be privileged for pentecostal metaphysics. Furthermore, the content of that history is soteriological and eschatological as it is the story of Jesus of Nazareth in whom we live, move, and have our being. As such, reality itself has a narratable structure of past, present, and future because God is Father, Son, and Spirit. Thus, pentecostal spirituality ought to enact and bespeak the narrative and triadic structure of the reality in which it is enfolded and with which it is identified. A triadic creation so understood is faithfully interpreted when construed by the roles of the three persons in the one mutual life that is the triune God. Let us look at the "roles" of said persons beginning with that of God "the Father, the Almighty, creator of heaven and earth, of all that is, visible and invisible."

That creation is a history means that reality as we experience it has a narratable beginning. Moreover, its initiation points to an Initiator as the Source of this eschatologically oriented reality who antecedently acts as Source within his own life. The Christian tradition points us to the Father as said Source.[37] "God is Father

---

37. For example, Origen says, "Now we hold ... that the Wisdom of God has her subsistence nowhere else but in him who is the beginning of all things, from whom also she is born. Since this Wisdom is the one who alone is Son by nature, she is therefore called *the only-begotten*" (*On First Principles*, 1.2.5, p. 47.). Furthermore, "As God the Father is indivisible and inseparable from the Son, it is not by emanation from him, as some

in that God is the *givenness* of reality—both for himself and for us."[38] Therefore, a Spirit-freed and so eschatologically oriented reality that is initiated by the Father as absolute Source—and utterly dependent on the Son—means that said reality must be contingent; and its contingency *begins* by the will of the Father. Chris Green puts it thus:

> We can know that God's Fatherhood is ultimate because of what the Scriptures tells us about Jesus's life: he lived and died over against God as the transcendent horizon of his and all other reality. The Jesus narratively described in the Gospels is one who knows himself and everything else only in relation to the Father's will—what already is true because of that will, and what in the end will be true because of that will.[39]

suppose, that the Son is generated." Rather, in Scripture "John also indicates that *God is light*, and Paul also declares that the Son is the *brightness* of eternal *light*. As *light*, then, could never exist without *brightness*, so neither can the Son be understood without the Father, for he is called *the express figure of his substance* and the Word and Wisdom" (*On First Principles*, 4.4.1. p. 563). Moreover, for Origen, "The Father-Son relation is distinct from and metaphysically prior to the relation between God and creation, and to his affirmation of the eternity of God's goodness and creative power" (Peter Widdicombe, *The Fatherhood of God from Origen to Athanasius*, p. 67). Later, John of Damascus says it succinctly, yet quite adequately, "We believe in one Father, the principle and cause of all things, begotten of no one, who alone is uncaused and unbegotten, the maker of all things and by nature Father of His one and only-begotten Savior, Jesus Christ, and Emitter of the All-Holy Spirit" (John of Damascus, *Expositio Fidei*, 1.8).

38. Green, *The End Is Music*, p. 22.

39. Green, *The End Is Music*, p. 22. In this quote, Green implicitly used "Father" to denote both the triune God and the Father as *persona* in relation to Jesus. Indeed, this also happens in Scripture. Considering that Green is writing on Jenson's theology, perhaps it would be helpful to briefly spell out how Jenson makes sense of this. For Jenson, a "person" (in his later work) is one whom others can address and from whom others may be addressed. Thus, persons are "social relations," and in the case of the triune God, social relations of origin constituted by mutual address and response. However, there cannot be a straightforward univocal identification between what person means in God, and in our experience; the clearest example is that one of the "persons" in God is "Spirit," and to be spirit is to be the spirit *of* "another one." "Person," then, as fitted to our experience would be better suited to the Triune God than one of his relational "constituents." "For a community to be capable of converse and so of personality there must be someone who can be addressed as the community. In the case of the Trinity, there is such a someone ... the Father is to be addressed as the God of Israel and ... the Trinity is the God of Israel" (*ST*.1.122). Father is the God of Israel and the *persona* who is addressed—with the Son, and by the Spirit—precisely so that the Trinity is personal to us. St. Thomas makes a similar argument when discussing the "Our Father" in his *Summa Theologiae* 1.33. When we pray to the Father we are at once joining ourselves to the Son's filial address *and* praying to the Trinity.

As such it must be one created *ex nihilo* as contingent realities cannot be the source of their own existence. Precisely, because "the cosmos is not a necessary being."[40] Nonetheless, this traditional doctrine imposes difficulty on our imaginations because nothingness as such is impossible to imagine, and so impossible to narrate.[41] This is the difficulty Israel is confronted with as they, in Genesis, dogmatically connect their own particular narrative as God's people to the unrivaled God who precedes, sustains, and fulfills all things. The Earth's pre-creative state as "formless and void" is not a description of a material reality which God has to either overcome or work with; rather, in order to make the beginning narratable, the Genesis story starts "before" the beginning by describing pre-creation in pure negations. Before there was anything at all, there was only God—sourced by the Father who begets the Son and "breathes" the Spirit who frees him to love the Son. As such, the doctrine of *creatio ex nihilo* envisages pre-creation as nothing other than the life of the triune God, and "speaks of a God who gives of his bounty, not a God at war with darkness";[42] creation is therefore not "prized from chaos so that God must then actively preserve creation against a chaos that somehow abides as its other side. But creation's other side is, quite simply, nothing at all."[43]

Considering the Father's role in the triadically structured creation, then, we may again say that the Father is the Source of creation. The Nicene Creed dogmatically asserts that those who gather and confess believe in "God, the *Father* almighty, maker of heaven and earth, of all that is visible and invisible."[44] Also,

---

40. Matthew Levering, *Proofs of God: Classical Arguments from Tertullian to Barth* (Grand Rapids: Baker Academic, 2016), p. 1.

41. Amos Yong's sympathies to this difficulty lead him to modify the traditional understanding of *creatio ex nihilo* from his perspectives of emergentism, the economy of salvation as phenomenologically experienced, and his reading of the creation narratives in Scripture. I part ways with him on this point.

42. David Bentley Hart, *The Beauty of the Infinite: The Aesthetics of Christian Truth* (Grand Rapids: Eerdmans, 2004), p. 258.

43. Hart, *Beauty of the Infinite*, p. 258.

44. It is important to note that this does *not* mean that the Father is sole creator so that the Son and the Spirit are not. To be utterly and necessarily original is indeed an important aspect of what constitutes deity, and because I am not positing anything implicitly subordinationist, it is here important to briefly note that (and how) Son and Spirit are Source. Following from what I have already said in conversation with Green and Jenson about "persons as relations of address and response" in a previous footnote, let us say: The Father speaking his Word is what constitutes the Son and calls for a response; that Jesus speaks (to God in response, to us in address) makes the Son like his Father; inasmuch as Jesus creatively speaks like his Father, Jesus is also Source of creation. Finally, the Father breathes the Spirit and just so is freed into the communal freedom that God *is*; inasmuch as the Spirit frees creation to be free for its constituents and for our future with and toward God, the Spirit is also Source of creation (Jenson, *ST*.1.119-24; Robert W. Jenson, *The Triune Identity: God According to the Gospel* [Philadelphia: Fortress Press, 1982], pp. 103–59).

the Genesis narrative dogmatically teaches that this Source creates by speaking "let there be …" and insofar as that address is aimed at something other than himself, space is given through this command for anything other than God to exist. However, what exists still perdures in him through the Son and by the Spirit. In combining the Genesis narrative with trinitarian theological reflection, we may describe creation as initiated by the Father's speaking, and the life of Jesus is the content of his "let there be …" Therefore, by the will of the Father, God creates soteriologically *for* the redemption of creation, which is possible only through the life of the Son, whose future is to be eschatologically joined to his church—that is, the *totus Christus*—by the Holy Spirit.[45] Creation, therefore, is not a past act but a standing and continuous relation that God has to creation as initiator, sustainer, and fulfiller. As such, creation is thoroughly a narratable and eschatological act of the triune God, initiated by the Father.

*The Son as Goal*
*Jesus as Uncreated*: It has thus far been argued that creation—precisely because it is a triune act of God—has a triadic structure in that it is a history that is initiated, mediated, and fulfilled. The narrative character of reality has thus been granted ontological status in that it is one story, one life lived in particular that precedes and envelopes the cosmic story, and so gives all stories within it their possibility, meaning, and fulfillment. That story is the soteriological narrative of Jesus, which for pentecostals, happens to fully encompass the full gospel narrative. As Vondey has noted, "The full gospel is soteriological from beginning to end" so that "salvation is a primary theological theme throughout Pentecostal theology."[46] To view all of creation through the eschatological lens of God's saving acts in Christ is indeed a pentecostal impulse. This impulse, combined with the positing of creation as an eschatological and triune act, compels us to now expound Christ's role in creation. Put differently, now that the Father's role in creation has been sketched, a pentecostal and trinitarian theology of creation leads us to explicate a construal of Jesus as cosmic creator. Having argued for the Father as the Initiator and Source of his own life, and therefore, of creation, the following will continue

---

45. For this reason, the triune name can logically be Father, Spirit, and Son. The Father is the Source, the Spirit becomes the freeing Guide toward the Goal who is Jesus *with* his people as the *totus Christus*. Put differently, the Father sends the Spirit to free the Son and his Body for their joint future which is to be the *totus Christus*. I have chosen to keep with the traditional Father, Son, and Spirit name of the Triune God as it is presented thus in both Scripture and the liturgical formulations of the triune name. While exploring the possibilities gifted to us by the naming of God as Father, Spirit, and Son is indeed a fruitful theological endeavor, the logic of the traditional name still holds for the purposes of this work.

46. Vondey, *Pentecostal Theology*, p. 37. It is for this reason, among others, that I have not deemed it *necessary* to explicitly account for all aspects of the fivefold gospel in my construct as soteriology sufficiently undergirds them all.

## 5. Toward a Pentecostal Theology of Being-in-the-Spirit

the task of interpreting creation soteriologically, and so eschatologically, by the roles of the three persons of the trinity by now focusing its attention on God the Son as creator.

*Jesus as Creator*: I want to now focus on Scripture to look at Christ's relation to creation for two reasons: first, scripture—specifically the New Testament—*explicitly* asserts the Christological determination of creation. Second, Scripture functions as the macronarrative in which pentecostal micronarratives (testimonies, personal experiences, and stories) are fitted.[47] Just so, the life of Jesus is *the* narrative in which our personal narratives and indeed the cosmic narrative of all creation find their meaning and coherence. As such, we now turn to Scripture's explicit references to Jesus' relation to creation as the appropriate norm for discernment on this point. I will first take a somewhat cursory look at three New Testament texts—Heb. 1:1-4; Jn 1:1-5; and Col. 1:15-20—which make such assertions.[48] I am aware that full-length monographs can be written on the implications of these texts alone, and so can they be written on what the whole of the New Testament has to say about Christ and creation. With that said, I am picking these three texts—one from Paul, one from the writer of Hebrews, and one from John—as representative of a diverse witness within the New Testament of the ways in which it speaks about Christ's relation to creation.

First, I will look at our Heb. 1:1-4 text to illumine the Son's role as creator:

> Long ago God spoke to our ancestors in many and various ways by the prophets, but in these last days he has spoken to us by a Son, whom he appointed heir of all things, through whom he also created the worlds. He is the reflection of God's glory and the exact imprint of God's very being, and he sustains all things by his powerful word. When he had made purification for sins, he sat down at the right hand of the Majesty on high, having become as much superior to angels as the name he has inherited is more excellent than theirs.

Through a straightforward but careful theological reading of the text, one can find four claims about the doctrine of creation—as a triune act—which the other selected New Testament texts further instantiate: (1) that God creates *through* the Son, and (2) the Son upholds all things by his powerful word. That the world is created and upheld by a powerful word alludes to Genesis 1, wherein God *speaks* creation into existence. That same word spoken in the beginning is being spoken now, and that word is and always has been that of the Son. This text also teaches that (3) creation is *for* the Son, as he is here identified as heir of all things. Finally, (4) this Son, who according to the claims so far adduced can only be divine, becomes a creature and acts in history to make purification for sins. Thus, the

---

47. Smith, *Thinking in Tongues*, pp. 62-3.
48. I must here note that the readings of these texts are in conversation with notes taken from a course wherein Chris Green offered his own readings of these same texts. I owe these insights to him.

doctrines of Incarnation and creation intersect. As a story lived in human history, the Son takes human nature itself and as an act of new creation, raises humanity to superiority over the angels, which indeed had not been the case prior to the act of Incarnation.[49] Creation, therefore, has always been aimed at Incarnation precisely because—as the whole of the full gospel proclaims—Jesus is savior.

*Jesus as Creature*: These claims about Christ and creation are repeated and further instantiated in the other New Testament texts I have pointed to. So, Jn 1:1-5:

> In the beginning was the Word, and the Word was with God, and the Word was God. He was in the beginning with God. All things came into being through him, and without him not one thing came into being. What has come into being in him was life, and the life was the light of all people. The light shines in the darkness, and the darkness did not overcome it.

The previous section labored to describe the work of the Father as initiator both within the life of God, and so with creation. Yet the work of creation that the Father initiates, as this Johannine rereading of the creation narrative of Genesis 1 insists, comes into being through the Son so that the history God creates is in and through the Son. Indeed, John is emphatic that *all* that is—visible and invisible reality, personal, human, cosmic, etc.—exists in, and only in the Son. As such, Jesus is not merely savior of humanity, but *cosmic* savior. Once again, the revelation of his life in history through the Incarnation makes a dramatic ontological difference for human existence. In Genesis 1, light is the first of what God commands to come into existence by his word, so that light in the Genesis narrative is what is most basic to creation itself. The light, in John's creation narrative is the life of the Son, so that the light which is utterly basic to creation in Genesis 1 is, and always has been, Jesus. The life of Jesus, I suggest from this text, is the light that illumines for humanity what it means to be human.

*Jesus as Creation*:  Finally, our last New Testament Scripture explicating Christ's relation to creation, Col. 1:15-20:

> He is the image of the invisible God, the firstborn of all creation; for in him all things in heaven and on earth were created, things visible and invisible, whether thrones or dominions or rulers or powers—all things have been created through him and for him. He himself is before all things, and in him all things hold together. He is the head of the body, the church; he is the beginning, the firstborn from the dead, so that he might come to have first place in everything. For in him all the fullness of God was pleased to dwell, and through him God was pleased to reconcile to himself all things, whether on earth or in heaven, by making peace through the blood of his cross.

---

49. C.f. Psalm 8:4-8.

Once again, in order to discern what Jesus means for creation, let us read this Scripture in conversation with Genesis 1 while keeping the previous New Testament texts in mind. First, in this text which contains Paul's doxological utterance, we read that God's beloved Son (v. 13) is the image of the invisible God. In Genesis, we read that Adam and Eve are made in the image of God. According to Paul, God's image itself is identified as Jesus.[50] Incarnation, then, is *not* about Jesus taking on our image as much as it is about God revealing to humanity the image it was created *for*. Once again, creation has always been aimed at Incarnation as a dramatic part of God's act of unifying all things to himself. Put differently, Incarnation is not God's "plan B" to "restore" what once was, but a dramatic moment in his moving us toward—by revealing himself to us, in Christ—the final cause of our being.[51] Maximus puts it this way: "And this is because it is for the sake of Christ—that is, for the whole mystery of Christ—that all the ages and the beings existing within those ages received their beginning and end in Christ."[52] Creation in Christ is both soteriological and eschatological.

Jesus as the firstborn of all creation, once again, is the one who shows us what humanity is meant for; so that, "Upon Jesus Christ ... has come the role marked out for humanity, and hence for Israel: Christ is *the firstborn over all creation* ... it is *in virtue of* this eternal pre-existence that the Son of God holds supreme rank."[53] What the history of Jesus is, then, is Jesus acting *as* humanity, not merely as *a* human being; so that, "Jesus is not *a* human being but *the* human being. What happens to him happens to human beings. It happens to all and therefore to us. The

---

50. It is worth noting here that this point is why we are better served as the church to abandon the "standard canonical narrative" as Simon Chan has suggested, because in it, "God's ultimate purpose for humanity is shown in his creating humankind in his own image and likeness" (see Chan, *Liturgical Theology*, p. 21). Instead, this text asserts that it is Jesus who antecedently is the image of God, firstborn of all creation, so that it is Jesus—not Adam and Eve—who reveals God's ultimate purpose for humanity.

51. See Athanasius, *On the Incarnation*. Also, Irenaeus, in his 34th Demonstration of the Apostolic Preaching, makes this point when talking about the life of Jesus from the point of view of his crucifixion. "And since he is the Word of God Almighty, who invisibly pervades the whole creation and encompasses its length, breadth, height and depth ... so too was the Son of God crucified, having been imprinted in the form of the cross in everything ... that he might demonstrate, by his visible form, his activity." Irenaeus goes on to say that it is the life of this Incarnate Jesus "who illumines the 'heights,' that is the things in heaven, and holds the 'depths,' which is beneath the earth, and stretches the 'length' from East to West, and who navigates the breadth of the northern and southern regions, inviting the dispersed from all sides to the knowledge of the Father."

52. Maximus the Confessor, *Questions to Thalassius*, 60.4.

53. Wright, *Colossians and Philemon*, p. 75 (emphases original).

name of Jesus embraces in itself the whole of humanity and the whole of God."[54] As Rowan Williams puts it, Jesus is at once "infinite act and finite embodiment."[55] Finally, we read from this text and others before it, that all created things are not only through him but *for* Christ. Creation as the act of the triune God is the Father gifting creation by the Spirit to the Son. Soteriologically, and so eschatologically, creation as gift is the Son perfecting said creation—that is, new creation—and gifting it back to the Father.[56] God gives and creates *ex nihilo* from his bountiful love so that all of cosmic history is inner-trinitarian gift.

A final and brief summation of what these texts claim about Jesus and his relation to creation: (1) God creates all things *through* the Son;[57] (2) creation is upheld and sustained *by* him and his word, so that *in* him all things hold together.[58] Moreover, as heir (3) creation is *for* the Son so that creation itself has been aimed at union with God in the Son by the Spirit. Thus, creation is a triune gift borne out of the triune God's infinite and bountiful love.[59] Finally, (4) this one through whom, in whom, by whom, and for whom all things exist takes on humanity by becoming incarnate,[60] and so lives a life in history as the definitive image of the invisible God,[61] thus being and revealing what humanity, and all things with it,

---

54. Dietrich Bonhoeffer, *Ethics*, p. 85. Bonhoeffer's statement is not a novel insight. For one human life to act salvifically on behalf of all humanity, all humanity must be assumed by one human life. Maximus the Confessor, reading Dionysius the Areopagite says in *Ambiguum* 5:

> Dionysius teaches that the God of all, having been made flesh, is not said to be "man" simply or superficially, "but as being that which in the entirety of its essence is truly man." Thus he teaches quite clearly that none of our natural human properties should be denied to God incarnate ... (Jesus) is that which in the entirety of its essence is truly man" ... we do not decree that He is a mere man, for this would be to divide the union that transcends thought. Thus when we call Him "man" it is not "insofar as He is the cause of men," but because in truth He who is God by nature essentially imbued Himself with our substance ... He became "that which in the entirety of its essence is truly man," clearly by the assumption of human flesh endowed with an intellectual soul, united to Him according to hypostasis ... For once the "Word beyond being assumed human being," He possessed as His own, together with His human being, its undiminished power of movement, which characterizes Him generically as a man, and which took on specific form through all that He performed naturally as man, because He truly became man ... he Himself, without change, truly became what human nature is, and in actual fact fulfilled the divine plan of salvation itself on our behalf.
> 
> (Maximus the Confessor, Amb. 5:2-4, 8)

55. See Williams, *Christ the Heart of Creation*, pp. 1-35.
56. Cf., 1 Cor. 15:24.
57. Heb. 1:2c; Jn 1:3; Col. 1:16c.
58. Heb. 1:3b; Col. 1:16-17.
59. Heb. 1:2b; Col. 1:16; cf. 1 Cor. 15:24.
60. Heb. 1:3b; Col. 1:20; cf. Jn 1:14.
61. Heb. 1:3; Jn 1:1; Col. 1:15.

are meant for. We have thus far sketched the eschatological character of creation explicitly through the roles of Father and Son. Finally, we turn our attention to *Creator Spiritus*.

*The Spirit as Guide*
*Introduction*: Considering the ubiquity of the Father and the Son's roles in creation adduced in the previous section, one might wonder if the Spirit's role is anything other than superfluous or derivative. This, of course, must not be the case, especially if this metaphysical construct claims to be pentecostal. Neither do I find it acceptable to tame Christological claims to "make room" for the Spirit. Moreover, considering the fact that this section has been about elucidating the lineaments of the one triune act of creation with special attention to the triadic structure of this one act, I want to once again explicitly affirm *opera trinitatis ad extra indivisa sunt*.[62] How I ground this theologically will be explicitly demonstrated in my engagement with Cappadocians below. That said, before suggesting what the Spirit's role in creation might be, it will be necessary to sketch the Spirit's relation to Israel's narrative, and the story of Christ with his people as its fulfillment. The aim of taking this crucial first step is to posit the Spirit as prevalently active in creation without cost to dogmatic Christological formulations. This first step will move through three phases: the first will be to explicate the role of the Spirit in the Old Testament; followed by a further explication of the Spirit's life in Jesus as revealed in the New Testament; finally, a brief look at Ascension and Pentecost will help discern the Spirit's relation to Christ, and therefore, to creation. Once this is accomplished, I will then be explicit about the Spirit's creative activity in our cosmic reality. The following sketch of the Holy Spirit is far from exhaustive but aims to be thorough enough to give what should amount to be a faithful account of the Holy Spirit in relation to Christ, the community of faith, and creation.

*"We Believe in the Holy Spirit ..."*: Christians confess belief "in the Holy Spirit, the Lord, the giver of life ... who has spoken through the prophets." Let me once again turn to Scripture as a norm in our first-level discourse to sketch the metaphysical implications of affirming the Holy Spirit who is Lord, giver of life, and who speaks through the prophets. In the Old Testament, life itself is utterly dependent upon the transcendent, elusive, yet all-inhering presence of the *ruach* of God. Indeed,

---

62. See, for example, Augustine's *De Trinitate* 1.2.7 wherein Augustine suggests that the triune life *ad extra* logically follows from his own immanent life, *ad intra*. To the point, Augustine's commitment to the one inseparable action of the "three" in the economy of salvation follows from his commitment to their ontologically inseparable unity; moreover, his commitment to the distinct action of the three follows from the eternal distinction of the persons by relations of origin. Jenson puts it this way, "The different ways in which each is the *one* God, for and from the others, are the only differences between them ... they are distinguished only by their relations to each other, there is only one step remaining—not however explicitly taken until centuries later—and that is to say that the hypostases simply *are* 'relations subsisting in God'" (Thomas, *ST*. 1.29.3-4). Jenson, *The Triune Identity*, pp. 105–6.

the Spirit of God creates life (Job 33:4) and *is* life (Ps. 104:29-30).[63] Furthermore, according to the Old Testament, God's Spirit not only creates and animates all life generally, but is further responsible for creating history by empowering leaders for political and *prophetic* action.[64] As early as Israel's pre-exilic history, he empowered Moses for such action as "The Torah's most explicit projection of his identity is as the prophet *par excellence*, the exemplar for all Hebrew prophets to come."[65] Through these pre-exilic leaders, the Spirit of God still creates life, but does so in creating a historical people of Israel by coming upon its leaders through his Spirit to evoke prophecy for the sake of throwing down the status quo[66] to make room for what he intends.[67] By the Spirit of the Lord, David acts just so in Israel's history, and as a prophet claims himself as one to speak promises for God (2 Sam. 1-7).

Ascribing prophetic speech and acts to the Spirit of God continues in the exilic and postexilic prophets. In light of where Israel finds themselves historically, their hope has become increasingly eschatological. We see this prominently in Isaiah[68] and Ezekiel, among other places. The book of Ezekiel begins with the presence of the ever-elusive, dynamic wind of God (1:4, 17, 20-21) which is later revealed as God's life-giving Spirit and evokes a vision of eschatological hope wherein God finally overcomes Israel's alienation from him (37; 39:29). In Ezekiel 37, the alienation from God as illustrated by a valley of dry bones is to be overcome by God's promise of the Spirit to bring resurrection to his people. God's Spirit once

63. One can read in this Psalm that there is a participatory element at work between our receptive lives, and God's life-giving Spirit: "The rhythm of life and death and the appearance of new life is the effect of the relation between the 'breath' (*ruach*) of creatures and the breath (*ruach*) of the Lord" (see James L. Mays, *Interpretation: Psalms*, p. 335).

64. In his monograph on the Spirit in the book of Judges, Lee Roy Martin notes the significant prophetic, political, and *historical* events that take place in Israel, pre-exile, when the Spirit of God comes upon a leader: "When the Spirit of the Lord comes upon Othniel (3:10) he goes to war and triumphs against the enemy. Clothed by the Spirit, Gideon gathers an army and wins a miraculous victory (6:34). Jephthah also defeats the enemy by the power of the Spirit (11:29)." See Martin, *The Unheard Voice of God: A Pentecostal Hearing of the Book of Judges*, pp. 4-5. When talking about Othniel, Martin points out that when the Spirit of the Lord came upon him, he delivers the Israelites from an eight-year oppression (3:7-11) and ushered in forty years of tranquility, further instantiating the fact that the Spirit of God dramatically affects and effects history (Martin, *Unheard Voice*, p. 85).

65. Moore, *The Spirit of the Old Testament*, p. 71.

66. Lest we be tempted to tame the Spirit, Moore reminds us that he "Plays a prominent role in the associations with madness. Perhaps it is easy to see why, since *ruach* is wind, the untamed and untamable energy and dynamic (is) controlled only by God ... such turbulence of spirit can seem rather wild, unnatural, abnormal, and even crazy to civilized society" (Moore, *Old Testament*, p. 64).

67. He not only does so with Moses, but with Saul, the last judge and first king, (1 Sam. 10:10-11; 11:6-7, etc.); and David: See 1 Sam. 16:13 wherein the spirit of the Lord comes mightily upon him to take over the role of judges *and* to speak as a prophet.

68. See Isa. 11:1-16; 28:5-6; 32:15-16; 34:16.

again evokes prophecy and is further revealed to be the ontological opposite of death,[69] bringing life and eschatological hope where death once ruled.[70] The Spirit, then, is simultaneously the object of ultimate hope to come, and its guarantee as God's people are borne along in history. Put differently, the Spirit inheres in all of history by uniting the promises made by God's past acts with their final cause—the content of said promises is eschatological union with God through the resurrection and the community that proclaims it.

According to the Old Testament witness, the Spirit is life, wisdom, and evokes prophecy. Israel's understanding of—and life with—the Spirit could be fulfilled only in a unified vision of the experienced Spirit of prophecy with the eschatological hope of said Spirit's outpouring. This union has both a messianic and communal component. Regarding the messianic, Isa. 11:2-9 promises Israel's triumph because there will be a final prophetic figure, a Spirit-bearer who will inaugurate that eschatological reality. Communally speaking, that Spirit-bearer's messianic mission is to share the Spirit that rests on him; that is, to pour out his Spirit to create a life-giving community—that is, the church—of prophets.[71]

*"The Testimony of Jesus Is the Spirit of Prophecy"*: The hope of the continuity of the Spirit's work in the life of Israel—as the prophetic, life-giving, eschatological Spirit—is to be embodied by *the* final prophet who will pour out the very Spirit he bears. As Stronstad observes, "A close reading of Luke's history of the origin of Christianity compels the reader to conclude that Jesus ministers, from first to last, as the eschatological, anointed prophet."[72] Moreover, the life of Jesus and the

---

69. Pentecostal OT scholar, Verena Schafroth notes the scholarly consensus on the close relationship between Ezek. 35:5, 6, 8, and 10 with Gen. 2:7 and the life-giving role of God's breath. However, Schafroth notices a subtle but important variation in Ezekiel, "While in the Genesis creation account, God was still the subject of the 'breathing,' it changes in Ezekiel to the spirit, which is unique in the OT. In this context, 'spirit' is the animating principle of life that makes a person a living being" (Verena Schafroth, "An Exegetical Exploration of 'Spirit' References in Ezek. 36 and 37." [JEPTA], p. 71).

70. Schafroth comments, "Ezekiel is brought to the valley plain (cf. 3:11; 8:4), which had been a place where judgment had to be suffered, but now becomes the place where God triumphs over death and serves as an impressive symbol of God's resurrecting power." This text is yet another instance of "spirit transportation in Ezekiel (cf. 3:12, 14; 8:3; 40:1), which is always induced by the 'hand of God,' an expression often used to describe God's possession, inspiration, and empowering of the prophet." See Verena Schafroth, 'Exploration of "Spirit,"' p. 70.

71. Jl 2:28; Isa. 59:21; Num. 11:29.

72. Stronstad continues to state this case rather strongly as he notices an *inclusio* in Luke's Gospel based around the theme of Jesus as eschatological prophet beginning with the inauguration narrative (Lk. 3:1-4:44) and ending in the retrospective affirmation of his vocation by his disciples (Lk. 3:22). Thus, says Stronstad, "everything which Luke reports Jesus as doing and saying are the works and words of the eschatological anointed prophet" (Stronstad, *The Prophethood of All Believers*, p. 3).

dramatically narrated events of his birth, baptism, and works are at every turn, by the power of the Spirit. As for his birth, Jesus was conceived by the Spirit as something new which marks his life as one who would be fully human, but not human in the same way as anyone else in history.[73] As stated above, Christ is not merely *a* human being, but assumes humanity itself. This life sourced through divine freedom and not mere contingency both affects and effects reality in a way that a merely contingent human life cannot. Thus, the Spirit's overshadowing of Mary, "is the creative power of God, in terms perhaps reminiscent of the hovering Spirit at creation (Gen. 1:2), in Mary's conception of Jesus the Spirit effects new creation. This overshadowing of the divine presence signifies that the conception of Jesus has an importance that is similar to that of the earlier creation of the cosmos."[74]

The identity of the Spirit as the agent active in the life of Jesus continues and is further instantiated in his baptismal narrative. In all four Gospels, the baptism of Jesus is unanimously the descent of the Spirit upon him.[75] Finally—as Stronstad rightly observes from the book of Luke—while everything Jesus says and does are the words and acts of an eschatological prophet, Matthew and Mark testify that Jesus' healing works are specifically done in the Spirit of God.[76] The important thing to note here is that the narrated life of Jesus is the fulfillment of Israel's hope for a Spirit-bearer whose history inaugurates new creation and the hoped-for eschatological reality. Moreover, Jesus does not bear this Spirit for his own sake but bears him to give him as eschatological gift,[77] which will consequently create a community of prophets that is, the church.

There is, therefore, a strong union between Jesus, *his* eschatological life-giving Spirit, and the creation of a prophetic church so that the acts and inspiration of the Spirit are at all times understood Christologically and so trinitarianly. Indeed, the testimony of Jesus is the Spirit of prophecy.[78] John Christopher Thomas's seminal work on the Apocalypse powerfully displays the intimate connection between Jesus's life, his Spirit, his community of prophets, and the world:

> In the throne room scene, the intimate relationship between Jesus and the Spirit is conveyed by the fact that the Lamb has seven eyes, which are identified as the Seven Spirits of God that are sent out into all the earth (5:6). The hearers

---

73. Commenting on Jn 1:13, John Christopher Thomas says, "John goes on to make it clear that this birth is not the result of physical, sexual, or human means but comes from God himself (v. 13). This activity will later be attributed to the work of the Spirit" (John Christopher Thomas, *He Loved Them until the End: The Farewell Materials in the Gospel According to John* (Cleveland: CPT Press, 2015), p. 35.

74. Stronstad, *The Prophethood of All Believers*, p. 41.

75. Mt. 3:13-17; Mk 1:9-11; Lk. 3:21-22; Jn 1:29-34.

76. Mt. 12:28; Mk 3:29-30.

77. Mk 1:7-8.

78. Rev. 19:10.

also know that his same Spirit is closely associated with the life and ministry of Jesus' own faithful witness. Not only is this borne out in the example of the two prophetic witnesses who are given of Jesus' witness to prophesy, who are the two olive trees and lampstands that stand before the Lord (11:3-4), and the apostles who are sent out in the power of the Seven Spirits before the throne (18:10), but also by the way in which the hearers are called to pneumatic discernment throughout (2:7, 11, 17, 29; 3:6, 13, 22; 11:8; 13:9-10, 18; 17:9-10). Thus it should be abundantly clear that the witness of Jesus and the Spirit of Prophecy are intricately connected to one another and in the Apocalypse cannot be understood apart from each other. That is to say that the witness of Jesus is quintessentially pneumatic, prophetic, dynamic, and active. The Spirit who goes out into all the world is the same Spirit that empowers the church's prophetic witness. The same Spirit that speaks prophetically to the church is the same Spirit that speaks prophetically to the world, and in 19:10 these ideas are united. The hearers would not likely discern that this is simply a matter of static equation between the witness of Jesus and the Spirit of Prophecy. For the community, participation in the faithful witness of Jesus is fueled by the Spirit of Prophecy. It too is active and dynamic. It is the kind of pneumatic witness that is very much at home in a prophetic community, a community where the prophethood of all believers seems to be a basic understanding.[79]

*Between Ascension and Pentecost*: Finally, brevity notwithstanding, a pentecostal account of the Spirit's relation to Jesus must account for the event of Pentecost, which is connected to the Ascension. Ascension and Pentecost bring to the fore the apparent tension between the "absence" and presence of God in the world, which further demands an account of the Spirit's relationship to Jesus. Regarding the relationship between Jesus and the Spirit in general, the foregoing attempted to demonstrate that there cannot be separation. As specifically revealed through the Ascension and Pentecost, a fruitful place to look is Jesus' farewell materials. Commenting on Jesus' farewell discourse in Jn 14:15-31, John Christopher Thomas notes throughout the text that Jesus is teaching the disciples that upon his "departure" the Spirit is to function as Jesus did in their midst. In the Fourth Gospel, the Paraclete is called the Spirit of Truth while Jesus is full of truth'[80] and is indeed identified as 'the truth'.[81] Moreover, just as the world did not receive Jesus, neither will it receive the Paraclete.[82] Finally, in the Fourth Gospel

> one of Jesus' primary roles is that of teacher (1.38; 3.2; 6.59; 7.14, 28, 35; 8.20; 11.28; 13.13, 14; cf. also 18.20; 20.16). Thus the Paraclete, the Spirit of Truth, the

---

79. John Christopher Thomas, *The Apocalypse: A Literary and Theological Commentary* (Cleveland: CPT Press, 2012), pp. 572-3.
80. Jn 1:14.
81. Jn 14:6.
82. Jn 14:17.

one who is sent by the Father, will do precisely what Jesus has done—teach! He will remind the disciples of the things Jesus said to them.[83]

By sending his Spirit, Jesus makes it known that he will not leave his people orphaned, but this is preceded by an astonishing promise that he will, in a sense, bring humanity with him when he ascends by the Spirit.[84] "At the Ascension Jesus goes up, with his humanity, to complete its deification. At the Ascension human nature ascends to be with the Father, to enjoy the trinitarian life."[85] That is, Jesus' ascending to God and deifying humanity *is* the act of him preparing a place for us in the Father by the Spirit.

Pentecost, then, is about the Spirit's descent upon believers as a foretaste and anticipation of the day that our inclusion in the life of God is fully realized. As Althouse puts it, "the Spirit of Pentecost is the guarantee of the eschatological consummation of that which has begun in Christ … As such, the present gift of the Holy Spirit is the guarantee that God will complete what he has begun."[86] Of course, Pentecost is not only about believers enjoying a foretaste of what's to come but also about the empowerment of believers to participate in Jesus' mission of bringing others into that life. As Vondey rightly states, "only through Pentecost can the church maintain an incarnation theology of Christ as God-with-us to continue beyond ascension."[87] He goes on to say, "the move of the church outward into history is therefore also a move forward eschatologically to the new creation. We can say that pentecostal ecclesiology is formed by the mission of the kingdom. More precisely, however, this eschatological mission is shaped by the day of Pentecost as the bridge in history between the ascension and the return of Christ."[88]

Before moving to the final step of explicating precisely how the Spirit might create cosmic history and act through natural processes, let me remind readers of what has thus far been constructed about the Spirit: (1) From the beginning, the Spirit is the elusive and animating force of life, often characterized as the wind and breath of God; (2) this life-giving Spirit creates history by coming upon leaders for prophetic and political action. Some of these pre-exilic and postexilic prophets, by the same Spirit, claim authority to speak promises on God's behalf. (3) As Israel's hope becomes eschatological, so do the promises that proceed from the mouth of her prophets as they await a Spirit-bearer who will pour out said Spirit and create a community of prophets. (4) In the New Testament, Jesus is identified as that Spirit-bearer whose life *is* the very Spirit of prophecy; (5) Jesus *apparently* leaves but does so only to take humanity with him by the room that the Spirit creates in the Father. Moreover, that Spirit which creates prophets and effects history is poured

---

83. John Christopher Thomas, *He Loved Them*, p. 37.

84. Jn 14:1-7.

85. Eugene F. Rogers, *After the Spirit: A Constructive Pneumatology from Resources Outside the Modern West* (Grand Rapids: Eerdmans, 2005), p. 206.

86. Peter Althouse, "Ascension—Pentecost—Eschaton," p. 238.

87. Vondey, *Pentecostal Theology*, p. 100.

88. Vondey, *Pentecostal Theology*, p. 249.

out at Pentecost on his prophetic community—joining the historical body to the Resurrected Christ—as eschatological witnesses so that "The Spirit continues to rest on Jesus's body, only now that body turns out to be the church. The church, moreover, under the direction of the Spirit, has as its task—in word and deed—to point to Jesus."[89] and she may be granted to do this, because and only because, the Spirit rests on her.

*Robert Jenson's Pneumatological Naturalism*
*Introduction*: My work on the Holy Spirit in Scripture has highlighted that the creative, prophetic, and cosmic Spirit of the Old Testament is indeed the Spirit of Jesus, and his Spirit has been given to his church as a foretaste of what God means for creation, and just so, for empowered participation in his continued eschatological mission in the world. The final step in this section on the work of the Holy Spirit in creation, then, is to further explicate what it might mean for the Spirit of Jesus and his people to be cosmically efficacious. It is at this point that I turn to Robert Jenson as primary interlocutor as he labors to do just that in a way that I find particularly helpful for pentecostals.[90] Pentecostals insist on the Spirit's immediacy, ubiquity, and activity in creation—as does Jenson. Furthermore, Jenson does not shy away from the vital role of the church for the cosmos—the offensiveness of its particularity, notwithstanding—which this work has also been committed to explicating. As such, I find Jenson to be a fruitful dialogue partner for this section.

Both the Old and New Testaments speak of the same Spirit of God, albeit with different emphases. In the New Testament, the Spirit is quite emphatically displayed as the creator of new life for God's people in particular,[91] while in the Old Testament the Spirit is more explicitly the universal and historical creativity. The church, precisely as the body of Christ, has been given his Spirit so that "it must be the particular Spirit of Jesus and of the church to whom we attribute cosmic efficacy; that is, we must assert the universal potency of events in one little religious group."[92] The claim is audacious, yet that fact must not tempt Christians to tame the Spirit's universality, nor particularity. Jenson seeks to practice the "hermeneutical courage" required of this task by conversing with cosmic pneumatologies within the Christian tradition in which he identifies two common themes, the Spirit is: (1) "the freedom of universal history" and (2) "the spontaneity of natural process."[93]

---

89. Hauerwas and Willimon, *The Holy Spirit*, p. 37.

90. These ideas can be found throughout his work, but I will be primarily engaging his piece entitled "Cosmic Spirit" as his aim in this piece is very near to mine: see Robert Jenson, "Cosmic Spirit," in Carl E. Braaten and Robert W. Jenson (eds), in *Christian Dogmatics: Volume Two* (Minneapolis: Fortress Press, 2011), pp. 165–78.

91. Of course, as Jesus pours out his Spirit upon all flesh, his particular people are expanded across ethnic boundaries.

92. Jenson, "Cosmic Spirit," p. 165.

93. Jenson, "Cosmic Spirit," p. 166. I have omitted the third, "the beauty of creation" as it is not necessary for our purposes.

*The Spirit of Jesus Is the Freedom of Universal History*: Jenson argues that the Spirit is the freedom of *universal* history, and grasping what he means by this requires a conceptual move away from the Greek notion of God as Mind, who merely *knows* what is given (such as, a cosmos), and toward a Hegelian notion of God as spirit who *acts* transformatively on what is given, enabling it to be. For Hegel, there is no gap between the existence of a thing and its being known by a "Universal Consciousness." Rather the existence of a thing *is* its being known and acted upon by said Consciousness. Jenson appropriates Hegel to say that "The world subsists in that it is transformed by a God who is—far from static mind—lively Spirit."[94] As such, the intelligibility of historical change does not depend on a mechanistic cosmos; rather, historical change—via creative processes, lively debate, or prophetic inspiration, for example—*is* the object of spirit.

Because God is triune, the conception of God as transforming Spirit whose objectivity is the world and the dramatic changes therein, requires that history also have a triadic structure. Recounting Hegel's arguments, Jenson notes that history displays a frequent occurrence of conflicts so severe so as to only be conceptualized as contradiction. Put differently, historical reality tends toward evoking its own negation so that history is made up of "thesis" and "antithesis." Yet, the intelligibility of history so understood *happens* when thesis and antithesis are embraced by a synthesis as the dramatic resolution which gives history its meaning. That is, historical synthesis is the oncoming of a surprising new thesis. There is a theological and cosmic connection to be made here. In Hegelian terms: "Universal Consciousness" (thesis) evokes the world (antithesis) as its object. In doing so, Universal Consciousness "finds its own meaning in this object, by the "transforming action to fulfill itself as Spirit and not mere Mind, and to fulfill itself as history and not mere cosmos. Thus, the Spirit not only creates but involves the world; the Spirit is the freedom *of* universal history."[95] Put succinctly, Universal Consciousness knows itself as spirit in the transforming action upon its opposite (the world).

For Jenson, gospelizing Hegel with trinitarian insights is not a problem. One simply needs to substitute Universal Consciousness for Father, and the world—as the Object in whom the Father finds himself—with Jesus. Here, Jenson adds a crucial step: "Absolute Consciousness finds its own meaning and self in the *one* historical object, Jesus, and *so* posits Jesus' fellows as its fellows and Jesus' world as its world."[96] He goes on to say that "If the risen Jesus is Lord, not only is he Lord of the church, but his will determines the history not only of believers but also of all nations (e.g., Eph. 1:20-23)."[97] The Spirit of the risen Jesus, which the church possesses as sheer gift poured out at Pentecost, is the freedom in which universal history, and historical synthesis occurs. It is this fact upon which

---

94. Jenson, "Cosmic Spirit," p. 168.
95. Jenson, "Cosmic Spirit," p. 168.
96. Jenson, "Cosmic Spirit," p. 169.
97. Jenson, "Cosmic Spirit," p. 169.

Christians may live in hope during the event of what might seem to be a historical impasse. When the Spirit of Jesus acts by bringing surprising resolutions in such moments, Christians may see these as penultimate foretastes of the Spirit's final transformation—or, the Spirit's Ultimate Synthesis. As a Christian, prophetic, Spirit-privileging community, pentecostals may view history eschatologically, that is, "as available to final triumph by its own structure."[98]

*The Spirit of Jesus Is the Spontaneity of Natural Process*: Pentecostals have insisted that nature ought to be redefined pneumatologically. Smith says that "implicit in the prayers of pentecostals is a richly pneumatological understanding of creation that affirms the Spirit's continued presence and activity in what we would call … 'nature' … So nature, in a sense, is 'charged' with the Spirit's presence. Nature, then, is always more than 'the natural.'"[99] Prayer, both petitionary and praise, is at the heart of pentecostal spirituality. In light of the aims of this work, the appropriate question is what kind of metaphysical vision ought to undergird the practice of prayer, so that a faithful vision of God's relation to creation may be sustained while rightly insisting that prayer is meaningful for Christian practice? A vision for the Spirit's work in history was just proposed, but how do we posit the free Spirit of Jesus as active in what is seemingly the regularity and predictability of natural processes as a deterministic vision of nature presupposes? We have seen that for pentecostals, nature ought to be understood in light of pneumatology. Therefore, I continue with Jenson as a model for a helpful way to do that. In what follows, I will simply lay out the striking implications of Jenson's thesis for prayer, and what that means we can and cannot say about the relationship of natural processes to the Spirit of Jesus

Let us continue with our conversation with Jenson. He asserts that the Spirit of Jesus is the spontaneity of natural process, which has counterintuitive consequences over against the reigning deterministic metaphysical presuppositions of our day. Beginning the conversation with the Christian practice of prayer illumines just why the picture modernity gives us of natural processes in reality cannot be coherently sustained where prayer is practiced. If said processes are indeed a network of causal determinisms, then prayer is petition to an agent *external* to this network, to *intervene* in it, which, as pentecostal scholarship has argued, an interventionist God presupposes a closed-off world—neither of which best coincides with pentecostal belief and practice in conversation with the classical Christian tradition. But if, indeed, the Spirit of Jesus is the spontaneity of natural process, nature does not subsist apart from personality; so that, in each event—or "actual occasion"—of our existence, we are confronted by someone's communicative and intrusive presence. Precisely because this personal presence is communicative, "we are involved in a conversation with Christ and so to his conversation with his Father. Our side

---

98. Jenson, "Cosmic Spirit," p. 170.
99. Smith, *Thinking in Tongues*, p. 40.

of the conversation is prayer."[100] Jesus joins us to his relationship, and so his discourse, with God when he invites us to pray "*Our* Father." Moreover,

> if the freedom of natural process is someone's Spirit, that someone can be addressed. We can meaningfully and reasonably ask, "Make it rain," because rain will or will not occur in freedom that is someone's freedom. And if the spirit of natural process is the Spirit of Jesus and his Father, he can be addressed in trust and joy, by petition and praise.[101]

This vision coheres with the pentecostal disposition of reality and its relationship to prayer: "By every actual occasion, the risen Lord says: 'There are possibilities. Ask' and 'There are marvels. Praise.'"[102] Finally, as an eschatologically oriented people, natural process as the Spirit of the risen Jesus implies that "natural process has not merely a direction but a goal. And since we know whose spirit it is … we know the goal: unconditional love."[103]

## Conclusion

The aim of the previous section was to display the eschatological orientation of pentecostals and how it ought to thoroughgoingly inform their understanding of creation. By utilizing insights gleaned from my reading of the larger ecumenical and dogmatic Christian metaphysical tradition, I looked at the triadic character of creation by discerning the distinct but inseparable roles of each person of the trinity. The Father is the *arche* of the divine life and functions just so as the Source of *all* that is. The Son is the one in whom, by whom, and for whom the Father initiates creation, and further the one in whom creation is sustained. The Spirit acts eschatologically and so transformatively on the Son, and just so acts on all of creation, through the church, in the same manner. While all creation is in Christ, in light of what I have argued in this section, the eschatologically oriented church has a unique way of being in creation. This will be unpacked in the following section.

---

100. Jenson, "Cosmic Spirit," p. 172.

101. Jenson, "Cosmic Spirit," p. 172.

102. Jenson, "Cosmic Spirit," p. 173. Indeed, Christian liturgical practice is communication with God and each other: confessing, petitioning, praising, and proclaiming. This account of the cosmic Spirit makes these acts which are the heart of Christian liturgy and spirituality, the most natural things for us to do as we are not asking God to unnaturally intervene into a cosmos made to otherwise function without him. This will lead us to a proposed liturgical renewal for pentecostals, below.

103. Jenson, "Cosmic Spirit," p. 172.

## A Foundational Ecclesiological Pneumatology

### Introduction

Once again, the overall aim of this project is to engage pentecostal spirituality and theology critically and constructively through conversation with the ecumenical, dogmatic, and Christian metaphysical tradition for the sake of constructing a pentecostal vision of the whole. In the previous section, I have argued that pentecostal self-identity is a storied one; it is a dramatic narrative of a people journeying toward the Consummation of New Creation. Utilizing the dogmatic Christian tradition, I argued that creation is itself triadically structured by the Triune God who is tri-personally active and creative in this history. Now that a pentecostal, narratival, and eschatologically oriented vision of pentecostal identity and the triune determination of creation have been traced, it follows that a coherent and recognizably pentecostal ecclesiology ought to be adduced as the church is the context wherein this identity and vision is discovered, formed, and enacted. This pentecostal ecclesiology must show how pentecostal spirituality works as an eschatologically oriented, identity-making, and embodied expression of the story about the one in whom all of creation lives, moves, and has its being. And Simon Chan's work has done exactly that. He rightly privileges the soteriological story of the triune God as revealed in Jesus—and thus, the people of God joined to him—as more basic, primal, and prior to creation itself. And he unpacks the ontological implications of what it means for the church to be the people of God, the body of Christ, and the temple of the Holy Spirit.[104]

### Simon Chan's Ecclesial Metaphysics

For Chan, ecclesiology presupposes a metaphysical conviction: the church's ministry depends upon the church's identification with Christ and participation in his being. This conviction may be at least partially uncovered by how one answers this question: Is the church primarily an instrument God uses to accomplish his purposes in creation, or is the church itself the unique expression of God's aims for creation? In Chan's view, the church embodies God's desire for creation, and is therefore not a mere instrument or "means of grace" in any technological sense. Instead, the church, as it were, "precedes" the world. Chan has this in common with others who hold to "communion ecclesiology."[105]

---

104. I must note here that Chan's ecclesiological ontological vision is not completely unique among other pentecostals; for example, see Yong's "Ephesian ecclesiology" in Yong, *Renewing Christian Theology*, pp. 178–82. I find Chan's ontological reflections of the church to be best suited for this work because he is a pentecostal who does ecclesiological work while being attentive to the story of Jesus with his people and explicates that story's inchoate metaphysical implications—it is that exact tendency that I aim to emulate.

105. Such as Karl Rahner, who argues, "Either history is itself of salvific significance, or salvation takes place only in a subjective and ultimately transcendental interiority, so that the rest of human life does not really have anything to do with it." Rahner continues, "If the first solution is the only really and genuinely human solution, then the church itself belongs

Chan's ecclesiology thus resists the often presupposed "standard canonical narrative"[106] of creation-fall-redemption-consummation.[107] For him, as for others in the communion ecclesiology tradition, the church's identity is known narratively. In other words, the church's ontology can be articulated only in a particular story, a so-called "meta-narrative." The story we ought to adopt, according to Chan, is this: "God created the world in order that he might enter into a covenant relationship with humankind. And he accomplishes this with the call of Abraham and culminates his elective purpose in Jesus Christ and the church."[108]

For many in contemporary pentecostal circles, as well as the wider evangelical tradition, "Creation becomes the basis for understanding the nature and role of the church." That, in turn, means that "the church is the subspecies of creation and must discover the clue to its identity within the created order."[109] According to this ecclesiological vision, the Incarnation is merely a *response* to human sin, and the church is merely *instrumental* in God's redeeming of creation and restoring it to its original purpose. Chan, however, wants to abandon this narrative and thus alter our ecclesiological self-understanding dramatically, shifting away from the merely functional, instrumental, and utilitarian. He wants to argue that the church is joined ontologically to Christ, who precedes creation, and just so exists as the unique expression of God's ultimate purpose for creation, and not merely one of

---

to the salvation history of God's grace not only as some useful religious organization, but rather as the categorial concreteness and mediation of salvation ... and only this makes church really church" (Karl Rahner, *Foundations of Christian Faith: An Introduction to the Idea of Christianity* [New York: Seabury Press, 1978], p. 345). For critical engagement with Rahner, see Miroslav Volf, *After Our Likeness: The Church in the Image of the Trinity* (Grand Rapids: Eerdmans, 1998).

106. Chan borrows this phrase from Soulen, who has a strong view of the deeply foundational and formative character of narrative in how we understand ourselves and Scripture. He argues that to overcome problematic theologies, we cannot simply address doctrines but the story that upholds them. "Christian doctrines presuppose a more basic storied account of God's relations with humankind, and it is this storied account that forms the bedrock of the church's convictions, practices, and character." See R. Kendall Soulen, *The God of Israel and Christian Theology* (Minneapolis: Augsburg Fortress Press, 1996), p. 16.

107. Here, humanity as made in God's image and likeness—with their inherent non-temporality, rationality, and capacity for communion with God—reflects God's original anthropological purpose until the Fall disrupts it. In this story, the Incarnation is a *response* to human failure. Christ's work is to redeem fallen creation and inaugurate the final consummation of God's original purpose in creation.

108. Chan, *Liturgical Theology*, p. 22.

109. Chan, *Liturgical Theology*, p. 21.

many means to that end.¹¹⁰ To accomplish this, Chan directs our attention to three biblical metaphors that denote the church's ontological relationship with the triune God; the church is the people of God, the body of Christ, and the temple of the Holy Spirit.

*The Church as the People of God*
First, the church's ontological reality as the people of God means that our story begins historically with the election of Abraham and his descendants precisely to be God's people. Creation thus provides the world-historical background in service of this main story of God's election of his people to bless all nations. Resisting supersessionism and displacement theology, Chan insists that God's election is irrevocable.

> If Israel serves only a functional purpose then the church, like ancient Israel, is just as dispensable. The church too could be superseded! If election of the whole people of God is not seen as an end itself for God's sake … the tendency is to see the church as simply one of a number of entities whose legitimacy is to be established solely based on their ability to serve a higher, all-transcending goal.¹¹¹

Said goal is typically set by whatever *zeitgeist* the people of God find themselves in. Thus, the church as the people of God means that the church is a people with a storied (and often imperfect and troubled) journey which precedes them, perdures through them, and moves toward a consummation which is eschatologically ahead of them.¹¹²

---

110. He nuances this a bit by saying that church can be thought of as a means of the renewal of all creation, but only insofar as this is understood in such a way that resists the instrumentalist sense of the word, wherein the church is seen as "an agent doing something for the world, carrying out an extrinsic mission; rather, it is a means of renewal in its very life, by its being the Body of Christ indwelled by the Spirit" (Chan, *Pentecostal Ecclesiology*, p. 27).

111. Chan, *Liturgical Theology*, pp. 25-6.

112. The fact that we understand our End as *eschatologically* "ahead" of us is no small matter. In this work, through my engagement with Chris Green, who is much clearer on the matter than is Chan, I acknowledge a distinction between *the* (big-*E*) End—an event that happens *to* time—and the many (small-*e*) penultimate end(s) that happen *in* time. The stories of this reality yield only penultimate ends which are succeeded by other beginnings which may yield yet more ends that are better, or far worse. Put differently, the narrative of progress is a myth, and thus it is impossible to know whether we are contributing positively or negatively to the world that proceeds us (see N. T. Wright, *Surprised by Hope: Rethinking Heaven, the Resurrection, and the Mission of the Church* [New York: Harper One, 2008], pp. 81-7, 98). Journeying toward an End that is eschatologically ahead of us, then, does not mean that we see our work as necessarily moving us toward better penultimate

### The Church as the Body of Christ

Second, the church as the body of Christ, says Chan, names an ontological reality and not a mere metaphor. As such, if the world wants to grasp the resurrected Christ as an object, it must look to the church who *is* Christ's bodily availability to it. Yet, there remains a distinction between Christ and his body, and Chan borrows from Jenson to clarify it. On the one hand, the church as *community* is precisely God's people to be object-Christ in the world; on the other hand, the church as *association* is also confronted by said object-Christ and subjected to correction from the same. The church, then, is always more than a gathering of people with like interests who choose to gather for self-imposed aims, even if those aims are to be an instrument of God's goodness in the world. Neither are the church's practices that constitute her of her own making. "The church is a communion ... and the church becomes the one body of Christ by eating and drinking the body and blood of Christ."[113] In other words, the church is gifted by God with practices by which Christ is first available to her, so that she may partake of Christ and be joined to him to be his presence in the world. The implications further extend to our understanding of tradition as "the life of the 'embodied Christ' through time. If Christ is the Truth, then tradition is the extension of the Truth through time until it reaches its eschatological fulfillment."[114] Christ is object to the world as the church, and object to the church as the community faithfully gathering and participating in the Lord's Supper and the practices around it. What makes this union possible is found in Chan's third image of the church.

### The Church as the Temple of the Holy Spirit

The final metaphor Chan employs to denote the church's ontological relationship with the triune God is that of the church as the temple of the Holy Spirit. The church as the temple of the Holy Spirit, says Chan, sees the church as a divine-humanity which is grounded in the story of the triune God and identifiable through concrete practices by which the Spirit accomplishes his sanctifying mission. Moreover, the joining of the Head to the body as the firstfruits of what will be fully realized at the Eschaton as the *totus Christus* is accomplished by the work of the Spirit. On this side of the Eschaton, this joining work of the Spirit is what makes the church's embodiment as Christ in this world possible, keeping her alive, dynamic, vibrant, and moving toward her appointed End.

---

ends; rather, it is an acknowledgment that all penultimate ends are finite and so always tend toward death. Therefore, we labor in anticipation and hope that God acts Finally to resurrect and envelop all finite reality and our penultimate stories in his Ultimate End. To be eschatologically oriented in just this way, then, is to hope in the decisive and Final Act of God. More on this below.

113. Chan, *Liturgical Theology*, p. 29.
114. Chan, *Liturgical Theology*, p. 31.

To speak of the church as the temple *of the Spirit* is also to recognize its essentially eschatological character, since the Spirit is the Spirit of the "last days." This eschatological dimension of church is usually carried by another image: the pilgrim church. The church is constantly on the move, in need of being transformed by the Spirit until it is completely restored at the consummation of the age.[115]

Just so, the personhood of the Spirit is posited in relation to its coming upon the church and opening up its eschatological future. Pentecost is what transforms God's elected community from the people of God to the body of Christ and the temple of the Spirit. Through Jesus, God is still acting in the world bodily by the continuing work of the Spirit which makes the church the body of Christ and its temple.

> The progress of dogma has the character of plot, the ongoing story of God's action in the world, and the story of the church is part of that development. But what is the church's story? It is the story centering on the Third Person of the Trinity: the sending of the Spirit. The coming of the Spirit, as noted earlier, constitutes the church by uniting the body to the Head. In this very act, as Jenson puts it, the "Spirit frees an actual human community from merely historical determinisms, to be apt to be united with the Son and thus to be the gateway of creation's translation into God."[116] The story of the church, therefore, could be said to be the story of the Spirit in the church ... This is why Pentecost is so vital to the continuing growth of the Christian story. Without telling the story of the church, which is the story of the Spirit in the church, we have an incomplete gospel.[117]

*Conclusion*

If Yong has constructed a "foundational pneumatology" to serve as the ground from which he accounts for the relationship between God and the world from a pneumatological perspective, perhaps what I have just offered in the previous section is the beginning of something like a foundational ecclesiological pneumatology. I have argued that pentecostal theology is liturgical theology which privileges the Spirit throughout so that it is necessarily thoroughgoingly eschatological. Perhaps then, this foundational ecclesiological pneumatology can be understood as the bedrock for the forthcoming constructive vision of reality. This bedrock, or foundation, privileges the particular Spirit of the Father and Son—the triune God—and said Spirit's work in (1) joining the Body to the Head (via Pentecost) so that the church may be Christ's ongoing bodily availability

---

115. Chan, *Liturgical Theology*, p. 32.
116. Jenson, *ST.2*, p. 179.
117. Chan, *Liturgical Theology*, p. 35.

to the world;[118] (2) opening the future to the church, bearing her along (via tradition) in history while she bears the world on her narratable journey toward eschatological consummation to be the realized *totus Christus*; and (3) gifting the church with practices and speech-acts—through which Christ first remains object to the church—to bodily and faithfully participate in items one and two, just noted above. This foundational ecclesiological pneumatology underwrites the claims this work has made about the metaphysical world-making character of the church's first and second-level discourses. Thus, in addition to my pentecostal metaphysical construct utilizing Smith's five categories as my scaffolding, this ecclesiological pneumatology will serve as my foundation.

*Summary/Conclusion*

In sum, through conversation with Chan's ecclesiology which focuses on the church's ontology, I reaffirmed the centrality of narrative for pentecostal self-understanding and uncovered that what often inhibits our ecclesiology is succumbing to a story in which the church is pigeonholed to be nothing more than one of many instrumental goods in the world. But, if the church is joined to Christ by the Spirit to *be* his body in and for the world, then the church both precedes creation with Christ, and exceeds creation in that it (imperfectly) embodies the union that God eschatologically intends for all things with himself. Therefore, church practice, and the narrative self-understanding it embraces, carries deep ontological weight.

## *I Am That You Are: The Radical Openness of God*

*Introduction*

According to the first section on a "radical openness to God" from the perspective of pentecostal scholarship, I adduced that thus far, scholars have understood the pentecostal proclivity of being radically open to God as a lived orientation in

---

118. Just so, "God's history cannot be lived, and his story cannot be told without the parts we play in it" (Green, *The End Is Music*, p. 21). We play our parts in God's history because we have been enabled to do so through God's initiative in the life of Jesus, which has transfigured us and the world. As Green also says, "God alters reality from within its deepest center, its innermost depths, opening it up fully to God and so to its own essence, its own fullness." In similar fashion, the church is called to live so that the world is "opened up to God who is not far off and whose kingdom is always at hand. Holy Week is a reminder that God is always working, doing what only God can do. But it is also a reminder that we are called to join in that always-ongoing work ... We're not meant to remain witnesses of the witness; we're meant to take in the experience, to absorb it and be absorbed by it, so that we're transfigured by the mystery." https://macrinamagazine.com/sermon/guest/2021/03/28/transfiguring-being/ (accessed 04/02/21).

which one expects God to act in surprising ways that are different and new, at least from the creature's perspective. It is here that I must draw our attention to the fact that—in light of my revisions for what it means for us to be eschatologically oriented—I will be revising the definition of "a radical openness to God" not in such a way as to say something completely different, but to add to it so as to make ontological reflection explicitly necessary.[119] That is, in addition to our expectation of God's surprises, to be radically open to God also means that our being—and that of all contingent reality—is such that we are wholly dependent on our participation in the life of the triune God for our very existence. As we will note below, there is a distinction in how the church participates in God, and how the world does. In the eschatological orientation section just above, we have already been primed for this as we have posited creation as God's dramatically narrated act of initiating, sustaining, and fulfilling a history by the unified act of God in which Father, Son, and Spirit have particular but inseparable roles. Just so, an explicit ontological account of the being of God as three in one will be here posited. Indeed, it is God toward whom our being is radically open—and from whom we receive it—and so a constructive account of the being of God is necessary to better illumine our own in relation to him.[120]

In arguing for such a disposition—in light of my foundational ecclesiological pneumatology, and in conversation with the norms drawn from Scripture and the greater historical Christian tradition—I will be positing a participatory ontology. I will start this reflection by attending to the triune being of God and follow it with an understanding of the being of creation in light of who God is. I will do the preceding in appreciative and critical conversation with what pentecostal scholarship has already said on these matters, as displayed previously in the work of Yong and Smith, among others. The remaining three elements of a pentecostal worldview will mostly be the implications of the work done in these first two elements.

Finally, to remind the reader once more, the final purpose of this monograph is to offer a constructive and critical engagement of pentecostal spirituality, and academic pentecostal theology through conversation with the greater ecumenical, dogmatic, and Christian metaphysical tradition; this effort is aimed at constructing

---

119. In Smith's five elements, he is more concerned with adducing a worldview rather than a metaphysics. As such there is not an explicit constructive ontology proposed within them. It is interesting to note, however, that in the same monograph he does posit an ontology, but it is in a different section placed outside of the five elements (Smith, *Thinking in Tongues*, pp. 86–105). Because this work is constructing an explicit metaphysical vision, it must include an ontology. And because I am using Smith's five elements as scaffolding, "radical openness to God" is the most fitting place for it.

120. Simon Chan reminds us, "Central to any spirituality is its conception of what is ultimately real ... Clearly, a proper conception of God—is essential to the development of an adequate Christian spirituality," which inevitably presupposes and implies a metaphysical vision of the whole. (See Chan, *Spiritual Theology*, p. 40).

a pentecostal metaphysics that, simultaneously, does justice to what is best in the first-level pentecostal experience while confronting that which is unfaithful. In service to the overall goal just described, specifically as it relates to my constructive and critical engagement with academic pentecostal theology, the following section, which posits a pentecostal ontology, will begin first of all in conversation with the historic Christian tradition, by briefly sketching Mediterranean antiquity's understanding of being—and the being of God—and denoting how St. Thomas conversed with and altered these notions in a way fitting to the gospel. Secondly, after following Thomas's lead regarding the one being of God, I look to the Cappadocians to elucidate how the one being of this God is conceived trinitarianly. Once the being of the triune God has been traced, I will posit an ontology of participation—conversing with those already produced by pentecostals—which aims to construct a coherent account of the being of the church, and subsequently the being of other creatures and their participation in the life of God. It is in this section that once again the church's unique ontological reality, distinct from—not just over against, but *for*—other creatures will be noted.

### "I Am": The Being of the One God

The history of Christian theology, we have said, can be read as a sustained effort to upset—or at least, reinterpret—the "common sensical" ways of talking about God, and thereupon, all of reality in a given context across time. This includes critiquing the contextually shared ways of talking about the nature—or better, the being—of things. Once again, this work is from a decisively Christian perspective; therefore, the answer to the ontological questions of existence—such as, "what is it to be?," "what is being?," and "what sort of being has ... ?,"—are best understood not through a general concept of being, but being as it may be understood by the revelation of triune God through the particular life of Jesus of Nazareth.[121] Just so, this section which posits an ontology of participation for creatures must begin with the being of God as evoked by the church in our first- and second-level discourse. Only from that starting point can we begin to make gospel sense of our being as eschatologically oriented and radically open to God.

For Christians, the question of God's being is imposed upon us, especially when the Nicene Creed is confessed in our first-level discourse as it begins with, "I believe in God, *the* ...," dogmatically asserting that God indeed *is*. For Christian metaphysics, this prompts the second-level question, in what sense *is* God? Or, what sort of being does he have—which later proceeds to the question(s) of what sort of being we have? More basic still, we may ask what is being in the first place? As odd as these questions may seem, once asked, they refuse to go away; and in our attempts to answer them we realize that they are neither esoteric nor inconsequential. One

---

121. This approach is consistent with my approach of doing metaphysics in an antecedently Christian way and follows from what I have constructed in the section above which gives ontological and temporal priority to Christ over against creation. I follow Steve Wright's scholarship on this point in *Dogmatic Aesthetics*, pp. 8–39.

only needs to turn this line of questioning upon oneself and the objects of one's experience to recognize this. As Christians, however, we must first labor to answer the questions, in what sense *is* God, or, what kind of being has he?

From its inception, Christianity was met with an antecedent discourse inhospitable to biblical faith—that is, Greek Hellenic theology—and was both dependent upon and opposed to what said discourse posited about the being of G/god(s). Replete with particular anxieties about time's contingencies due to its underlying narrative, Greek theology developed an understanding of what the being of "God" must be so as to stymie the problems of being-in-time.[122] As such, the "God" they posited was one who was utterly removed from, and untouched by time so as to be immortal, and just so the ground of Hellenic temporal being was a timeless one. The Greek God so described cannot be an object of our experience in this everchanging existence, and so was described by the negation of predicates such as "impassible," "invisible," etc. Dualistic reality with two utterly separate kinds of being was thus imposed: one is the lesser and inferior one, subjected to time's contingencies, while the other kind of being was the superior one, untouched by the same. And so, in late antiquity the desperation of the human condition comes to be understood by the unscalable chasm between God's being in eternity, and humanity's being in time—just so, the search for a third kind of mediatory being ensued. Consequently, beings which were god-like but thought of as existing in time—so as to be graspable—were narrated via mythological stories wherein these mediatory beings were varied by a hierarchy abstracted from true, timeless, and invisible deity. Christians entering into this discourse had to be clear about the being of Jesus so that he is not mistaken as merely another mediator of many, however great.

Finally, then, what is being for ancient Greek thinkers? First of all, to truly be is to be unaffected by time's contingencies, so that *true* being is the all-embracing *aion*;[123] while *temporal* being derives from such completion in varying qualitative

---

122. There is indeed a stark contrast of narratives. The life of Israel is narrated as wandering tribes seeking protection and rescue from oppressive civilizations, while the civilization of Mycenaean Greece was overthrown by such northern Dorian tribes. As the Ionians sought to restore Greece, they were well aware of the fragility of historical contingencies and longed-for protection therefrom, thus invoking a deity of timeless eternity. Such histories of Greek religion can be found in the following: Jane Ellen Harrison, *Prolegomena to the Study of Greek Religion* (Cambridge: University Press, 1903), esp. chapters 1, 7; Martin P. Nilsson, *A History of Greek Religion*, trans. F. J. Fielden (Oxford: Claredon Press, 1925); and Werner Jaeger, *The Theology of Early Greek Philosophers* (Oxford: Clarendon Press, 1947). For a brief, yet helpful historical sketch of time and eternity, see Alan Padgett, *God, Eternity, and the Nature of Time* (Eugene: Wipf and Stick, 2000), pp. 38–54.

123. True being is divine—which is autonomously and completely self-satisfied so as to be impassible and unmoved—the *aion* which embraces the *telos* of all that is temporal and contingent. From this motionless and timeless completion, contingent beings—to varying degrees—derive their own being. See Joseph Owens, *The Doctrine of Being in the Aristotelian Metaphysics: A Study in the Greek Background of Mediaeval Thought* (Toronto: PIMS, 1951), pp. 435–54, 463–4.

degrees.[124] Second, being is the form (*eidos*)—that is, a pattern or organizing inner principle which gives particular beings substance and shape—such as, the form of a tree, a house, a human, and a god.[125] A form itself remains untouched by time's contingencies, while time still may affect the particular beings which participate in the form. While true being is divine and so unaffected by time, form is indeed knowable and seeable—so that, to be is to be knowable and seeable in varying capacities.

Being as posited by the Greeks could not be accepted by Christian theology. From the outset, Christianity's narrative identity begins with Israel *not* seeking protection from change, but in hoping for it. "Whereas Yahweh was eternal by his faithfulness *through* time, the Greek gods' eternity was their abstraction *from* time. Yahweh's eternity is thus intrinsically a relation to his creatures ... whereas Greek gods' eternity is the negation of such relation."[126] Indeed, the Christian God

---

124. In Aristotle's thought, however, it is not quite clear just how his God relates to substances as efficient cause, as Aristotle's thought is focused on the final cause of things. In other words, there is no account of how the Unmoved or Prime Mover is self-diffusive as efficient cause. "Substances in the heavens and in the sublunary world love and desire the Prime Mover as ultimate first cause ... But it is not clear how in Aristotle's metaphysics the actuality of substantial form is related to that of the Prime Mover. The latter is but a remote first cause that imparts motion exclusively by final causality, not by efficient causality ... once the first cause is denied efficient and formal causality and limited to final causality, the individuation of composites is severed from the Prime Mover," therefore, "Aristotle's God is desired and loved as the ultimate final cause but this God is utterly indifferent to the sublunary world—'thought thinking itself,' a purely self-directed energy." Pabst, *Metaphysics*, pp. 22–3. See also, Joseph Owens, "The Relation of God to the World in the *Metaphysics*," pp. 210–18.

125. Gilson helpfully puts it so, "Forms are the intelligible core of visible reality." He points to an animal as an example and argues that by mere chemical analysis at a strictly material level, nothing is revealed which suggests that its material cause could not as well enter the composition of beings of an entirely different sort. Just so, a conception of form is necessary as the "inner principle which accounts for its organic character, all its accidents, and all the operations it performs." Therefore, the form "is the very act whereby a substance is what it is, and, if a being is primarily or, as Aristotle himself says, almost exclusively *what it is*, each being is primarily and almost exclusively its form ... The distinctive character of a truly Aristotelian metaphysics of being ... lies in the fact that it knows of no act superior to the form, not even existence." See Étienne Gilson, *Being and Some Philosophers* (Toronto: PIMS, 1952), p. 47. Finally, forms require matter for their actualization, unless they are more noble forms which do not require composition. In their lack of need for compositions, these noble forms fully possess being so as to be instantiated in themselves. See Owens, *The Doctrine of Being*, pp. 426–34.

126. Robert Jenson, "The Nicene-Constantinopolitan Dogma," in Carl Braaten and Robert W. Jenson (eds), *Christian Dogmatics: Volume One* (Minneapolis: Fortress Press, 2011), p. 116.

as revealed through the Incarnation is God *with* us. We are thus radically open to the surprises that a life with him may bring; just such a distinction demands a revisionary understanding of being and beings. Thomas Aquinas (*et al.*) does not evade the concept of being. Rather, he appropriates it while conversing with Plato, Plotinus, and Aristotle and others, and reinterprets them in light of the gospel, thereby attempting to answer the question of what it means for the Christian God to be. I will follow his example.

For Aristotle, there is no act of being superior to form, and form which does not require a material cause is necessarily divine. For Thomas, however, the incorporeal nature of angels means that a form without material properties does not necessitate its divinity. Thomas thus overcomes Aristotle's composition of form and matter wherein form is the highest act of being, and instead joins form and matter together and fits them under what he calls "essence." Being (*esse*: act of existence, or act of being) can *consist* of essence—either composed of form and matter, or form without matter (as in the case of angels)—but it (*esse*) does not *necessitate* it. Aristotle posited that in knowing the *what* of a thing (its essence), the *that* or *why* of a thing is thereby implied. This marks a great point of departure for Thomas, who says that contingent and composite beings genuinely are, but do not contain, the reason for their existence within themselves, and as such have their being from beyond themselves. That is the composite and contingent condition of all creatures.[127]

God, however, as necessary and uncomposed means that his existence and essence are identical, so that *what* he is guarantees *that* he is. His existence *is* his essence, and he is the only one for whom this is true.[128] "I am who I am" says

---

127. The essence-existence doctrine of St. Thomas is the centerpiece of his entire metaphysical system; therefore, the intricacies of this doctrine have been the object of much technical debate among Thomists. I follow Gilson (and others such as Geiger, Fabro, de Finance, and W. Norris Clarke) in that I find it best to say that essence and existence are not a distinction of two proper things. According to Gilson, Thomas "often said that essence and existence are united in the thing (*re*) Thomas never understood this as a composition of two *res*, or things … Thomas was trying to make it clear that this composition was not a mere composition of two abstract notions, but, rather, of two elements inherent in the metaphysical structure of actual being" (Étienne Gilson, *History of Christian Philosophy in the Middle Ages* [Washington, DC: CUA Press, reprinted 2019], p. 421). God, of course, is not composite and so, for him and only him, his essence *is* his act of existence.

128. According to Wippel's reading of c. 4 of Thomas's *De ente et essential* (c. 1252-6): "Thomas's point is to show that it is impossible for there to be more than one being in which essence and *esse* are identical. If we grant the fact of multiplicity, then all existing things, with this single possible exception, essence and *esse* must differ." See John F. Wippel, *The Metaphysical Thought of Thomas Aquinas: From Finite Being to Uncreated Being* (Washington: CUA Press, 2000), p. 146. Wippel is heavy-handed on the distinction between the essence and *esse*. Just how *real* this distinction is at the heart of the Thomist debates about the essence and *esse* in Thomas. Per my engagement with Gilson (*et al.*) in the previous footnote, I prefer to think of them as two connatural elements in actual being over against two distinct *res*.

Yahweh to Moses (Exod. 3:14), and "Before Abraham was, I am" says Jesus to the Jews (Jn 8:58).[129] Therefore, God is the sheer *Ipsum Esse Subsistens* (Subsistent Act of Existence). As such:

> He is not a "being," at least not in the way that a tree, a shoemaker, or a god is a being; he is not one more object in the inventory of things that are, or any sort of discrete object at all. Rather, all things that exist receive their being continuously from him, who is the infinite wellspring of all that is, *in whom* (to use the language of the Christian Scriptures) all things live and move and have their being. In one sense he is "beyond being," if by "being" one means the totality of discrete, finite things. In another sense he is "being itself," in that he is the inexhaustible source of all reality, the absolute upon which the contingent is always utterly dependent, the unity and simplicity that underlies and sustains the diversity of finite and composite things.[130]

The account of St. Thomas's understanding of God's being just adduced stresses his transcendental unity by rejecting composition of any sort in God. God is simple, he is who he is. I want to insist here that to say that God is simple is *not* to say that

---

129. Thomas himself connects these two texts using the name he deems most appropriate for God—"He who is" (*Summa Theologiae*, 1.13.11)—in light of the ontology just described: "For eternal existence knows neither past nor future time, but embraces all time ... Thus it could be said: *he who is, sent me to you, and I am who I am* (Exod. 3:14) ... When speaking of himself, in order to show that he was not made as a creature is, but was eternally begotten from the essence of the Father, he does not say, I came to be, but *I am* he who *in the beginning was the Word* (Jn 1:1); *before the hills, I was brought forth* (Prov. 8:25)." (Thomas, *Commentary on John*, C.8 L.8 [emphases original]). See also Matthew Levering, *Scripture and Metaphysics: Aquinas and the Renewal of Trinitarian Theology* (Malden: Blackwell Pub., 2004), pp. 47–74. I follow this tradition, arguing alongside Levering that "Trinitarian theology ... persistently calls into question the alleged opposition between metaphysical analysis and scriptural exegesis." (Levering, *Scripture and Metaphysics*, p. 8). I thus reject Rhys Kuzmic's suggestion to follow Marion—who argues that ontology is unscriptural idolatry—for constructing a pentecostal ontology in Rhys Kuzmic "To the Ground of Being and Beyond: Toward a Pentecostal Engagement with Ontology," in Nimi Wariboko and Amos Yong (eds), *Paul Tillich and Pentecostal Theology* (Bloomington: Indiana University Press, 2015), pp. 45–57. For problems with Marion and the modern attempts to overcome metaphysics, see David Bentley Hart, "Remarks Made to Jean-Luc Marion Regarding Revelation and Givenness," in David Bentley Hart (ed.), *Theological Territories: A David Bentley Hart Digest* (Notre Dame: University of Notre Dame Press, 2020), pp. 26–44.

130. David Bentley Hart, *The Experience of God: Being, Consciousness, Bliss* (New Haven: Yale University Press, 2013), p. 30 (emphases original).

God is monadic but that he is perfect unity. God is triune. As such, I wish to retain Thomas's notion of divine simplicity precisely by tracing it along the lineaments of God's triunity.[131]

### "The Holy One of Israel": God's Life as Being-in-the-Spirit

St. Thomas taught us that God is *Ipsum Esse Subsistens*—that is, the act of being, or the subsistent act of existence—so that "God" cannot be a referent for a form of any sort. Moreover, we have said both here and in the previous chapter that God is action; he *is* in that he acts *ad intra*, and we *are* in that he acts *ad extra*. He is active, talkative, and relational within himself; we exist in that his action, communication, and relations have been opened to include us. God is not a static or monadic agent, neither is he merely a mind nor untouched timeless infinity who passively and remotely knows things as they exist through mere observation. Put succinctly, we have argued that God is not a mind who statically knows, but a Spirit who dynamically acts and transforms. Whatever follows from here, we are compelled in our first-level discourse to say about God's being that God is relational, God is one, and God is active. How then, may we affirm God's tri-personality—as we are likewise compelled to—in light of what we have said?

Considering that part of my work is aimed at constructing a pentecostal metaphysics that does justice to what is best in the first-level pentecostal experience, I will be privileging God's dynamic "threeness" because, as Chris Green rightly suggests, what we experience in pentecostal worship—specifically in prayer as

---

131. Because pentecostals tend to think of God as active and dynamic, I will be following something reminiscent to what Lincoln Harvey calls the "renaissance theologians" who essentially "depict a God who is eternally to-ing and fro-ing in self-relation, with the tri-personal gospel event of dynamically mutual differentiation being posited as the unsurpassable life of God's substantial reality." See Lincoln Harvey, "Essays on the Trinity: Introduction," in Lincoln Harvey (ed.), *Essays on the Trinity* (Eugene: Cascade Books, 2018), p. 3. In other words, God's being is identified by the *action* that happen*s* *within* the one life of the three, which upsets some "deeply held assumptions, most notably the commonly held belief that 'Being' is splendidly singular, unmoving, and unchanging, and pretty much un-anything at all" (Harvey, "Essays on the Trinity," p. 3). The problem this vision seeks to attack is that the doctrine of the Trinity remains peripheral to much of the first-level discourse of the church. I am thus eager to assist in attempting to move toward remedying Rahner's diagnosis (via Harvey, "Essays on the Trinity," p. 6 n. 14): "despite their orthodox confession of the Trinity, Christians are, in their practical life, almost *mere* 'monotheists.' We must be willing to admit that, should the doctrine of the Trinity have to be dropped as false, the major part of religious literature could well remain virtually unchanged." (Rahner, *Trinity*, pp. 10–11).

we are gathered at the altar[132]—is "one presence of threeness," or perhaps, the three-fold internal structure of *one* dynamic *life*. Following Del Colle's insights[133] and a slightly modified version of Coakley's insights[134]—and further allied to his readings of Rom. 8:26-27 and 1 Cor. 2:9-16—Green argues that because God's

> triplicity is the being of the one God revealed to us savingly in the gospel, we can speak of that presence as the presence of the Father in Jesus Christ who is made experienceable for us by the Holy Spirit, *or* as the presence of the Holy Spirit, drawing us into the Father's embrace of the Son, *or* as the presence of Jesus, baptizing us in the Spirit who reveals to us the Father's heart.[135]

In pentecostal prayer at the altar we can experience the unique ways each *hypostasis* draws into the one life of God. Following this logic, the above sub-section sought to adduce God's *one* presence or, *one* life, and what follows will be an explication of the "threeness" of that one presence, or life.

If Green is right, then faithful pentecostal experience of God is shaped trinitarianly, and pentecostals can look to the New Testament to see how this logic has always been at work in the life of the church. This logic along with the reading of Scripture within the life of the church has historically served to correct our course toward trinitarianism against the threats of the theology of Mediterranean antiquity.[136] Be it through Paul, John, or the letter to the Ephesians, etc., or our praying the "Our Father" and confessing the creeds, the language of the Christian faith is determined by trinitarian logic and the triune naming of God. Historically speaking, the tacit trinitarian theology of the church was forced to become explicit due to the pressure of Arius' denial of eternal generation in favor of understanding

---

132. It appears that Green is assuming that this altar around which pentecostals are gathered in prayer will culminate in Eucharistic celebration. While the different ethnographic research efforts on modern pentecostal worship (displayed in previous sections) show that this cannot be assumed full stop, Green's argument tacitly anticipates the need for the forthcoming proposed scripted liturgy. In this same essay, Green argues that "our experience of God is inseparably bound up with our theological accounts of that experience," therefore, "we need to fill our worship with prayers and songs, sermons and testimonies that attune us to the dynamics of God's triune presence by attending carefully to the trinitarian grammar witnessed in the Scriptures and affirmed in the Christian tradition" (Green, "In His Presence," pp. 198-9). I will argue that this is precisely the gift that an at least partially scripted liturgy might give us.

133. Ralph Del Colle, *Christ and the Spirit: Spirit-Christology in Trinitarian Perspective* (New York: Oxford University Press, 1994).

134. Sarah Coakley, "Living into the Mystery of the Holy Trinity: Trinity, Prayer, and Sexuality," *Anglican Theological Review* 80 (1998), pp. 223-32.

135. Green, "In His Presence," p. 194.

136. Jaroslav Pelikan, *The Christian Tradition: A History of the Development of Doctrine* (Chicago: University of Chicago Press, 1971), 1.108-20, 172-277.

the Son as *not* unoriginated, and thus positing him *explicitly* as a creature. Arius' vision was anathematized; and once the Council of Constantinople reaffirmed Nicaea, Athanasius' *homoousion* had won the day.[137] Thus, Christianity's entanglement with the alien metaphysics of antiquity was severed; there is only God and creatures, *sans* semidivine mediators.[138] Furthermore, there is no God "himself" to be abstracted or rescued from the life of Jesus, and as such, neither modalism nor subordinationism are acceptable formulations of God's being. Acceptance of Nicaea and its trinitarian implications, however, did pose important and difficult questions about the being of God. If there are no semidivine mediators or ways to abstract one true God from the godhead so that Father, Son, and Spirit simply and equally *are* God, how do we not then become tri-theists? Here, we take a look to the Cappadocians to assist us in answering this question and to complete our constructive thought on the being of God.

By the late fourth century, subordinationism still held some influence. What was needed was a way to differentiate Father, Son, and Spirit without qualitatively ranking them, and simultaneously avoiding both tritheism and modalism. After 370, the Cappadocians were just the ones to deliver, and their innovations began—just as it did for St. Thomas—in conversation *with* and modification *of* antecedent discourse. The philosophical tradition had been using *hypostasis* (ὑπόστασις) and *ousia* (οὐσία) almost interchangeably to mean "that which is" or "something that is"—and up until Cappadocians, Christian theology had followed suit. The Cappadocians untangled these terms so that *ousia* named the *one* deity of God while *hypostasis* named the particularity of the three.[139] In the inherited

---

137. See Frances M. Young, *From Nicaea to Chalcedon: A Guide to the Literature and Its Background*, 2nd ed. (Grand Rapids: Baker Academic, 2010), pp. 40–72; Lewis Ayers "Athanasius' Initial Defense of the Term ὁμοούσιος; Re-Reading the *De Decretis*," *JECS* 12 (2004b), pp. 337–59; David M. Gwynn, *The Eusebians: The Polemic of Athanasius of Alexandria and the Construction of the "Arian Controversy"* (Oxford: OUP, 2007); Widdicombe, *The Fatherhood of God*, pp. 159–222; J. N. D. Kelly, *Early Christian Creeds*, 3rd ed. (London: Continuum, 2006), pp. 242–62; John Behr, *Formation of Christian Theology Volume 2: The Nicene Faith Part 1* (Crestwood: SVS Press, 2004), pp. 117–22, 163–259.

138. Leonard Hodgson, *The Doctrine of the Trinity*, pp. 113–41.

139. See Basil the Great's letter to Count Terentius, 214.4 wherein he states:
Ousia has the same relation to hypostasis as the common has to the particular. Every one of us both shares in existence by the common term of *ousia* and by his own properties is such a one and such a one ... in the same manner ... the term *ousia* is common, like goodness, or Godhead, or any similar attribute; while hypostasis is contemplated in the special property of Fatherhood, Sonship, or the power to sanctify. If then they describe the Persons as being without hypostasis, the statement is *per se* absurd; but if they concede that the Persons exist in real hypostasis, as they acknowledge, let them so reckon them that the principle of the homoousion may be preserved in the unity of the Godhead, and that the doctrine preached may be the recognition of true religion, of Father, Son, and Holy Ghost, in the perfect and complete hypostasis of each of the Persons named.

philosophical tradition, *ousia* tended to be used for the what of a thing, while *hypostasis* described the particularity of a thing as distinguished from the others who share the same what-ness. Gregory uses men like Stephen and Luke—and for the sake of consistent three-ness, I will add Paul—to make this concept lucid. Stephen, Luke, and Paul are particular instances (*hypostasis*) of the humanity (*ousia*) which they share. For the Cappadocians, deity is what is common to Father, Son, and Spirit—the three hypostases—who are relationally identified over against each other as unbegotten, begotten, and proceeding.[140]

If Stephen, Luke, and Paul are three humans, would this not imply that Father, Son, and Holy Spirit are three gods? No, say the Cappadocians, for two main reasons. First of all, what distinguishes one human person from another belongs to their individual accidents—like say, their familial origins, physical attributes, and location in space—and not their shared humanity. So that, if Stephen, Luke, and Paul had different accidental characteristics than what they possess, it would make no difference to humanity itself; indeed, neither would humanity as such be fundamentally nor ontologically altered should they not have existed at all. On the other hand, *that* God *is* Father, Son, and Spirit is not merely accidental. Rather the distinct relations between the three belong to their joint possession of one deity.[141] God the Father is the Source of the Son and the Spirit's deity, God the Son is the recipient of the Father's deity, and God the Spirit is the act of reception of deity to the Son from the Father.[142] Just so, the relational distinctions between the three belong to God's *ousia*.

Second, I remind you of Thomas's insistence that "God" does not name a form. For Gregory, in similar fashion, neither does "God" name the divine *ousia*. God and *ousia* are not to be conflated. Instead "God" names the mutual, divine, and unified *action* of Father, Son, and Spirit which constitutes their one life as God. God's one being is the *life* lived as the relational and mutual action of Father, Son, and Spirit. As such, "there are not existent persons existing at the end of each relation: the 'persons' simply *are* the relations. The Father *is* the begetting, speaking, and sending of Jesus, the Son. Jesus *is* the begotten, spoken, and the sent. The Spirit *is* the breathed forth, and the poured out." Therefore, "all there is to God we might say, is the event of these relationships. There isn't a divine being (much less three divine beings!) that sometimes decides to act."[143]

---

140. This is put succinctly and clearly by Gregory of Nazianzus in *Orations* 31.9.

141. See Gregory of Nyssa's elegant treatment of the matter in *Against Eunomius*, 2.2. For a concise treatment more proclamatory in tone, Gregory of Nazianzus in his *Orations* 34.10: "If all that the Father has belongs likewise to the Son, except Causality; and all that is the Son's belongs to the Spirit, except his Sonship, and whatsoever is spoken of Him as to Incarnation for me a man, and for my salvation, that, taking of mind, he may impart his own by this new commingling; then cease your babbling ..." Once again, the joint acts of Father, Son, and Spirit *are* the deity of God and could not have been otherwise.

142. See Gregory of Nyssa's letter to Ablabius, *On "Not Three Gods."*

143. Green, *From His Fullness*, p. 130.

How, then, is this God whose being is discourse, act, and event, personal? The answer lies in understanding that the life of a person is simultaneously many acts, events, and conversations bracketed by one coherent narrative so as to be one act, one event, and one conversation. At a human level, Norris Clarke argues that "one's life must take the form of a *journey,* unified by a final destination or goal. To be a good story, a meaningful story, it must be a *unified story.*"[144] As such, "my human life takes the form of an unfolding story"—constituted by events, actions, and conversations—"with a point to it."[145] I am a person in that my acts are *faithful* to myself, which is ultimately determined by the point of my story. As a creature, the meaningfulness and faithfulness of my story is not one of my inventions. That is, "I do not have this faithfulness in myself; I have it in the coherence of God's intention for me."[146] If I do not honor God as the one in whom my life as a person has an aim and so a storied continuity, I will succumb to the myth of my life as an uneventful continuity—that is, a story-less existence, borne along by the meaningless sequence of time. God, on the other hand, is triune. As *triune person* the coherence and faithfulness of God's life is first grasped within himself, "so that all acts cohere to make the one act that he personally is."[147] Just that is the difference between God's triune personality and our monadic personhoods. Our dramatic coherence is narratively gifted to us by an intention outside of our own—so that our lives cohere only insofar as we live faithfully in and beyond ourselves—while God's triune personality is his own coherence. As such, God is utterly free to relate to us personally as Scripture demonstrates without violation to himself. "He changes his mind and reacts to external events, he makes threats and repents of them, he makes promises and tricks us by how he fulfills them. If we understand this language fundamentally inappropriate, as 'anthropomorphic,' we do not know the biblical God."[148] Indeed,

> Persons do all these things, precisely to be personal, and in that the true God is personal they are ontological perfections, not deficiencies. The criterion of the triune God's self-identity is Jesus, just in his openness to his fellow human beings. Therefore, that God listens to us and responds to us, far from being a condescension, is the very way he is faithful to himself.[149]

Put succinctly, the triune God is the coherently personal, eventful, and talkative faithful action in himself, and thereupon toward us. Having said that, we are now compelled to adduce the being of all else in relation to the triunely personal and active being of God.

---

144. Clarke, *The One and the Many*, p. 64.
145. Clarke, *The One and the Many*, p. 124.
146. Jenson, *ST*.1, p. 222.
147. Jenson, *ST*.1, p. 222.
148. Jenson, *ST*.1, p. 222.
149. Jenson, *ST*.1, p. 222.

## "The Lord, Your God": Being-in-the-World as Ontological Participation

### Participatory Ontology and Pentecostal Spirituality

Regarding the being of creatures, James K. A. Smith has argued that as Christians "we should affirm some version of a participatory ontology."[150] I agree with Smith on this point, and believe that a participatory ontology which affirms the sacramental existence[151] of all things is in alignment with pentecostal sensibilities of living in a world wherein transcendence inheres in immanence, so that the world is primed for the Spirit's manifestations in such a way that God's acts are not "interventions" in a reality otherwise created to get along without him.[152] When

---

150. Smith, "Will the Real Plato Please Stand Up?," p. 72.

151. It is indeed valuable to highlight the covenantal relationship between God and the created world, and with humanity in particular; that said, I want to stress with Hans Boersma that we must insist on a *sacramental* link between God and the world as it "goes well beyond the mere insistence that God has created the world and by creating it has declared it to be good. It also goes beyond positing an agreed-on (covenantal) relationship between two completely separate beings." Instead of beginning and ending with covenant absent of an ontology which overcomes the separation, "A sacramental ontology insists that not only does the created world point to God as its source and 'point of reference,' but that it also subsists or participates in God ... In other words, because creation is a sharing in the being of God, our connection with God is a *participatory*, or real, connection—not just an *external*, or nominal, connection." Hans Boersma, *Heavenly Participation: The Weaving of a Sacramental Tapestry* (Grand Rapids: Eerdmans, 2011), p. 24. This serves as an intentional correction to the theologically problematic modernistic proclivity to tacitly posit a God and world relationship which assumes Scotus's univocity of being, and Ockham's nominalism.

152. With that said, at least as I read him, Smith can be quite puzzling in his constructs as he proposes not *an* ontological vision, but what seems to me to be two visions—depending on whether he is speaking as a pentecostal, or from the Reformed tradition. For example, when speaking from the Reformed tradition, Smith critiques RO's "suspension of the material world" claiming that it devalues the material world. Moreover, Smith argues that this suspension model derives from their Platonic ontology, which he finds it to be incompatible with Christianity, see *IRO*, pp. 197–206. Here, Smith names Plato's ontology as used by RO as "ultimately pagan" and therefore, incompatible as a resource for Christian ontology. Moreover, Smith says that RO directly connects itself to Plato and so his pagan dualisms. According to Smith, RO's model devalues the material world and God because it understands materiality as only instrumentally good, and also it implies that creation cannot be itself without God's constant "reaching into" it. He thus offers a Reformed—and Leibnizian-Deleuzian—caveat to reassert the dignity of creation *as* creation over against RO's vision which he believes has occasionalist sympathies. See Smith "Will the Real Plato Please Stand Up?" A charitable read of this conflict in Smith would be to say that depending on who he is speaking as, he merely shifts emphasis on transcendence (pentecostal) or immanence (Reformed). While the question of who gets Plato right or wrong in their back-and-forth on the matter is beyond the scope of this work, I must simply note here that

Smith explicitly identifies himself to be speaking *as* a pentecostal, he recommends RO's "suspension (of immanence in transcendence) model"—albeit in light of Yong's pneumatological assist[153]—as a good option to move toward a pentecostal ontology.[154] I will be following Smith's recommendation by way of what many influential contemporary Thomists have already utilized.[155] For now, I must continue with what pentecostals have thus far proposed regarding an ontology of creatures in relation to God and each other. I will thus converse with what pentecostals have said on this matter, while offering my own reflections in light of what I have previously proposed about the relation between God, creation, and the church in my constructive section.

Adrian Pabst, a newer contributor to RO, pushes back heavily on the notion of Plato being hopelessly dualistic, claiming that to be a misreading of him. While he is not responding to Smith directly, Pabst's reading of Plato differs significantly from that of Smith. See Pabst, *Metaphysics*. For a helpful essay which traces the back-and-forth between Smith and RO, see Brendan Peter Triffett, "*Processio* and the Place of Ontic Being: John Milbank and James K. A. Smith on Participation," *The Heythrop Journal* 57 (2016), pp. 900–16.

153. Wherein, once again, the Holy Spirit is the agent in which the material world is suspended, so that all of the material world is pervaded by the Spirit.

154. For example, when writing as a pentecostal, Smith says that RO's vision is best suited for pentecostals because its "dynamic, participatory ontology refuses the static ontologies that presume the autonomy of nature … we might say that nature is always already suspended in and inhabited by the Spirit such that it is always already *primed* for the Spirit's manifestations." Smith, *Thinking in Tongues*, p. 101.

155. W. Norris Clarke, "The Meaning of Participation in St. Thomas," in W. Norris Clarke (ed.), *Explorations in Metaphysics: Being-God-Person* (Notre Dame: University of Notre Dame Press, 1995), pp. 89–101; J. F. Wippel, *The Metaphysical Thought of Thomas Aquinas: From Finite Being to Uncreated Being* (Washington, DC: Catholic University of America Press, 2000), pp. 94–131; R. McInerny, "Saint Thomas on *De Hebdomadibus*," in Scott MacDonald (ed.), *Being and Goodness: The Concept of the Good in Metaphysics and Philosophical Theology* (Ithaca and London: Cornell University Press, 2001), pp. 74–97. In following this tradition more closely, I will not be following Milbank's (and thereupon, RO's) understanding of participation in St. Thomas. Triffett, ("Ontic Being," p. 903), helpfully distinguishes Milbank and Thomists like so:

> On Milbank's account of created being, a divine principle is infused into each creature; the creature receives its proper being by virtue of receiving and participating in an "alien" gift. But for Aquinas, to say that creatures have being by way of "participation" is simply to say that (a) the formal content of the finite being proper to each thing is pre-eminently included in the original plentitude of divine being (pure *esse*) and that (b) creatures need to be actively sustained by God throughout their existence. In this account of created being there is no mention of (c) divine *procession* and infusion … What proceeds from God to creatures in the act of creation is not some indwelling divine gift, but rather the non-divine, innate being of things.

Suggesting a participatory ontology is not unique to Smith.[156] Yong also affirms that all of reality participates in God, and simply adds a pneumatological assist to Smith's participatory ontology—which Smith happily receives—suggesting that it provides a trinitarian vision to Smith's ontology and resources it theologically (through the biblical phrase, "the Spirit poured out on all flesh"), rather than merely philosophically (e.g., through revisions on Plato).[157] Once again, Yong argues that "the Spirit poured out on all flesh" at once: provides a trinitarian ontology, overcomes the perceived bifurcation between transcendence and immanence, and overcomes the ontological distinction between the church and the world. Smith, receives Yong's assist, but denies that Yong's chosen text overcomes distinctions between the church and the world as I have previously noted in detail in the chapter that deals with their engagement. In dealing with the issue of ontological distinction between the church and the world, Smith employs the metaphor of the intensity of participation in which he argues that all participate in God by the Spirit for their existence, but some beings and communities—namely, Christians and the church—participate in him more intensely (or soteriologically).[158] Andrew K. Gabriel complements this by coming at it from the other direction when he says that it is the Spirit's activity in these communities and persons which is more intense.[159]

Considering that Yong's pneumatological assist in terms of its biblical resource was helpful but also found to be a bit wanting in that it utilized a reading of an Acts 2 text in such a way so as to minimize the particularity of the Spirit

---

156. For Vondey, for example, at Pentecost the presence of the Spirit intensifies throughout all of creation so that at that event the cosmos is baptized in the Spirit for the purposes of cosmic redemption. "Nevertheless, while all of creation can be said to participate in the presence of the Spirit, not all elements of the cosmos participate in the divine presence with the same intensity" (Vondey, *Pentecostal Theology*, p. 165).

157. Once again, Yong claims that "the gift of the Spirit to 'all flesh' underwrites the ontological participation of all creation in the divine presence and activity that sustains the world, thus providing a 'pneumatological assist' to a sacramental principle which revalues the material world" (Yong, "Radically Orthodox," p. 247). I think Yong overstates what "the Spirit poured out on all flesh" can accomplish here. Following Smith (as detailed in my section on their interaction), I think that reading the text as an outpouring upon all of humanity as such is a stretch, in that Acts 2:17a seems to be referring to the Spirit's outpouring without respect for ethnicities or nations to create a *church* that will be representative of all of humanity. Furthermore, as I will note in a following section, Yong advocates for a theory of emergence and supervenience which does not quite fit with a metaphysics of participation.

158. Hans Boersma also uses the language of intensity when comparing the Eucharist's participation in God in comparison to God's sacramental presence in the rest of reality, in *Heavenly Participation*, p. 52.

159. Andrew K. Gabriel, "The Intensity of the Spirit in a Spirit-Filled World: Spirit Baptism, Subsequence, and the Spirit of Creation," *Pneuma* 34 (2012), pp. 365–82.

and thus overreached its universal import, I aim to provide a more thorough theological—and so biblical and ecclesiological—assist to it in light of what I have said thus far in my own construct.[160] That is to say, what I have argued in the previous chapter regarding the Spirit of Jesus *with* his body, and this joint relationship to creation honors both the universal efficacy of the Spirit, *and* its particularity as the Spirit of Jesus with the church. With that said, I find it to be useful for both Smith and Yong regarding their ontologies.

Now, we continue with the pentecostal ontology so far provided. Gabriel helpfully poses this ontological problem of distinct participations as a pneumatological one which is imposed upon us by Scripture. Given that Scripture affirms both the Spirit's ubiquity in all of creation *and* his *subsequent* fillings in history, "it seems necessary to make some sort of distinction, for example, between the presence of the Spirit in a tree and the presence of the Spirit in a believer. The distinction should not, however, consist in saying that there is a different Spirit dwelling in these two places." He goes on to insist that "there is only one Spirit who is present in both creation and redemption, though in different ways … (sustaining, creating virtue, giving wisdom, regenerating, justifying, sanctifying, empowering, renewing) according to the intensity with which the Spirit is present."[161]

Intensity of the participation of beings in God or intensity of the Spirit's presence has proven to be a helpful metaphor for pentecostals to make ontological distinctions in creation.[162] Here, I will explicate my own complementary metaphor in light of the arguments made in the previous chapter which has already set the stage for what is to follow. As a more thorough biblical resource to Yong's "Spirit poured out on all flesh," I offer my previous biblical survey of the Spirit's activity in creation, with Christ, and in the church as a resource. For the sake of recapitulation, I pointed readers first to the Old Testament which says of the Spirit that he both creates life and *is* life, thus highlighting the dependency of all that is on this life-giving Spirit. This life-giving Spirit of God, moreover, creates history by filling prophetic leaders to speak promises on God's behalf, thus throwing down what is to make room for what God *intends* in history. Post-exilic prophecy shows that the Spirit's inspiration of prophetic speech to "make room for what God intends" has become more explicitly eschatological. Just so, Israel's understanding of the Spirit is to be fulfilled in a unified vision of the history-creating Spirit of prophecy with the eschatological hope of the Spirit's outpouring. There is a *messianic* and communal component to this fulfillment: it is messianic in that there will be a final Spirit-bearing prophet who will initiate that eschatological reality; and it is *communal* in that the said Spirit-bearer's messianic mission is to share that Spirit which rests on him to create a life-giving community of prophets.

---

160. To be fair to Yong, he does have an account of the Spirit's ubiquity in and through creation (Yong, *All Flesh*, pp. 280-3), but for his "pneumatological assist," he focuses primarily on the Acts 2 text.

161. Gabriel, "Intensity of the Spirit," p. 377.

162. Recently in Vondey, *Pentecostal Theology*, pp. 164-5.

In the New Testament, I showed that Jesus emerges as the eschatologically anointed prophet whose life is the content of Israel's hoped-for eschatological reality. Jesus bears the Spirit precisely to give him as eschatological gift, and the fruit of that outpouring is new creation, witnessed to by the community of prophets that is the church, who is also created via that same outpouring. At Pentecost, then, the Spirit descends upon believers to join us to Christ to be his body and availability to the world, and moreover descends as a *foretaste* and *anticipation* for when our inclusion in the life of God—that is, our salvation—is fully realized. With that said, I will here offer a new metaphor to supplement the understanding of the church as participating more intensely in the life of God by the Spirit: the church then, is ontologically an *eschatological step ahead* of the world, in the story of God drawing all things to himself.[163] Specifically, "It is through the eucharistic celebration, therefore, that the church herself becomes a sacrament of the eschatological reality of the fullness of Christ."[164] This is true of us not pridefully, but rather, missionally and mediatorially. The church witnesses to the world by embodying and being what God intends for all of creation. Further still, the church is not set apart (holy) merely to show the world, but to bear the world. That is, the Spirit bears the church along (via tradition with proper nourishments) in history so that she can bear the world along with her on her narratable journey toward eschatological consummation to be the realized *totus Christus*. The Spirit intensely participates in the church, and the church intensely participates in the Spirit for her being, and just so, the being of the church is to be an eschatological step ahead of the world in its narratable journey into God's eschatological embrace.

*Being-in-the-World*
I have just attempted to supplement Smith's participatory ontology while resourcing Yong's pneumatological assist with my pneumatological survey of Scripture. The result of which was the positing of the uniqueness of the church's being in the world as an eschatological step ahead of it. How then, might we say that creatures who are not specifically the church participate in God for their existence?

The doctrine of participation imposes a *task*; a task not so much of committing a homogenous body of propositions to memory as much as it is central to the church's ongoing effort to find better ways to make sense of what it means to be a creature in relation to the biblical God. Historically, outside of Christian discourse, this has manifested as the problem of the one and the many, the problem of universals and particulars, or, the relation of the infinite to the finite. For Christians, however, we have already identified the God appropriate to Scripture and our first-level

---

163. This holds in light of what I have said in the beginning of my eschatological orientation section. That is, that the church is the firstfruits of new creation and that one of the ways of understanding what liturgy is for the worshipers is an identity-orienting eschatological *journey* into the life of God. By the Spirit, the assembled church publicly embodies and beholds what is to become of it, the *totus Christus*—for herself, and the world.

164. Boersma, *Heavenly Participation*, p. 189.

discourse as the triune, supra-formal, self-diffusive, perfect, and complete *Ipsum Esse Subsistens*, so that neither Plato's nor Aristotle's conception of infinity nor perfect form could be adopted full stop by the Christian tradition. Just so, for the doctrine of participation we are compelled to follow St. Thomas's basic structure once again.

Thomas's doctrine of participation sought to provide a theory for rendering intelligible the common possession of a given attribute in many subjects "by reference to a higher source from which all receive or participate in some way the perfection they possess in common."[165] It manifests as explanations for "the sharing of all the members of a species in the same specific form, the sharing of many specific forms in the same genus, and the sharing of all being in the same transcendental perfection of existence received from the one supreme Source, God."[166] While Thomas has been thought to be for Aristotelianism and against Neoplatonism,[167] as independent historical studies of both Thomas and Aristotle have continued—his *synthesis*, and original appropriation of the two have become more apparent.[168] He models for us, once again, what it looks like to evangelize antecedent discourse. Taking a brief look at how he does this is helpful for better understanding his doctrine of participation.

---

165. Clarke, "Participation in St. Thomas," p. 92.

166. Clarke, "Participation in St. Thomas," p. 92.

167. See Étienne Gilson, *The Christian Philosophy of St. Thomas Aquinas* (Indiana: Notre Dame Press, 1956) esp. ch.1 "Existence and Reality" and Gilson, *Being and Some Philosophers*.

168. In particular, I am thinking of the initial work done by Clarke in the following two essays, originally published as: W. Norris Clarke, "The Limitation of Act by Potency in St. Thomas: Aristotelianism or Neoplatonism?," *New Scholasticism* 26 (1952), pp. 167-94; W. Norris Clarke, "The Meaning of Participation in St. Thomas," *Proceedings of American Catholic Philosophical Association* 26 (1952), pp. 147-57. Although these works were respectively written in 1952, the historical work Clarke has done in displaying the importance of Neoplatonism in St. Thomas's doctrine of participation has continued to prove useful—especially against what has been argued by the likes of Gilson *et al.* that Thomistic metaphysics is decisively for Aristotle and *against* Neoplatonism. There have been many who have since (like Clarke) understood St. Thomas as dependent on Plotinus' vision of participation, that is, Mark D. Jordan, *The Alleged Aristotelianism of Thomas Aquinas* (Toronto: PIMS, 1992); and Rudi A. te. Velde, *Participation and Substantiality in Thomas Aquinas* (Leiden: Brill, 1995). Kerr offers a helpful and brief overview of these different schools of thought in his monograph, Fergus Kerr, *After Aquinas: Versions of Thomism* (Oxford: Blackwell, 2002), pp. 9-10, 48-50, 70-1. Finally, a more recent monograph on metaphysics (2012) when discussing participation in St. Thomas follows Clarke's lead on exactly this point. See Pabst, *Metaphysics*, pp. 201-71. Finally, it is important to note here that Clarke was not the first to see this. He was seeing what other well-known Thomists were during that time in Ireland, and Continental Europe (specifically, France, Belgium, and Italy).

First, his engagement with Neoplatonism. Thomas found Plotinus useful in that he had posited a participation and limitation structure of the universe wherein creatures were limited participants of an infinite plenitude of perfection. However, due to the Christian *distinction* between creator and creature, Thomas could not fully adopt Plotinus's emanationist metaphysics. For Christians, there is only one triune source. *Ergo,* Thomas emptied the emanationist proclivities of Neoplatonism and its vast hierarchic procession of concretized or reified universal concepts and "substituted as the fundamental ontological perfection of the universe the supra-formal act of existence, participated first directly by essential form, as limited potency in pure spirit (angels and hosts, etc.), then dispersed, so to speak, in material beings by being communicated through specific forms to their multiple participations in matter."[169]

A "vertical" participation structure so described means that creatures—as participants in existence beyond themselves, and also somehow distinguished from each other—are necessarily composite. The weakness of Neoplatonism is its ambiguity in dealing with the *unity* of the being of composite participants. Recognizing this, Thomas synthesizes Neoplatonism with its problem of ambiguity on the unity of being, with the Aristotelian notion of act and potency which deals precisely with the unity of being throughout time and change. There is still a disconnect here, however, between the vertical and the horizontal. To connect act and potency in time and space with the vertical notion of participation, we must remember that God is not composite and as such is pure actuality. If God is pure act, potency is what *limits* said act within a receiving subject to be precisely *a* creature. Potency as that which *limits* a received perfection in a subject is the original idea of Thomas, which connects act and potency to the vertical structure of participation. At the same time, potency denoted the "horizontal" unity of a being throughout change in time and space as the principle of continuity. To close this brief reflection on Thomas's original synthesis of Neoplatonism and Aristotelianism for the sake of constructing a doctrine of participation, perhaps it would be helpful to quote a Thomist in his definition of the foundational metaphysical co-principles, act and potency. Act is "the actuality or actual presence of some positive mode of perfection"; and potency is "any potential subject that receives and limits an act, and is the principle of continuity underlying and determining the limits of actual changes it can go through."[170]

Through Thomas, participation along with act and potency has been identified as the metaphysical principles of finite being. To conclude my reflections on the dependency of creatures on God via Thomas's doctrine of participation, I must here remind the reader that unlike God, *what* creatures are (essence) does not necessitate *that* they are (existence). Any finite being, or finite act of existence has some determinate character, and its essence is precisely that which determines the character that it has via its potency. The existence (act) and essence (potency) of a

---

169. Clarke, "The Limitation of Act by Potency," p. 80.
170. Clarke, *The One and Many,* p. 159.

finite being are both derived from God's creative action so that "God not only gives finite beings their existence but *communicates* to them their essence. They not only exist in virtue of act, but they also express his nature."[171] This not to say that finite beings are only parts of God. Pantheism is not here suggested. Rather, in the order of *essence* each finite being "is a reflection or 'imitation' of what God is, contracted to the finitude of the creature's existential act,"[172] so that the nature of a being and all that exists analogously[173] expresses God's nature.[174]

Looking now at the order of *existence*, God is the *causa prima* and the *causa in esse*. A metaphor which would serve to illustrate God as the constant wellspring of being upon which created reality has total ontological dependency as its *causa in esse* is to see this relationship as comparable to:

> a candle's or lamp's flame to the light it casts out into a room at night: should the flame be extinguished, in that very instant the room would fall dark ... (so that) the cause of being is not some mechanical first instance of physical eventuality that, having discharged its part, may depart the stage; rather, it is the unconditional reality underlying all conditioned things in every instant.[175]

*Being-in-the-Spirit*

Finally, we must briefly look at how the ontological dependency of creatures may be traced within a God who is Father, Son, and Holy Spirit. Both *that* creation is, and *what* its constituent creatures are, depends wholly on the space that the triune God makes for us in his life. This is depicted in the prologue of the fourth Gospel as it "fuses together the vision of the divine creative act as both unconditional hospitality for, and a loving communal discourse with, the other. It depicts the act of cosmic creation as proceeding from the Word that speaks it forth while being turned toward God" (πρὸς τὸν θεόν, Jn 1:1).[176] Consequently, "the orientation of the creative speech is not directed outside the divine reality

---

171. E. L. Mascall, *Existence and Analogy* (London: Longmans, 1949), p. 122.

172. Mascall, *Existence*, p. 122.

173. According to Thomas, the perfections in caused things as they relate to God are predicated analogously, and not univocally nor equivocally. For a brief and lucid, yet thoroughly adequate explanation of the doctrine of analogy, see Joseph Owens, *Elementary Christian Metaphysics*, pp. 86–93.

174. For a more thorough treatment on the metaphysical composition of finite being which details the distinction between finite beings in the order of essence, see Clarke, *The One and Many*, pp. 42–160. See also how Clarke distinguishes between real beings and artifacts in pp. 64–8.

175. Hart, *The Experience of God*, p. 104.

176. Daniela Augustine, "Creation as Perichoretic Trinitarian Conversation," in Stephen John Wright and Chris E. W. Green (eds), *The Promise of Robert Jenson's Theology: Constructive Engagements* (Minneapolis: Fortress Press, 2017), p. 100.

but rather remains in the inner communion of the Trinity itself. Thus creation takes place (and dependently perdures) *within* the perichoretic intimacy of the trinitarian life as a trialogue of loving interface with one another."[177] That lively, loving, and active communication between Father, Son, and Spirit is so excessive it has "spilled over" so that creation is the hospitable effect of that loving excess.[178] "In a gift of unconditional hospitality, the proto-communal Trinity becomes the immediate dwelling place of others as the very environment in which they live and move and have their being (Acts 17:28)."[179] Furthermore, "God (being love) pours himself forward toward the existence of the other through the kenosis of the Word and the Spirit so that creatures may come to be (as materialized *logoi* spoken by the *Logos* and animated by the Spirit who circumscribes them in the self-giving, life-sustaining generosity of love)."[180] Finally then, in tracing a participatory ontology with respect to a God who is triune, we may say that creatures are in that the capacious and excessively loving triune relations, actions, and discourse have been spilled over toward what is other than Father, Son, and Holy Spirit. Creatures are in that they live, and move, and have their being in such a life. That life itself *is* God, the wellspring of being. The church is in that it participates in that life more intensely by being an eschatological step ahead of the rest of creation, historically manifesting, witnessing to, and foretasting what God intends for all things.

*Conclusion*

Above, I argued that pentecostals are not only radically open to God in a practical sense but are further so in an ontological sense thus opening my inquiry to ontological reflection. Pentecostals have argued for a participatory ontology to be best suited for us, and I agree. I aimed to pursue a participatory ontology by first adducing a vision of the being of God, first following Thomas, then the Cappadocians. I then set out to posit an understanding of the being of creatures by first looking at what pentecostals have said on the matter. I reminded readers of my earlier findings that Smith recommends RO's suspension model wherein immanence is suspended in transcendence and Yong adds pneumatological assist to say that that which immanence is suspended in, is the personal presence of the Holy Spirit. I resource Yong's pneumatological assist biblically with what I have said about the Spirit in creation in my Eschatologically oriented section, and in light of this I discovered that the difference between the being of the world and the being of the church is that the church participates more intensely in the Spirit (and vice versa) in that it is an eschatological step ahead of the world. To denote the

---

177. D. Augustine, "Trinitarian Conversation," pp. 100–1 (emphasis mine).
178. Rowan Williams, "The Deflections of Desire: Negative Theology in Trinitarian Closure," in Oliver Davies and Denys Turner (eds), *Silence and the Word: Negative Theology and Incarnation* (Cambridge: Cambridge University Press, 2002), pp. 115–35.
179. D. Augustine, "Trinitarian Conversation," p. 101.
180. D. Augustine, "Trinitarian Conversation," p. 101.

being of the world in greater detail following this insight, I made a move to follow St. Thomas's doctrine of participation closely. All beings participate in God as their essences analogously reflect God's nature, while their existence itself remains wholly dependent upon the triune God. I then reminded readers that because God is triune, to participate in the life between the Father, Son, and Spirit means that he opens space in his life and loving embrace to include others than himself. We are in that God's attention, action, and discourse have been turned to another than himself.

I conclude with this quote from Vladimir Lossky which does a superb job of concisely stating what I have argued thus far in my constructive sections:

> The world was created from nothing by the sole will of God—this is its origin. It was created in order to participate in the fullness of the divine life—this is its vocation. It is called to make this union a reality in liberty, in the free harmony of the created will with the will of God—this is the mystery of the Church inherent in creation. Throughout all the vicissitudes which followed upon the fall of humanity and the destruction of the first Church—the Church of paradise—the creation preserved the idea of its vocation and with it the idea of the Church, which was at length to be fully realized after Golgatha and after Pentecost, as the Church properly so-called, the indestructible church of Christ. From that time on, the created and contingent universe has borne within itself a new body, possessing an uncreated and limitless plentitude which the world cannot contain ... The entire universe is called to enter within the Church, to become the Church of Christ, that it may be transformed after the consummation of the ages, into the eternal Kingdom of God. Created from nothing, the world finds its fulfillment in the Church, where the creation acquires an unshakable foundation in the accomplishment of its vocation.[181]

This is in alignment with what we have said about the church as the people of God, the body of Christ, and the temple of the Spirit.

## *Deep Calls Out to Deep: Re-Enchanting Nature and Rediscovering Creation*

### *Introduction*

We have now arrived—in the constructive portion of this work—at the third element of a pentecostal worldview. In service of the greater purposes of this thesis, I will be constructively and critically engaging academic pentecostal theology on its "enchanted theology of creation" through conversation with the

---

181. Vladimir Lossky, *The Mystical Theology of the Eastern Church* (Crestwood: SVS Press, 1976), pp. 112–13.

greater dogmatic Christian metaphysical tradition to lead us toward constructing a pentecostal metaphysics that will honor what is best in pentecostal experience while identifying and thereupon shedding that which is less faithful.[182] In the two categories of "eschatological orientation," and "a radical openness to God" engaged above, we have posited a Holy Spirit-infused reality which dynamically draws all things toward their eschatological final cause in and through Christ *with* the church, as willed and sourced by the Father. What we have yet to account for constructively, however, is the presence of other spirits, neither divine nor created, but nonetheless beneficial or troublesome to creation. Fittingly, Kärkkäinen has named such a vision a "'plural' pneumatology" which accounts for the role, effects, and ontology of said spirits who work with or against the Spirit of God.[183] Heavenly hosts, satan, and demons, are all present in the pentecostal imagination and work benevolently for, or malevolently against, God's creatures. The pentecostal imagination is primed to understand the world as a spirit(s)-filled cosmos wherein corporeal and incorporeal agents interact with, and exercise influence over against each other. In what proceeds, I will be engaging appreciatively and critically with Yong's ten speculative theses for a pluralistic cosmos—along with the philosophies, theories, and precommitments that undergird them—as he is the primary pentecostal theologian to construct a comprehensive vision of the being of spirits in the material world and how they interact therein. He does so with an eye toward global perspectives while wanting to remain informed by the modern sciences.

### *The Liveliness of God and Gaps in Scientific Explanation*

Yong's theology and metaphysics, I would argue, are animated by a search for "open spaces": first, metaphysical open spaces wherein nature itself contains "ontological gaps"[184] and is oriented toward a (Peircean) "teleology" which directs the natural world and its governing laws to evolve, thus creating "open spaces" for the emergence of novelty, surprise, and qualitatively distinct realities.[185] Just there is where he locates "pneumatological/eschatological divine action" when seeking mutual formation with modern sciences. Second, in an effort to discern

---

182. Once again, "best" in the sense that it is ecumenically promising and does not run counter to what the classical Christian tradition has said about God and creatures; furthermore, "best" as described per my engagement with Smith's categories.

183. Kärkkäinen, "Spirit(s) in Contemporary Christian Theology," pp. 29–40

184. For example, he looks for the possibility of divine action in "open spaces" in the causal nexus of the world. See "How Does God Do What God Does?," pp. 56–8; *The Spirit of Creation*, pp. 77–101.

185. Through Peirce's "Thirdness" he argues there must be "a kind of final cause to draw evolutionary process forward, one that (is) neither random nor mechanistic but sufficiently *open-ended* so as to allow for the emergence of novelty." Yong, *Spirit of Creation*, p. 120 (emphasis mine).

truth in a world thus constituted, Yong argues for epistemic openness to make room for dialogue. For Yong, the principle of openness is found in pneumatology. Hence, his foundational pneumatology accounts for the God–world relation in "hope to arrive at the rudiments of a universal rationality, albeit one that is consciously anti-totalitarian precisely because … it is pneumatological."[186] The pneumatological character of this God–world account aims to create space for a "diversity of tongues"—read: traditions, cultures, discourses, methods of inquiry, burgeoning plurality—in the quest for truth about reality.[187] It thus "proceeds from what Peirce called a 'contrite fallibilism' wherein all knowledge is provisional, relative to the questions posed by the community of inquirers, and subject to the ongoing process of conversation and discovery."[188] Just so, Yong is ever attentive to mutually informing dialogue with other disciplines, and his primary posture is that of openness. As will be noted below, said openness can come at the cost of clarity and precision in his own constructs. Thus, a close reader of Yong might find ambiguity in his work depending on who he is speaking to, with, or as—which, at least it seems to me—is a price that Yong is happy to pay so long as his underlying conviction that he remains receptive to other disciplines, dialogues, and perspectives stays intact.

In Amos Yong's first thesis seeking an account of divine action in the natural world, he argues that "Pentecostal Christians do not have to embrace classical Christian construals of the God–world relationship insofar as these have attempted to define divine action according to the terms of Aristotelian efficient and material causes."[189] Considering that I am a pentecostal and that my metaphysical vision adheres to classical Christian construals of the God–world relationship, a response is in order; and it is a response that will lead us into deeper engagement with Yong's work. First, while Yong is more than welcome to question classical Christian construals of the God–world creation as methodologically normative for pentecostals, the alternative construct that he or anyone else provides must not fundamentally alter what Christians believe about the nature of God. Put differently, the alternatives he provides ought to preserve what needs to be preserved about the God–world relation in order to speak faithfully about the gospel. Part of what this section will accomplish—in conversation with what I have already constructed above—will be to demonstrate that he does not do this convincingly. Second, Aristotelian efficient and material causes are not at all classical Christian attempts to make sense of divine action in the world, at least not as Yong describes it. This will be unpacked as this section progresses.

For now, as I see it, there is a deeper fundamental issue that must be addressed first which will illumine the reasons for my pushback on Yong's statement, and

---

186. Yong, *SWC*, p. 84.

187. This is also the basis for Yong's pneumatological theology of religions one will find in Yong, *Discerning the Spirit(s)*, and Yong, *Beyond the Impasse*.

188. Yong, "On Divine Presence and Divine Agency," p. 168.

189. Yong, "How Does God Do What God Does?," p. 63.

his metaphysics. I will begin with a quote from the same essay that very subtly illustrates it. Yong claims that "It was the *scholastic embrace* of Aristotle that led to the emergence of the empirical method of early modern science."[190] A statement like this may seem banal enough to gloss over, but I want to pause here for the sake of seeking precision which should yield greater illumination for the discussion that follows. We must not overstate the consonance or continuity between premodern philosophy, and the modern empirical method as undergirded by mechanical philosophy.[191] By the time Aristotelian and Scholastic philosophy passed through the filter of modern thought, enough subtle adjustments had been made to render preceding ideas unrecognizable from their original intent. All too often, contemporary thinkers reject—and in some cases, accept—premodern philosophical notions following from the modern misconstruction. For example, as it pertains to scholastic metaphysics via St. Thomas, "A distinctive conception of causation, essence, form, matter, substance ... and other basic metaphysical notions underlies all of Aquinas's arguments ... and it is a conception very much at odds with the sorts of views one finds in Descartes, Locke, Hume, Kant, and other founders of modern philosophy."[192] Whether or not contemporary philosophers explicitly identify themselves as dependent upon the founders just mentioned, "their thinking about the metaphysical concepts just noted nevertheless tends, however unconsciously, to be confined within the narrow boundaries set by these modern thinkers." Consequently, "when they come across a philosopher like Aquinas, they unthinkingly read into his arguments modern philosophical presuppositions he would have rejected."[193]

---

190. Yong, "How Does God Do What God Does?," p. 52.

191. To Yong's credit, Aristotle is rightly often thought to have laid down the metaphysical foundations of physical and biological science. Beginning with the fact that "Aristotle's priority of substance over being privileges essentiality over existentiality," which means he "laid down the main conceptual foundations that *mutated* into the supremacy of (transcendental) ontology over theology." (Pabst, *Metaphysics*, pp. 9–10 [emphasis mine]). The problems with Yong's statement are subtle and two-fold. First, the *scholastic embrace* of Aristotle that Yong mentions is overstated—particularly through Thomas, who fitted Aristotle into a Neo-Platonist and Christian synthesis already present in Classical Christian metaphysics. See Clarke, "The Limitation of Act by Potency," pp. 65–88. Second, "the founders of the mechanistic-cum-mathematical conception of nature were driven by 'wishful thinking' and 'uncritical confidence' of just the sort of which they accused the Aristotelian Scholastic tradition they sought to overthrow; final causes and the like were regarded by them as "sources of distraction (which) simply had to be denied or removed." See E. A. Burtt, *The Metaphysical Foundations of Modern Science*, unabridged reprint of the 2nd revised edition published by The Humanities Press, Inc., 1951 (Kettering: Angelico Press, 2016) pp. 305–6 via Feser, *Aquinas*, pp. 41–2. That is to say, neither did the empirical method of early modern science receive Aristotle without serious revisions.

192. Feser, *Aquinas*, p. 8.

193. Feser, *Aquinas*, p. 8.

## 5. Toward a Pentecostal Theology of Being-in-the-Spirit

The metaphysics of Aristotle as received and developed by St. Thomas are by some accounts at odds with the metaphysics that later came to be assumed by many who championed the scientific method. This is not inconsequential. The founders of modern science just named, and the pioneers of inductive empirical methods—*a la* Galileo, Boyle, Newton, Bacon, and others—were given tacit conceptual grounding by the severance of transcendence from immanence of the late medieval period. Key contributions to this unhinging were Duns Scotus's univocity of being and William of Ockham's nominalism,[194] both of which run directly counter to Thomas's doctrine of analogy and realism. Following from the univocity and nominalism that took hold in the thirteenth and fourteenth centuries, and the scientific method's subsequent scrupulous refusal of any recourse to formal and final causes—what began as a helpful method of conceptually bracketing out these "higher causes" from physical nature for the sake of narrowing investigative focus, soon turned into a metaphysics of its own, commonly known as materialism, naturalism, and in some cases, physicalism. That which was not useful for a reductive and inductive methodological *investigation* of physical reality was effectively banished from all reality, *per se*.

The supposed metaphysics of modernity became one in which natural systems are all assumed to function as mechanical processes. Within such a "vision of the whole" devoid of "higher causes," the modern notion of causality itself is reductively misconstrued from that which was bequeathed by premodern thought.[195] "At the

---

194. See Gilson, *History of Christian Philosophy*, pp. 505-11; Dupre, *Passage to Modernity*; Pickstock, "Duns Scotus," pp. 116-48; Pabst, *Metaphysics*, pp. 272-303. Hans Boersma calls these two ideas the two blades that constitute the scissors of modernity, which were used to cut off the transcendence from immanence that were once woven together as a "sacramental tapestry." See Boersma, *Heavenly Participation*, pp. 68-83. Clarke says,

> With the advent of Ockham and the Nominalist tradition the atmosphere began to change. The fact of causal efficacy and the necessity of the principle of causality were by no means denied by Ockham. In fact, they are essential to his system, with its constant recourse to the unshackled omnipotence of First Cause. But the heavy dose of empiricism in his metaphysics and epistemology, in particular the denial of real relations and the resultant atomizing of the created universe into self-enclosed things each of which is separated from every other, made it impossible for him to give any metaphysical analysis or justification of causal efficacy.

(Clarke, "Causality and Time," p. 30)

195. In his monograph on the causal principle in modern science, Mario Augosto Bunge calls the modern use of causality *the* bewildering confusion which prevails in contemporary philosophy and science. Mario Augosto Bunge, *Causality: The Place of the Causal Principle in Modern Science* (Cambridge, MA: Harvard University Press, 1959). For some brief sketches which point out the historical landmarks of this development, in addition to the works just cited, see J. S. Wilkie, "The Problem of the Temporal Relation of Cause and Effect," *British Journal for the Philosophy of Science I* 1.3 (Nov., 1950), pp. 211-29. One

heart of the new scientific metaphysics is to be found the ascription of ultimate reality and causal efficacy to the world of mathematics, which world is identified with the realm of material bodies moving in space and time."[196] Always, in a world thus described, "A cause precedes its effect in time."[197] As such, modern mechanical metaphysics reduces "all real causality as an exchange of energy through antecedent forces working upon material mass."[198] Yong's dialogue with modern science has him adopting an "adapted" version of this notion of causality. "From a scientific point of view ... there is a need for a new view of causation that includes but is not limited to mechanistic causes, and that invites analysis of causal processes across the spectrum of the natural and human sciences."[199] It is adapted, at least partially, in the sense that he follows Peirce's Thirdness which posits a "final cause" that directs and opens nature to novelty. However, the modern notion of causality itself remains intact. For Yong, "cause" still tends to function as a kind of force on nature or material mass, but it does not act thus only antecedently or efficiently as it does for other modern thinkers. More on this later.

Contrastingly, Aristotle's αἴτιον[200] and the scholastic notion of *cuasa* as displayed in Aristotle's connected fourfold nexus of causality—material, formal,

---

can also find it throughout E. A. Burtt, *The Metaphysical Foundations of Modern Science* (Kettering: Angelico Press, 2016). Insofar as some Thomists followed this tendency—such as the Baroque Thomists and the proceeding Neo-Thomists such as Garrigou-Lagrange—I follow Lonergan who names their reading of Thomas's notion of causality as anachronistic. See Bernard Lonergan, *Grace and Freedom: Operative Grace in the Thought of St. Thomas Aquinas* (Toronto: University of Toronto Press, 2000).

197. Paul Weiss labors from this premise in his work: Paul Weiss, *Modes of Being* (Carbondale: Southern Illinois University Press, 1958), esp. pp. 40, 42; cf. *Nature and Man* (New York: H. Holt, 1947). Such is simply a twentieth-century restatement and application of what has already been established by early modern philosophers. Most notably David Hume, *Treatise of Human Nature,* I.3 sec. 2, 14; and *Enquiry Concerning Human Understanding,* sec. 7.2; and despite his more nuanced approach, Immanuel Kant, *Critique of Pure Reason,* 2nd ed., trans. Norman Kemp Smith (London: Macmillan, 1929), p. 469; where he explicitly states that the "causality of this cause, that is, the *action* of the cause, is antecedent in time to the effect which has *ensued* upon it" (emphases original). For Kant, there is no lapse in time to be wedged between cause and effect. However, sequentially there is indeed an order between the two.

198. David Bentley Hart, "Science and Theology: Where the Consonance Really Lies," *Renovatio* 2.1 (2018), p. 14.

196. Burtt, *Metaphysical Foundations*, p. 300. Worth noting considering this quote, and in light of who Yong engages; C. S. Peirce was a mathematician.

199. Yong, *The Spirit of Creation*, p. 95.

200. "Meant literally 'responsible for.' It came from law courts. A 'cause' of x is anything that makes a difference to x, that makes it x rather than y, anything that accounts for and thus explains x. A full explanation of any x includes these four dimensions." See Peter Kreeft, *Socrates' Children: The 100 Greatest Philosophers*, vol. 1, *Ancient Philosophers* (South Bend: St. Augustine's Press, 2019), p. 125.

efficient, final—are better rendered as "rational relations."²⁰¹ This series of rational and causal relations was not a failed premodern attempt at modern physical science, but rather, it was aimed at "describing the inherent logical structure of anything that exists insofar as it exists, and reflecting a world in which things and events are at once discretely identifiable and yet part of the larger dynamic continuum of the whole."²⁰² Indeed, the cosmological architecture of the world this reflected was a Ptolemaic one, which saved the appearances of the cosmos by providing a picture of reality in which all things are intricately and delicately related; a *universum* (read: "turned toward unity"), whereby the harmonious dance of the heavens constituted by spheres, stars, and planets were all congenially moved, and irresistibly drawn toward the divine.²⁰³ Within this cosmic framework, Aristotle's material, formal, efficient, and final causes as received and developed by Thomas²⁰⁴ were "a simple logical picture of reality in which both stability and change can be recognized and described … (they) were intrinsic and indiscerptibly integral relations, distinct dimensions of a single causal logic" whereas the modern tendency treats them as "separated forces only in accidental alliance."²⁰⁵ Neither does the modern shedding of the Ptolemaic worldview, nor the modern corrections of Aristotle's *Physics* necessitate the abandonment of classical theological metaphysics.²⁰⁶ In a modern world thus

---

201. Other ways to denote this causal action in this framework—especially when synthesized with Neoplatonist participation as St. Thomas did—is as "existential influx," whereby causal action is a "pure dynamic 'overflow' or 'gift of being,' as Gilson has called it, from cause to effect," or "transconceptual existential fecundity, of the dynamism beyond local motion at the heart of causal action" over and against the modern "persistent attempts to reduce efficient causality to something besides *the action of real existents*." (Clarke, *Causality*, p. 35; cf. Étienne Gilson, *Spirit of Medieval Philosophy* [New York: C. Scribner and Son, 1936], p. 95.

202. Hart, "Science and Theology," pp. 17-18. Indeed, for a thing or person to exist materially is already to be beyond a strictly material explanation. In St. Thomas's use of *hylemorphic* compounds allied to his doctrine of essence and existence—*what* something is does not necessitate *that* it is—matter "all by itself" is pure potentiality, and without being joined to a higher formal cause, does not exist at all.

203. For a concise yet thorough sketch, see C. S. Lewis, *The Discarded Image* (Cambridge: Cambridge University Press, 2013).

204. Thomas joined Aristotle with the Christian Neo-Platonist synthesis which connected Aristotle's Act and Potency with the metaphysics of participation; thus, Aristotle's causal nexus was explicitly connected to transcendence. I will mention more about this in a footnote below. See Clarke, "The Limitation of Act by Potency."

205. Hart, "Science and Theology," p. 18. Through the modern unhinging of the world from transcendence, causal relations could only be talked about *per accidens*; whereas for premodern thought, causal relations were at once *per se* and *per accidens*.

206. Regarding the accepted Ptolemaic astronomy, St. Thomas himself says, "the suppositions that these astronomers have invented need not necessarily be true; for perhaps the phenomena of the stars are explicable on some other plan not yet discovered

severed from transcendence—methodologically and actually—all things no longer participate in God; rather, God's being came to be conceived univocally and thus adventitiously as the supreme cosmic mechanic who either observed or intervened (mainly, as an "efficient cause," misconstrued) in a world created to get along without him. In such a picture of a God–world relationship, new notions of just how open nature and free creatures are to God turned into a zero-sum game of competitive agency.

I bring this to our attention to situate Yong and his engagement with classical theism, premodern philosophical categories, and his understanding of divine action in dialogue with modern science. Considering his apparent ambiguity (noted below) and vast body of work, I can only point to his discussions on these matters and attempt to articulate what they seem to suggest. At the very least, what I hope to contribute through this engagement for pentecostal theology is a raised awareness that we ought to take better care not to dismiss classical Christian theology without seriously considering the arguments raised from its first and second-level discourses, which we ought to share as Christians; if we are to shed their theology and metaphysics, I would hope it is because we find better ways to articulate it in light of our Scripture and its reception, our creeds, prayers, praxis, etc. and not because we have sought to be informed, or worse, have granted hegemony to modern methods to tell us what is ultimately real and true. We continue deeper into Yong's questioning of the normativity of classical Christian construals of the God–world relation.

*Questioning Yong's Questioning of Classical Metaphysics*

Yong points to Thomas's resistance of the idea that there can be an infinite regress of what Yong calls "cosmological causes," and says that cosmological causes according to Thomas require an "ontological first cause to explain why there was the … sequence of causation at all."[207] Therefore, according to Yong, Thomas's fourfold Aristotelian notion of causation—and specifically, final causation which "resides within living organisms"—required a First Cause. He then asks how the Thomist ontological "First Cause" interacts with secondary causes, and answers by way of "concordance"—whereby God, being the ontological cause, works in tandem with the secondary agents in the material world. So, for Yong, "double

---

by men" (*Sententia de Caelo et mundo*, II.17; cf. *ST* I.32.1). Thus, Feser argues, "Aristotelian physics is one thing, and Aristotelian metaphysics another, and they do not stand or fall together … there is no essential connection between the metaphysical notions and the scientific examples, and the former can easily be restated in terms of better examples." Moreover, Scholastic thinkers did not deny the possibility of empirical scientific advance, "as if they thought the science of their time infallible." Feser, *Aquinas*, pp. 38–9; cf. Edward Feser, *Aristotle's Revenge: The Metaphysical Foundations of Physical and Biological Science* (Neunkirchen-Seelscheid: Editiones Scholasticae, 2019).

207. Yong, "How Does God Do What God Does?," p. 53.

agency" and "concordance" are Thomas's way of making sense of God acting in and through free creatures.[208] Perhaps there is not much here to be quibbled with in Yong's account at this point; however, he follows his account of the medieval ideas of concordance and double agency and argues that they "have become central features of the classical theological tradition, especially once Reformation theologies adapted the idea of God as First Cause providing for, sustaining, and concurring with secondary causes."[209] But in the same way that it was a mistake for Yong to credit the scholastic embrace of Aristotle as the catalyst for the modern empirical method without accounting for radical revisions of the preceding metaphysical concepts, so is it a mistake to assume that Reformation theology received premodern classical theology without the same (mis)construals; indeed, not even Catholic theology was immune to this same tendency as we will see below. To be fair to Yong, he did call them "adaptations," although that's not quite strong enough of a word. The biggest issue in this case is that he (rightly) denies the arguments of the Reformers but understands this denial as at once a denial of "classical Christian theology." Once again, precisely because the Reformers found themselves on the other side of the modern (mis)construals of classical metaphysics, we must not overstate the continuity.

Yong says that Vernon White is representative of Reformation theology's contemporary restatement of the classical theological tradition, including its idea of God as "First Cause" (or primary cause). From this assumption, Yong presents White's picture of providence and attributes it to classical theology.

> Given divine concurrence with every event, White defends a robust theology of providential action such that there are no accidents in the universe. Within

---

208. It turns out, as usually happens when engaging such a vast tradition, that the picture provided is not quite as straightforward as described. Dominicans moving into the twentieth century—such as Garrigou-Lagrange and Jean-Herve Nicoalas *et al.*, representative of a significant school in contemporary Thomism—were working from Domingo Báñez, John of St. Thomas, and Diego Alvarez. For the latter, *praemotio physica* featured prominently as a way of naming God's moving of the creature's will without violating the creature's freedom. It denotes God as first efficient cause of all physical actions, but because he acts as such transcendently and not within the physical world of cause and effect, humans are free to physically act in a way that they choose, despite that choice already being predetermined by the eternal will of God. In other words, God, determining an act as primary cause does not violate human freedom insofar as he does not act thus antecedently in the contingent sphere of secondary causes; if God is not efficient contingent physical cause, the creature is free, and God is sovereign.

209. Yong, "How Does God Do What God Does?," p. 53. Yong notes in this footnote: "Protestant Reformation theologians like Luther and especially Calvin emphasized causality as *preceding* rather than concurring with secondary causes, while counter-Reformation theologians like Francisco Suarez leaned toward emphasizing concurrence of divine and creaturely causation."

this overarching theological framework, evil events are those permitted by God in order to bring about greater good that is currently incomprehensible to human minds except through the eyes of faith … Many theologians remain unconvinced that *this classical theological account of God's action in the world* suffices with regard to the problem of evil or the paradox of creaturely freedom … The theology of concurrence or divine agency seems to either require that God "builds in" ahead of time God's involvement both in the prayers themselves and in God's responses to them, or leads to the conclusion that God's ontological action is a superfluous level of explanation once cosmological causes are identified and Occam's razor is applied.[210]

As italicized in the quote above, Yong calls Vernon White's Reformed account of God's providence a "classical theological account," which, I argue, it is not. Before laying this problem on the shoulders of the reformers, however, Catholic Baroque Thomists were just as receptive to modern metaphysical (mis)construals without critique, leading them to problematic ideas about providence.[211] For example, in Domingo Báñez' (1508–1604) vision of *praematio physica*—which is purposed to preserve a proper understanding of the qualitative difference between divine and human action—God as primary cause gets reduced to what God efficiently predetermines; and as long as he does not directly act as the physical cause of an effect in the contingent world, creatures are "free" to act in the way already predetermined. Simply put, predetermination, in this vision, is what it means for God to act as the qualitatively distinct primary cause. Thus, creatures are "free," and God is absolved from any direct evil act. Baroque *Praematio physica* may very well be symptomatic of the invasion of modern mechanical philosophy, which posits efficient causality as the cause *par excellence*. When received uncritically by theology, it grounded God's transcendence in a more "respectable" kind of

---

210. Yong, "How Does God Do What God Does?," pp. 53–4 (emphases mine).

211. I must note here that the problem hardly began with the Baroque Thomists or Báñez. They are simply a modern example, symptomatic of what Hans Boersma has identified as a fivefold theological shift in Catholic ontology which began unfolding over centuries, constituted by: (1) the Gregorian Reform of the late eleventh century, whereby the earlier ontology regarded authority as intrinsically connected to church life and practice rather than imposed by extrinsic secondary agents; (2) debates about the nature of Christ's presence in the Eucharist, also in the eleventh century; (3) the overall discovery and privileging of nature in the twelfth and thirteenth centuries via the rediscovery of Aristotle in the High Middle Ages; (4) the fourteenth and fifteenth centuries' increasing bifurcation between the authority of Scripture and that of the church; and (5) finally, in light of the previous four, it seemed almost inevitably to lead to the sixteenth-century separation between nature and the supernatural. See Hans Boersma, *Nouvelle Théologie & Sacramental Ontology: A Return to Mystery* (Oxford: OUP, 2009); cf. Boersma, *Heavenly Participation*. These were all theological issues that contributed to the severance of immanence from transcendence.

causality: efficient supremacy. "And even spiritual freedom was reduced to the physical effect of a prior external force."[212]

However, the classical doctrine of creation is not about God creating static essences which must be predetermined by yet another act of God to be able (or "permitted") to act thus and such. Rather, in, through, and with the life of Christ, God gives being to both potency and act, which precisely as real beings possess and impart actuality to potentialities according to their proportionate secondary causal powers.[213] This is what it means for God to be primary cause—the ontological *causa in esse*, the hidden, inward, and ever-present cause, causing all causes *as* causes, drawing all things to himself, and whose transcendence is not achieved by negation of his "opposite." When God creates *real* beings[214] from nothingness, he donates being to that which in and of itself is nothing at all. God as primary cause must not therefore be redefined to be confused with efficient predetermination, relegating God to be the supreme efficient cause who reigns over immanent forces that merely express what he predetermines. Neither should one divide "primary causality into two distinct moments: creation and 'additional' predetermining impulse of the will"[215] as modern theology has tended.

The critiques of the metaphysics of the Baroque Thomist *praematio physica*—insofar as their metaphysics and theology are quintessentially modern—also hold for what we see in its modern variants, such as in prominent Protestant Reformation theologians. Said Thomists are a bit more nuanced versions of the voluntarist accounts of providence we see in the likes of Calvin. According to Yong, "Luther and especially Calvin emphasized divine causality as preceding rather than concurring with secondary causes ... while counter-Reformation theologians like Francisco Suarez leaned toward emphasizing the concurrence of divine creaturely causation."[216] However, I contend that Suarez is as susceptible to modern thought and thus *not* representative of classical metaphysics or its understanding of *causa* precisely because his understanding of "being" was univocal, and therefore, Suarezian "cause" cannot be in alignment with premodern thought. "Unlike the patristic and medieval metaphysics of relationality and participation, Suarez's

---

212. David Bentley Hart, "Providence and Causality: On Divine Innocence," in Francesca Aran Murphy and Philip G. Ziegler (eds), *The Providence of God* (London: T&T Clark, 2009), p. 42.

213. Known in the Scholastic tradition as the principle of proportionate causality. See Aquinas, *ST* I–II.63.3; I.4.2; I.6.2.

214. A real being "can ... express itself in action, is the center ... of its own characteristic action. I know *myself as real* because I am aware of myself as acting—thinking, deliberating, desiring. I know *other beings as real* because I am aware of their acting on me, actively responding to me ... determining me in ways I cannot control just by thinking about it but must submit to and cope with. Real beings *make a difference* in the real world." (Clarke, *The One and the Many*, p. 31. [emphases original]).

215. Hart, "Providence and Causality," p. 40.

216. Yong, "How Does God Do What God Does?," p. 65 n. 9.

system redirects focus away from the actuality of effects that intimate the first cause towards the univocity of being … Ultimately, Suarez cuts the links between creation and final causes and identifies God's creative action with *efficient causality alone*."[217] The point I am making here is simple. Yong seems to overstate: the continuity between premodern metaphysics and their modern counterparts, and subsequently, the continuity between classical theological accounts of divine action and the modern Reformed "adaptations."

Yong's questioning of classical metaphysics, then, seems at least in part to be based on these overstated continuities. It would perhaps be more precise to say that what he challenges is a Reformed—albeit not all within this tradition hold to it—understanding of providence undergirded by the (mis)construals of modern transcendental ontology.[218] When not explicitly challenging it, Yong makes use of many hallmarks of classical Christian theology and metaphysics.[219] However, ultimately, Yong's constructive metaphysical vision is deeply dependent upon C. S. Peirce's triadic metaphysics along with the concomitant modern redefinition of "cause" and thus "final cause"—*especially* when looking to engage modern science. Hence despite his sporadic use of classical Christian metaphysics, he ultimately adheres to a metaphysics that is at odds with the classic tradition. I do find it curious that Yong does this because he explicitly points to the modern redefinition of cause as a problem: "Yet the problem for any scientific account of divine action is that final causes were eclipsed during the Enlightenment when causality was reduced to quantifiable terms of physical events (efficient causes)."[220] While Peircean final causes might overcome purely inductive investigation that privileges efficient causes, they do not overcome redefining causality in quantifiable terms precisely because they

---

217. Pabst, *Metaphysics*, pp. 329–30 (emphases mine). Suarez even went so far as to divide being between infinite and finite, thereby subjecting both God and humanity under "being" as the enveloping category for both. See Boersma, *Sacramental Ontology*, p. 105.

218. And, as I have shown, Báñezian Thomists are also susceptible to those same misconstruals.

219. He does this explicitly in an essay on divine action in dialogue with modern science, in which he lays out seven speculative theses for a pentecostal pneumatological theology of divine action. For example, he says in his third thesis that "God is not embodied … God is the source and goal of all things"; and in his seventh thesis, he says that pentecostals must resist the seduction to imagine God "as an agent among agents." Elsewhere, Yong insists that "The triune God is the only necessary, transcendent … reality." (Yong, *The Spirit of Creation*, p. 208). Also, in his response to Smith's engagement with Radical Orthodoxy, Yong affirms a participatory structure to the God–world relationship offering a "pneumatological assist" to—which does not aim to correct, but resource—Smith's sacramental ontology. However, this is a very Yongian approach to dialogue—that is, to resource his dialogue partners without utilizing his own constructs outside of the conversation to bring correction. When speaking constructively, Yong's metaphysical vision is Peircean, emergentist, and Whiteheadian.

220. Yong, *Spirit of Creation*, pp. 87–8.

are still conceived through "pure nature" to be ever-evolving laws or "habits" that pull or direct nature and its constitutive processes toward their end; thus causality is still understood to be an exchange of energy through forces working upon material mass. The issue, then, is not *merely* the modern privileging of efficient causality to the exclusion of formal and final causes; more basic to that, I have argued, is the preceding (mis)construed redefinition of causality as such. With this in mind, we look at Yong's constructive metaphysics in conversation with Peirce.

*Eschatology and/or Teleology*
Peirce's triadic metaphysics looks at nature and its laws as paradigmatic for all reality. Yong seemingly takes on this fundamental conviction of Peirce, but because Yong is a Christian, he *theologizes* from this philosophical conviction with the aim of accounting for God's action in nature. Thus, for Yong following Peirce, the material world itself must contain a coherent and "scientifically plausible account of miraculous divine action *vis-à-vis* the laws of nature."[221] Peirce's triadic metaphysics is a way of looking at nature and its laws beyond the mechanical philosophy devoid of final causes by way of his triadic metaphysics, specifically within the category he called "Thirdness."[222] There must be "a kind of final cause to draw evolutionary process forward, one that (is) neither random nor mechanistic but sufficiently open-ended so as to allow for the emergence of novelty."[223] Final causes such as these are conceived of as habits that direct physical processes toward a final state. These habits—or laws—of nature themselves are not static, but they too are subject to evolve. This possible evolution of laws of nature (habits) Peirce calls "developmental teleology."[224] For Peirce, these laws and habits of nature evolved to strengthen themselves into "generalizing tendencies," which gave way to mind, association, and habit taking. Further, under the category of "Thirdness," consciousness in nature is thought to be accounted for through the generalization of natural law from which mind—by way of "developmental teleology"—emerged. The efficient causality of mechanical philosophy and the predictability of nature are thus met with Peircean teleology and final causes which are novel, unpredictable, and irreducible to preexisting causes. In short, "for Peirce the laws of nature are habitual tendencies that function teleologically like final causes."[225] These final or

221. Yong, *Spirit of Creation*, p. 118.
222. Yong, "Natural Laws and Divine Intervention: What Difference Does Being Pentecostal or Charismatic Make?" *Zygon* 43.4 (December 2008), pp. 974–81.
223. Yong, *Spirit of Creation*, p. 120.
224. In light of what I argued in the previous section about the modern redefinition of what causes are—that is, an exchange of energy through forces working upon material mass—it seems Peirce's understanding fits this quite well, except because Peirce has not banished final causes from his picture of nature altogether, final causes are understood to be the ever-evolving laws or "habits" that pull or direct nature and its constitutive processes toward their end.
225. Yong, *The Spirit of Creation*, p. 124.

end states and evolving laws are where Peirce finds room in the natural world for the emergence of novelty, surprise, and qualitatively distinct realities such as mind and consciousness; and, in the natural world thus conceived, this is where Yong finds room for divine action in conversation with modern science.

For Yong, Peirce's triadic metaphysics—especially under his category of "Thirdness" with its assumed modern (re)definition of (final) causality—provides room in the natural world for a pneumatological and charismatic view of divine action that understands the Spirit as active in the laws of nature, and also transforming it "in anticipation of the general shape of the coming kingdom."[226] The natural world and its evolving laws yield clues that it will one day be transformed eschatologically and is thus open to divine action; this leads him to correlate eschatology with (Peircean) teleology in some of his writing, specifically when dialoguing with modern science and attempting to discern divine action in the natural world. He says, for example, "miracles or divine activity in the conventional pentecostal understanding do happen today, although they are empirically inexplicable and thereby *only eschatologically comprehensible*. Given the empirical language of science, the language of faith is not fully translatable—hence my attempts to correlate 'eschatological' with 'teleological' language."[227] So strong is the correlation for Yong that in some cases he will refer to his proposal as an "eschatological-teleological theology of divine action."[228] What "science"—undergirded by Peirce's Thirdness—might comprehend as the evolutionary process of the emergence of novelties, then, Christians might comprehend as eschatological divine action. Both teleology and eschatology are "modes of reasoning" or explanations of novelty, surprise, and unpredictability in nature which cannot be grasped or made sense of by reductive accounts of "science"—in other words, they cannot be made sense of *sans* Peircean "final causes." Novelty, surprise, and unpredictability in nature are where Yong locates pneumatological divine action which points to God's purposes in bringing about the coming kingdom.[229] Put succinctly, eschatology is "a theological rendition of final causality"—that is, a hermeneutical read on novelty and surprise in nature as God's divine action.[230]

---

226. Yong, *The Spirit of Creation*, p. 125.
227. Yong, "How Does God Do What God Does?," p. 66 n. 23.
228. Yong, *The Spirit of Creation*, p. 73.
229. In his own words:
> There is a growing awareness that scientific explanations are impoverished apart from perspectives informed by final causality, that anti-reductionistic science in some ways invites teleological reflection, and that even the predictability of scientific explanation seems to assume a teleological mode of reasoning … I suggest that the pentecostal account of eschatological divine action functions for theology similarly to ways in which teleological accounts function for science.
> (Yong, "How Does God Do What God Does?," p. 62)

230. See Thesis 1 in "How Does God Do What God Does?," p. 63.

5. Toward a Pentecostal Theology of Being-in-the-Spirit 145

The preceding sketch of Yong's "eschatological-teleological," or "pneumatological theology of eschatological divine action" raises some crucial questions. First, does his (Peircean) "final causality," teleology, or "proleptic anticipations" point to the same *reality* or *realities* that eschatology does—within the context of the "science" and theology dialogue—with the difference mostly being a matter of hermeneutics according to the methods of the respective disciplines?[231] Following this, I am led to ask if indeed there is a differences between eschatology and teleology as such in Yong's vision, is it one of only slight variance? Or (least likely) is the difference absolute? If the difference is absolute, how can we meaningfully say that these distinct hermeneutical disciplines discerning absolutely distinct realities are mutually informative?

*Creation and/or Causation*
In the first part of Thesis 6 of Yong's seven theses for a "pentecostal account of eschatological divine action," he says that "Scientific discourses would also be recognized as *hermeneutical enterprises* without invalidating scientific explanations from any number of disciplinary perspectives. *So long as they remain at or within their appropriate levels of analysis*, the entire range of scientific findings will not threaten pentecostal claims."[232] Ergo, "science" must be chastened to speak only about the realities to which its methods grant it access. The question is, is eschatology one of those realities? Elsewhere, following Polkinghorne, Yong argues that Christians are shaped by church participation toward a "liturgy-assisted-logic" and just so, are resourced to understand realities *not* susceptible to historical or empirical investigation—such as incarnation and resurrection (read: eschatological realities). Here, it seems eschatology is out of bounds for scientific discourses. Yong affirms that when discussing events that are at once eschatologically transformative and historical such as the resurrection, we *cannot* simply discern those divine acts by way of historical and empirical investigation because the resurrected body of Christ and thereupon our future resurrected bodies do not belong within the natural order *as we know it*; rather, these "miracles" are *eschatological realities* fitted to God's re-creation. Based on the eschatological vision in conversation with Green posited above, I would wholeheartedly affirm this, and simply take what seems to me to be the next step and say: therefore, science as a culture and discipline equipped to inductively investigate physical nature—precisely *as we know it*—cannot tell us anything about eschatological realities which have to do with new creation. Moreover, that new creation has

---

231. Animated by his desire to see Christian theology translate its convictions "into public discourse accessible to those without the community of faith and to provide some means to clarify the validity of these interconnections besides just saying 'The Bible says so,'" he goes on to say that "what we are calling for is a mutual context, a context as wide as the creation itself and amenable to the languages of the natural world, of the sciences, and of theology." (Yong, *All Flesh*, p. 283).

232. Yong, "How Does God Do what God Does?," p. 63 (emphases mine).

been inaugurated can only be known by faith and thus cannot be known through empirical discipline.[233] But of course, Yong seems to say no such thing. He insists, as we noted earlier, that the material world must contain a scientifically plausible explanation of "special," "miraculous," or "eschatological" divine action *vis a vis the laws of nature*. Here, he seems to think that conceiving laws of nature as open to novelty ("teleology") is a way into this. Moreover, to insist that "science" and theology are mutually *informative* (although he admits they belong to distinct venues of inquiry), he has to say that teleology and eschatology as "modes of reasoning" strongly correlate. Does that mean, then, that teleology and eschatology at least come close to speaking about the *same* reality? If so, how close? If the sciences made room for "final causes" in their methods, would they be receiving (or at least evolving toward) what theology calls eschatology?

It is possible, then, that Yong would say that pentecostals can learn from Peircean final causes what it means for God to act eschatologically in the natural world, as we (can) know it. But didn't he also argue that eschatological realities (e.g., resurrection and incarnation) do *not* belong to the world as we know it, and therefore they cannot be historically investigated? Yong seems to be ambiguous on this point. In addition to his arguments around a liturgy-assisted logic above, he says "if the resurrection of Jesus is God's final albeit proleptic response to sin, suffering, and death, then it stands as the ground for hope that the future is nonextrapolatable from the currently known laws of nature."[234] Perhaps *currently* is the operative word in the previous sentence, so that what Yong wants to say is that if we leave space (via Peirce's "developmental teleology") in nature for *evolving* laws, then what emerges will be novelties that either witness to, or perhaps will evolve to become, or perhaps just *are* eschatological realities. He also says, "Insofar as Jesus' life, death, and resurrection are pneumatologically constituted, to that same extent the eschatological transformation of the fundamental conditions of nature is also pneumatologically accomplished."[235] Again, it might be that through the eyes of faith, the pneumatological and eschatological transformation of nature from theology's perspective, just *is* "developmental teleology" from the perspective of the sciences.[236]

As a final example, Yong says "the evolutionary or developmental aspect of Peirce's theory of natural laws (developmental teleology) allows for the proleptic interruption of the coming kingdom (novelty and surprise) in the here and now, even while we await the teleological transformation of creation as a whole into the eschatological rule of God."[237] Here, we are back to what appears to be a *distinction*

---

233. Hence, if a pentecostal wants to become a scientist and square that with her or his faith, I would strongly advise following Smith's *methodological* naturalism/materialism over against Yong's nonreductive naturalism/materialism. More on this later.

234. Yong, *The Spirit of Creation*, p. 90.

235. Yong, *The Spirit of Creation*, p. 91.

236. For another example, see: Yong, *The Spirit of Creation*, p. 96.

237. Yong, *The Spirit of Creation*, p. 130.

not only of discourse but of the reality about which each discourse is bespeaking. Thus, I am led back to my original question that began this inquiry in the previous paragraph: does Yong's Peircean "final causality," "developmental teleology," or "proleptic anticipations" point to the same *reality* (or *realities*) that eschatology does—within the context of the science and theology dialogue—with the difference mostly being a matter of hermeneutics according to the methods of the respective disciplines? If indeed there is a difference between eschatology and teleology in Yong's vision, is it one of only slight variance? Or is the difference absolute? If the difference is absolute, how can we meaningfully say that these distinct hermeneutical disciplines discerning absolutely distinct realities are mutually informative? Whatever the unambiguously clear answers to these questions might be, it is mostly clear that Yong's project looks for space in the natural world for the emergence of surprise or novelty. The different ways of naming that novelty, its "causes," and evolution—teleology, final causes, ontological gaps, space for SDA, etc.—are fitted to the project of enchanting *nature* as modernly conceived. Nature and its laws are paradigmatic and therefore must be "open" for God's action if our God is and acts. As such, his activity to some extent must be—or at least be undergirded by theories that make it possible—empirically verifiable, and theology can provide its hermeneutic utilizing its own resources on what is verified. For Yong, novelty thus conceived also means that that which is emergent is irreducible to its parts. Perhaps, then, we have arrived at Clayton's theory of emergence which—when undergirded by Peircean metaphysics and Yong's pneumatology—we may say undergirds Yong's enchanted theology of creation. We are finally on the matter at hand.

*The End(s) of Emergence Theory*

In a previous chapter where I engaged Yong more thoroughly, I noted that he relies heavily on an appropriated version of Philip Clayton's philosophy of emergence which he connects to Nancey Murphey's supervenience.[238] Unfortunately, I cannot follow Yong here for several reasons which follow from this main one: neither nature, natural processes, nor the laws thereof serve as my paradigm for reality.[239]

---

238. Yong's vision and use of the emergence theory is now shared by some of his students as the beneficial means of positing a metaphysical and ontological vision of spiritual realities. David Bradnick, *Evil, Spirits, and Possession*; David Bradnick and Bradford McCall, "Making Sense of Emergence: A Critical Engagement with Leidenhag, Leidenhag, and Yong," *Zygon* 53.1 (2018), pp. 240–57.

239. Per contra, I have argued that according to the biblical witness, history and narrative have ontological primacy over and against the cosmos and the natural processes which constitute it. Moreover, I have argued that natural processes are an encounter with the freedom of the *personal* Spirit of Jesus. Thus, natural processes can be personally addressed through prayer; neither is prayer an invitation for the Spirit to invade a process he is otherwise uninvolved in.

My work does not reason toward its conclusions by way of methodological induction (*via* modern scientific methods) to which I must point to (or add) directing and evolving "causes" to find space in nature for eschatological-teleological special divine action. Rather, the claims in my project are intentionally limited to be *deduced from* the claim that the God of Israel has raised his Son Jesus of Nazareth from the dead by the power of the Holy Spirit—as bespoken and enacted in a pre-rational, narratival, affective, and relational pentecostal spirituality.[240] To the point, when Yong looks to engage divine action in multidisciplinary perspective, he is forced to focus on "*naming* or *recognizing* events *as* divine action … since to affirm the possibility of divine action in general without being able to identify divine action in particular would be vacuous."[241] In other words, Yong has to define some activity in the world as divine action, and others as not. But who or what decides what constitutes (particular) divine action in the first place? I have argued that *all things* are created by, subsist in, and are consummated through Christ by the Spirit as willed from the Father. Ergo, I see creation through the logic of incarnation;[242] so that, "Although talk about God's 'incarnation' cannot avoid the deployment of the concepts 'divinity' and 'humanity,' because the incarnate one is *Jesus,* in practice all talk of 'divinity' and 'humanity,' must be reconstructed on the basis of his concrete form of existence."[243] When we do not look at creation

---

240. The differences here go much deeper than those between inductive and deductive reasoning. Indeed, that difference is merely symptomatic of the *cultural* difference between the two. Smith rightly argues that science is a cultural institution meant to study nature, which has its own network of practices, environments, instruments, methods, and has a history (Smith, "Room for Surprise"). Insofar as modern science is a *culture,* it is one that methodologically and latently incubates within itself tacit metaphysical presuppositions *and* its inchoate modern (mis)contruals of "causes" as we have noted. More issues with the culture of science are illumined by further questions: "what, for instance, constitutes reason; what the limits of knowledge are; what questions ought to be asked; which methods of inquiry should be presumed to reflect reality, and which should be regarded only as useful fictions. And it is here, at the level of culture, that the truly irreconcilable conflicts between scientific and theological thinking are inevitably found" (Hart, "Science and Theology," p. 14). I am noting this difference so heavily because I think Yong tends to be overly optimistic of just how mutually *informing* modern science—with its distinctive culture—and theology can be. Even the insistence that science account for final causes in the natural world would not solve the problem of the impossibility for even numerous quantitative steps to yield realities that are qualitatively distinct. Which is why a (guarded) *methodological* materialism via Smith seems to be the best approach for a pentecostal practicing science.

241. Yong, "How Does God Do What God Does?," p. 66 n. 17.

242. Specifically, through a Cyrillian Chalcedonian Christology which privileges the one *person* of Jesus as the locus of the hypostatic union so that the emphasis is not on parsing two natures, but on the union of one life.

243. Ian A. McFarland, *The Word Made Flesh: A Theology of the Incarnation* (Louisville: WJK Press, 2019), p. 216.

based on incarnation, we mistakenly presuppose some knowledge of divinity apart from Jesus to which he either measures up, thus affirming his divinity, or does not, thus affirming his humanity. Instead, I want to say that it is not natural anomalies or "novelties"—according to various disciplines—that determine what constitutes divine action over and against human or natural action. Rather, it is Jesus who reveals that whether he is sleeping on a boat or commanding the storm, *both* acts are found in one concrete life and are at once—ἀσυγχύτως, ἀτρέπτως, ἀδιαιρέτως, ἀχωρίστως—divine and human, or, divine and "natural."[244] Just so, through the metaphysics of participation and the logic of incarnation just described, nature is always (super)natural and is thus always open to divine action. The Spirit of Jesus is the spontaneity of natural process, we have said. Therefore, God does not create a static cosmos of natural laws in which he must intervene or act through "open spaces"; rather he creates a history of God with his people so that God goes forth in all beings and in all beings returns to himself. Nature and its laws do not reveal this to us, for nature is not what it is intended to be until it is consummated. Eschatology and creation, we have said, are one *decisive* act.

Second, I cannot privilege nature because decay and death are necessary for its persistence, and evil is ubiquitous. Following Chris Green's theses on his theology of evil, I want to say that because of what evil does to nature, it cannot be treated as a reliable witness or source for understanding all of reality, nor God's will for creatures because "Evil, however it was unleashed, has wounded all things at their heart."[245] For Green, "*nothing ... that creatures experience is exactly what it should be or would have been if not for 'the fall.'*"[246] He goes on to say that while believers are right to praise God for the marvels and gifts of rain and sunshine, these are also corrupted in that they can also

> bring the sorrow of floods and droughts as well as the joy of harvests. The same goes for all that is "natural." Perhaps it is best to say that everything that is, is from God; but nothing that is, is what it would have been if God had had his way perfectly. In a word, "nature" is not in harmony with its own nature.[247]

For that reason—combined with my privileging an eschatologically oriented narrative and history as more basic than the cosmos—I want to *sub*sume "nature" under the narrative of God's triune and eschatological act of redemption and let that

---

244. Chalcedonian adverbs: without confusion, without change, without division, without separation.

245. Green, "Breathing Underwater: Re-forming the Wesleyan Theology of Evil," *Wesley and Methodist Studies* 13.2 (2021), pp. 175–95.

246. Green, "Breathing Underwater."

247. Green, "Breathing Underwater"; Indeed, nature is a kind of thing that gives way to and is accomplished by violence and mass extinction; it is the process which advances *because* of warfare and disease in which thousands upon thousands are squandered for the sake of fashioning a single durable or more complex type.

inform my theology of creation, rather than letting nature as understood through the modern sciences do that work for me, Peircean teleology notwithstanding.

Third, and finally, I find the emergence theory adduced by Clayton and endorsed by Yong—*strong* emergence and *weak* supervenience—to be problematic in terms of coherence. It seems to me that the basis upon which said theory of emergence stands is what Yong—following Murphy and others—calls a "nonreductive materialism" which runs the risk of being self-refuting.[248] Either one is a materialist, or one is not. The difficulties of emergence—at least it seems to me—cannot be overcome simply by developing a novel grounding of "nonreductive materialism," which essentially begs the question.[249] The explanations of what a nonreductive materialist might be reveal it to be a category seemingly ready-made in anticipation of precisely a theory of emergence.

Clayton understands emergence theory as suitable for explaining how *all* reality (including consciousness, mental, and spiritual realities, save for God) is constituted and interrelated while submitting its reifiability to the empirical methods of modern science.[250] He must do so at the exclusion of formal and final causes precisely because the said culture he aims to be conversant with has done away them as required by their *methods*. The issue, however, is not the method itself; the method helpfully narrows the focus of scientific researchers via an imposed set of systematic constraints and limitations so that they can concentrate

---

248. Yong, *The Spirit of Creation*, p. 60. A nonreductive materialist is itself a contradiction in terms which can only be overcome through the assumption that several quantitative steps can overcome a qualitative difference—this is the definition of a pleonastic fallacy. Simply put, one cannot move from matter to spirit by a series of physical geometrical steps, even when resourced by Yong's theology which I will critique below. Smith has a preferable option of *methodological* naturalism which is "a pragmatic, working assumption in science that acts *as if* the universe were a closed, autonomous system ... so metaphysically speaking I might be a *super*-naturalist ... and yet as a scientist working in the lab I might approach the material universe *as if* it were merely natural" (Smith, "Room for Surprise," p. 41). This is a helpful way for a pentecostal to practice medicine or be a scientist. I would simply remind the pentecostal who is doing this, that practices and discourse about what those practices mean for reality are deeply formative and tacitly and often explicitly turn into a metaphysical vision. It is not mere happenstance that most enveloped by the culture of modern science are agnostic or atheist. It is essential then—as it is for everyone else in whatever line of work they might be in—to stay in practice with the church to remain in tune with her *counterinterpretations* of reality.

249. In the definition of nonreductive materialism itself, we find that it is primed for emergence theory in that "it makes room for more complex phenomena, that cannot be simply reduced to physical and chemical processes ... it claims that included in the ... natural universe ... are things that cannot adequately be explained by natural processes ... for instance ... 'mind' ... is a unique, distinct reality that *emerges from* physical and chemical processes but cannot be adequately explained by them" (Smith, "Room for Surprise," p. 41).

250. With the usual Peircean teleological caveats. Yong, *The Spirit of Creation*, pp. 144–5.

their investigations on clearly delineated objects, or at least different aspects of those objects. The issue comes when a helpful method metastasizes into a metaphysical vision of what *all* of reality actually is. A picture of reality devoid of formal and final causes, classically conceived, leaves profound explanatory gaps, and emergence theory does not seem to solve it. With modernity's exclusion of formal and final causes,[251] emergence attempts to fill the *lacuna* left by what these pre-modern higher causes logically provided, while simultaneously keeping with the precommitment to pure methodological induction. The only option available, then, is an attempt to posit consciousness, mental, and spiritual realities through strictly materialist means.[252] These spiritual and mental realities *must* be emergent from a more basic material reality, and thus a material monism[253] wedded to a mechanical philosophy is assumed. Accounting for non-physical—and *qualitatively* distinct—realities through strictly materialist means is a logical impossibility, thus committing a kind of "pleonastic fallacy."[254] For a materialist

---

251. Boersma, *Heavenly Participation*, pp. 68–83; Hart, *Experience of God*, pp. 64–76.

252. This is largely assumed by those who adhere to a metaphysics informed by the scientific method. Peirce is a unique contributor to this assumption. However, following Hart, I want to challenge this assumption and argue that "No empirical inventory ... will ever disclose for us either the content or the experiential quality of an idea, a desire, a volition, or any other mental event. This being so *we have no better warrant for saying that the brain produces the mind than that the mind makes use of the brain*" (Hart, *Experience of God*, p. 159 emphases mine).

253. This is a *material* monism which sees all created beings as emerging from a single *materia prima* so that even "mental" and "spiritual" beings emerge from such. Adrian Pabst connects this kind of monism to the modern project of "transcendental ontology" whereby essentiality and substance are transcendentalized and given primacy over existence. This tradition largely follows from Duns Scotus and William of Ockham who "attempt to tie together individual, empirical reality with universal, conceptual intelligibility" (he traces this rather closely in Pabst, *Metaphysics*, pp. 383–444). I on the other hand have argued for a metaphysics of participation, which understands all being—visible and invisible—as unified and participating in one creative act of existence. Therefore, over against what mechanical philosophy allied to monism says, undergirded by a participatory ontology I want to say: matter is more than merely mass and force, and material actions are more than exchanges of energy accomplished by undetermined movement. A metaphysics of participation also pushes against a Cartesian dualism which posits mind and body as two ontologically distinct yet somehow conjoined kinds of substance.

254. Clayton adopts a vision of "irreducible emergence," wherein the logical incoherence most explicitly presents itself. Yong says of Clayton that he "favors *weak supervenience* together with *strong emergence*, arguing that mind and higher-level properties are in principle irreducible to brain and lower-level parts because the former concern *qualitatively* and *ontologically* distinct realities" (Yong, *The Spirit of Creation*, p. 148 [emphases original]). This is the precise definition of the "'pleonastic fallacy': that is, the belief that an absolute qualitative difference can be overcome by a successive accumulation of extremely small and

committed to empirical reifiability, the notion that properties can emerge with no continuity with at least the calculable properties of its ingredients does not explain mental and spiritual beings. Neither is it sufficient to assert that random quantitative properties—however great and complex—can somehow cause higher qualitative ones to appear via "emergence," or Peircean "developmental teleology."

Because I am not eager to follow Clayton and Murphy via Yong, we are therefore "obliged to assume that the formal determinations of organic complexity ... are already present in (primitive) causes in at least latent or virtual form ... and so we are obliged to assume that whatever rational relations (read: causes) may exist in organisms (form and finality) are already present in those seemingly random states."[255] Put differently, "everything that enters into the structure of a living system is already constituted by those rational causal relations that cause discrete purposive systems to arise"[256]—but, of course, one cannot come to this conclusion through sheer induction. As necessary as that method is for important scientific discovery and advancement, we need to be clear about its limits and thus not grant it (or its understanding of nature) hegemony for providing a picture for *all* of reality. Recognizing these limits, we may say that "higher" causal relations are *not* merely accidental accretions; instead, they are intentional participations in God who is Father, Son, and Spirit. Emergence and supervenience, then, are not necessary for the pentecostal imagination and thus I exclude them from my metaphysics in general, and my enchanted theology of creation in particular—Yong's theological assistance notwithstanding.[257]

---

entirely relative quantitative steps" (Hart, *Experience of God*, p. 98). Indeed, a version of this fallacy seems to lie at the core of Clayton's argument. What is his theory of the emergence of mind from brain if not essentially a version of the pleonastic argument that "a sufficient number of neurological systems and subsystems operating in connection with one another will at some point naturally produce unified, self-reflective, and intentional consciousness?" (Hart, *Experience of God*, p. 156).

255. Hart, "Science and Theology," pp. 21–2.

256. Hart, "Science and Theology," p. 22.

257. Yong concedes that he does not possess the expertise to dispute Clayton's interpretation of the scientific data, and proceeds to offer biblical support for the sake of contributing to "a more robust theological vision both in terms of correlating aspects of emergence theory with the biblical witness and in terms of the mutual illumination that I believe can occur between a metaphysic of emergence and a pneumatological theology" (Yong, "*Ruach*, the Primordial Waters," p. 190). Yong's "canonical-pneumatological" reading of Genesis 1 and 2 does little to quell the issues I laid out with Clayton's "irreducible" emergence and supervenience theory. Indeed, Yong's aim is to theologically resource said emergentist metaphysics by offering a kind of novel reading of the Genesis creation narratives; and while I credit him for his innovation and creativity, it is still a house built on the sinking sand of emergence and supervenience. So committed is Yong to fitting the Genesis narratives to emergence that he radically modifies the classic doctrine of *creatio ex nihilo* to posit said narratives as a kind of archetype for it. For example:

Through the sketch above, we have discovered that foundational pneumatology, Peircean and emergentist metaphysics, etc. are the theories that undergird Yong's ten theses for a pluralistic cosmos. Contrastingly, the underlying convictions which ground my brief reading of Yong's theses will follow from two basic affirmations, the first of which is a restatement of what I have already argued early on in the constructive section of this work. The second of these affirmations denotes the implications for that which, or those whom, ontologically resist the truth of the first. The first underlying affirmation is simply that God *is*, thus creatures—visible and invisible—dependently are. The second is that *nevertheless*, there is evil. This will not be a thorough examination of Yong's ten theses. I will simply offer affirmations, denials, and brief reasons for them considering what I have already laid out in detail above. Moreover, some more thorough engagement awaits in my final section on liturgical renewal that will follow.

*God Beyond Being: Revising Yong's Theses for a Pluralistic Cosmos*

*Thesis 1: The Triune God is the only necessary, transcendent, and purely spiritual reality.*

The main points of my contention here have to do with trying to discern what Yong might mean by a *purely* spiritual reality. Yong rightly points to Jn 4:24 which states that "God is spirit"; however, that does little to support the notion that God is a "*purely* spiritual reality." For one thing, I find it problematic to refer to

> I propose that the link between *tohu wabohu* and *mayim* is suggestive of both the chaos of disorder and randomness (the vacuum) and the primordial plentitude (or plenum), arguably combining to anticipate the chaos of modern science with its unpredictable and nonlinear movement from simple perturbation of potentialities and possibilities to complex outcomes. The *ruach Elohim* is shown to be transcendent to, but also implicated in the stirring of primeval chaos. We therefore see the creation emerging from out of the primeval chaos through processes of division, distinction, differentiation, and particularization, beginning with the separation of light from darkness and continuing with the separating out of species of plants and types of animals, each in its own kind.
>
> (Yong, "Ruach, the Primordial Waters," pp. 194–5)

Yong also contends that "focusing on the work of the Spirit provides us with an eschatological framework for understanding divine action and hence invites a teleological orientation that is guided by a general vision of the kingdom as revealed in the life of Christ" (Yong, *Spirit of Creation*, p. 133). For Yong, divine action in the material world is both eschatological and empirically observable, which is precisely what I have argued above that eschatological realities cannot be. Considering what I have posited regarding *creatio ex nihilo* and eschatology, unfortunately, I cannot follow Yong here, in terms of both methodology and outcome.

God as a "reality" at all because as I have shown above, the classical Christian tradition this work follows argues that God is "beyond being" in that he is neither an agent among agents in the universe, nor is he "being" construed as the totality of finite particulars. Furthermore, I also think it is a mistake to posit God as "purely spiritual" as that raises the question of what Yong could mean by this considering the doctrine of the incarnation and its insistence that "the word became flesh." What, then, is the source and rationale for Yong's language of using "*purely*" as a qualifier? I affirm Yong's language of "necessary" in that all that is, is wholly dependent upon God for its existence as *creatio ex nihilo* and the classical metaphysics of participation insists. Finally, I affirm Yong's language of transcendence with a caveat that for clarity's sake, I must make explicit that I follow the classical Christian tradition when I say that God is transcendent in immanence and immanent in transcendence which follows from the logic of incarnation.

Finally, I will simply restate what I have argued in the previous two chapters on creation. Reality is primarily a history and not merely a cosmos. It is indeed a narratable history in which we participate, and is initiated, sustained, and fulfilled by the God who is Father, Son, and Holy Spirit. The character of its fulfillment, and thus its very nature, is determined by the moral intention of God. God is the *one* source of being so that it is his, and only his, will, intention, and love—that is, triune relations—that grounds the world and the beings in it.

*Thesis 2: The creation narrative reveals that the triune God creates all things as good and brings about order and complexity by Spirit and Word*

That the triune God creates all things as good, I affirm. However, I cannot affirm what Yong might mean when he says that God brings about order and complexity by Spirit and Word, because he works from a modified vision of *creatio ex nihilo* (noted above) which I do not hold. Instead, I want to say that God creates all things *ex nihilo*, and the fourfold rational causal relations are part of that same act. We have said that God does not first create static (nor chaotic) substances upon which he subsequently acts to bring about action and order. Neither is creation a past event; rather, things subsist in, through, and toward God's intended End, and that act is precisely what it means for God to create *ex nihilo*.

*Thesis 3: God is the primordial source of the transcendentals, for example, the good, the beautiful, and the true, but the dialectically oppositional aspects of the axiological, alethic, aesthetic, moral, and spiritual dimensions of the world only fully emerge in the cosmos with the appearance of Homo sapiens, supervening upon their relationships.*

*Thesis 4: The emergence of spirit in humanity intensified further the spiritual dimension already latent in the very fabric of our interrelational cosmos.*

## 5. Toward a Pentecostal Theology of Being-in-the-Spirit

These theses (three and four) and their explicit dependence upon the metaphysics of emergence and supervenience, I deny. I have argued in greater detail above that the explanatory gaps of qualitatively distinct substances cannot be overcome by several inductive quantitative steps, however great or complex.

*Thesis 5: Angelic spirits, then, are emergent benevolent realities that minister the salvific grace of God to human lives.*

Yong's angelology is indeed also dependent upon his metaphysics of emergence, which I have already mentioned that, unfortunately, I do not affirm. Moreover, Yong's theology of divine action at its heart seems to be about locating and naming the realities that touch the material world that are beyond reductionistic explanation. Under classical theological categories, Yong's work on divine action is better fitted to angelology than it is to theology proper, precisely because Yong is intent on naming particular anomalous events or actions as divine. In my final section on liturgical renewal, when discussing our worship as taking place with the angels and archangels, the reader will note how the classical vision of angels aligns with what Yong calls divine action.

For now, considering that this work addresses pentecostal spirituality by way of the dogmatic tradition, on this point, we will be following John of Damascus as he is the first of the Scholastics that essentially summarizes what the fathers have said about angels. I thus briefly engage him as a way of sketching the angelology of classical Christian metaphysics. The Damascene is also helpfully succinct thus honoring the elusive and apocalyptic difficulties of describing their forms precisely, yet adequately accounting for their reality in Scripture, in worship, and in our lives. The Damascene, in book two, chapter three of his *Expositio Fidei*, gives a helpful and brief exposition on angels which is generally representative of what the Christian tradition has taught about them. They are *creatures* of God who are "intelligent beings" whose nature is gifted to be immortal in the sense that they have no "natural" end, and yet angels remain utterly dependent on God for their being so as to remain wholly contingent creatures. Formally, they are bodiless and immaterial—that is, devoid of material cause—but not properly so, as that designation belongs solely to God. Rather, their "immateriality" is such only relatively to that of the visible world which we inhabit. Nor does their immateriality necessitate omnipresence as they do indeed move or "travel" from place to place. Moreover, when they appear to witness to—or indeed, to *be* and manifest—the word of the Lord on earth, we can and do see them but not as they are; rather, we see them only in forms appropriate to our conditions as the kind of beholders we are, says John of Damascus. Hence Scripture contains apocalyptic and elusive language to describe their appearances. In brief summation, angels are heavenly, spiritual, and immaterial creatures of God who manifest on earth—in such a way as to be visible and graspable under our conditions—as God's word of eschatological inbreaking and opportunity.

*Thesis 6: Demonic spirits, then, are divergent (as opposed to emergent) malevolent realities that oppose the salvific grace of God in human lives.*

While I affirm that demons and satan do not possess "being" nor positive perfections, I do so without the conceptual framework of emergence. Instead, I want to say the fact that there is evil of any sort is nothing less than an affront to the being of God and his relation to creation. All things are wholly and ontologically dependent for their existence on the triune God from whom all things subsist, and toward whom all things find their fulfillment. However, the presence of evil looms and Christian revelation and tradition teach that somewhere out there, or "down there," and around us is a subject-presence who hates all things; so that, to encounter him or succumb to his schemes comes at a detrimental cost to the identity of that which has been deceived. This universal hatred and detrimental subjectivity—contra Yong and others committed to the theory of emergence—is *antecedent* to our hating detrimental actions. Following Green, I want to say that we sin, we err, and make poor choices (willfully or otherwise: by thought, word, and deed) that work against our own personhood and that of our neighbors precisely because we have been first sinned against.[258] Even in the Garden, prior to anyone having done anything, evil asserts itself. According to the Genesis account, evil *did* exist in the Garden before the fall—Adam and Eve simply lacked knowledge of it. Therefore, "the-way-of-things is *not* right, has never been right so far as can be known … God made a good creation, to be sure, but because evil arose from the beginning and wounded the wisdom that is at the heart of all things, creatures always, everywhere have experienced the creation as fallen."[259] Evil's cavernous and detrimental "presence" has always "appeared" or "manifested" in its destruction of positive perfections. One need look no further than the violation of personhood of the man at the Gerasenes, and the subsequent restoration of his humanity and soundness of mind upon being freed from "Legion"; moreover, the immediate effect of the unclean spirits "entering" the swine was their beeline toward their own destruction.[260] Biblically, we can say that "Despite their ubiquitous harassments, there is no explicit reference to demons, or to their chief ever manifesting as specters or as corporeal beings."[261] Just so, evil has been traditionally conceived as the *privatio boni*, a no-thing devoid of any positive perfection or goodness of its

---

258. Contra Yong, who says "Sin enters the world through the destructive choices and behaviors of self-conscious human beings who refuse to worship God, who live in enmity with others, and who become estranged from the created environment" (Yong, *The Spirit of Creation*, p. 211).

259. Green, "Breathing Underwater."

260. Mk 5:1-7; Lk. 8:26-37.

261. Guthrie, *Gods of This World*, p. 17; Guthrie further demonstrates that in Scripture "There is a disproportionate set of manifestation stories in that angels manifest frequently to observers, but demons never do" (pp. 174–6).

own, and so its being can only be talked about and witnessed in abstraction from what is good. I intend to follow this tradition.

Who or what is this subject-presence or presences, and what sort of personhood has he, or have they? The Old Testament witness is quite scarce on the matter. We meet *ha satan*, or the satan (the accuser) in the mythical account of Job wherein he is the accuser who brings offenders to trial as a prosecutor in God's heavenly court. We see his accusatory existence again in Zechariah 3. In addition to being an accuser, he is also a deceiver. According to the account in Chronicles, he incited David to take a census which resulted in Israel's judgment. So then, David was deceived which resulted in judgment, much like the snake's deception in Genesis 3 resulted in the same (albeit at greater cost). Finally, we catch some allusions to this figure in the sea monsters of Daniel's apocalyptic vision. The sort of personification this deceptive force of evil, or the satan, has in the Old Testament "is important but not that important." What we can say from the Old Testament witness is that "the origin of evil itself remains a mystery; and the satan when he (or it) appears is kept strictly within bounds."[262]

N. T. Wright helpfully summarizes the "personal" nature of the satan and his demonic spirits in the New Testament. Specifically, in the Gospels, they "tell the story of the deeper, darker forces which operate at a *suprapersonal* level, forces for which the language of the demonic, despite all its problems, is still the least inadequate."[263] These "demonic forces" operate not only against persons, but against institutional (political and religious) powers. Wright, sees an appropriate way of identifying "the satan"—which he understands as naming an office as opposed to a proper personal being—in the New Testament as "the *quasi*-personal 'accuser' which is doing its best to drag Jesus down into the trap into which Israel, like the rest of the world, has already fallen."[264] He goes on to explain his preference for the terms "subpersonal" and "quasi-personal" "as a way of refusing to accord the satan the full dignity of personhood while recognizing that the concentration of activity (its subtle schemes and devices) can and does strike us as very much like that which we associate with personhood."[265] The aim of this nondivine and nonhuman subpersonal force is the death and destruction of all things. And so, he tempts, deceives, and "enters" into things which are, precisely to orient them toward destruction in his efforts to thwart God's intention of new creation which re-orients all creatures toward the Father, in Jesus, by the power of the Holy Spirit.

What makes this "power of death" and his personhood so difficult to grasp is precisely that he refuses to be an object-presence in and for the world. God is God because he is triune and is therefore truly self-sufficient in that he can find his "I" in himself, by himself. The Father is freed by the Spirit to find himself

---

262. N. T. Wright, *Evil and the Justice of God* (Downers Grove: InterVarsity Press, 2006), pp. 71-2.
263. Wright, *Evil*, p. 81.
264. Wright, *Evil*, p. 75.
265. Wright, *Evil*, pp. 111-12.

in the Son. Creatures, however, are not triune, and so are *not* self-sufficient to intend ourselves, by ourselves. I only know my "self" in a community of existents whom I act upon as subject, and who act upon me as object. I intend, engage, and dialogue with others and they do the same to me; just so, I know myself as existent. While God is self-sufficient and could have either not created at all or could have done so and remained ungraspable as a sheer subjectivity to creation—he is benevolently self-diffusive and so not only creates but gives of himself to be intended by his creatures in Christ Jesus. As such, God is *fully* self-sufficient, personal, and embodied.

Perhaps then, a way into explaining, albeit not exhaustively, what the devil might ontologically and personally be is by trying to answer the question of what ails him. The devil wants to be like God: self-sufficient and therefore *able* to be *only* an evasive yet determinative subject-presence in the world. However, he is not triune and so cannot find himself, by himself, but needs others to do so. He thus has no object in which to see or find himself, and just so has no self. "A subjectivity that refused all embodiment would be a pure and utterly compulsive hatred, and nothing else at all. The devil ... is unwilling to inhabit anything; this unwillingness is his being."[266] Once again, the aim of such a subpersonal existence can only be to make those who do exist be like him, which is precisely why his aim and ultimate power is death. A life after death, without bodily resurrection would be an ontological being like the satan; making one an ungraspable, un-intendable subject-presence. Of course, Jesus' overcoming of death through a bodily resurrection in which all creation will participate, denies satan the ultimate realization of his aims. Penultimately, however, we experience the world as subjected to death and decay, and so we experience the nonbeing of satan and his spirits.

In summation, the origins of evil remain a mystery as it asserts itself from the beginning so that creation has always been aimed at, and in need of, salvation. Satan and his spirits, as pure evil, are as real as evil is, but are equally mysterious in their origins. Whether or not one wants to hold that these spirits are "fallen angels" is not a matter of dogma. There is not a decisively scriptural or traditional teaching that asserts that this *must* be the case.[267] It is rather a teaching that stems from rightly wanting to assert creatures as good. If these spirits are creatures, then they were once good and became bad. If that is the case, what else—according to this theologoumenon—could they have been but fallen angels? In our attempts to make some sense of this difficulty, or fill in these gaps of explanation, what we cannot say is that these subpersonal, quasi-personal "beings" are the antithesis to God in an equal and opposite way. Neither are they ontological existents in the way anything in our reality recognizably *is*. Evil, the satan, and his spirits are pure privation. He,

---

266. Jenson, *ST.2*, p. 132.

267. However, see Guthrie, *Gods of this World*, pp. 17–21, in which he argues that "there is good indication in Scripture that the demons were once good angels who sinned and thus abandoned their original position of authority. By doing so, God condemned them to exile" (p. 20; he provides exegetical treatment of relevant texts here and in n. 26).

or they, tempt, scheme, and enter into true creatures precisely for the sake of their death and destruction with his ultimate aim to make all that is, like him.

> *Thesis 7: The good news is that the triune God continues to work to redeem the world incarnationally (Word) and pentecostally (Spirit) and in this dispensation, such is being accomplished through the church.*

To this thesis, I offer my affirmation and a caveat. We have said that the church is not merely an instrument of the God's redemption but *is* the penultimate (and so imperfect) expression of God's redemption in the world. Insofar as this thesis might bring us to understand the church as one instrument among others, I would apply said caveat and otherwise affirm this thesis.

> *Thesis 8: Negatively put, the redemptive work of the church involves participating in the life and ministry of Christ by the power of his Spirit and naming, resisting, and where appropriate, exorcising the demonic and delivering the oppressed from its destructive powers.*

To this thesis, I simply give my full affirmation.

> *Thesis 9: The eschatological redemption of the triune God will involve concrete and material bodies.*

As already alluded to in my reflection on Thesis 6 and will expand upon here: bodiless "resurrection" is not good news for the Christian. Indeed, a bodiless subjective presence is precisely the kind of non-life the satan has, and indeed is the kind of non-life he aims for all creation to have through death. Christ's overcoming of death and the resurrection of his *body* in whom all creation lives, moves, and has its being, is the overcoming of death so as to leave it behind altogether. We have been so joined to this life that what the Father means for the Son, he means for all creation. From the outset of this work, and all throughout, we have insisted that this is a *Christian* metaphysical vision which necessarily presupposes that the Father has raised his Son Jesus from the dead by the power of the Holy Spirit. It is through the lens of that truth that reality is read and understood for the eschatologically oriented Christian. As such, the proclamation of Genesis that creation is good is not a claim of our present experience, but a proclamation of faith that it is good because of the resurrection God intends for it. From the beginning, the material world has needed saving, and Christ's resurrection is the triune God's guarantee that it will be saved; just so, and *only* so, creation—and its constituent materiality, bodies, and beings, visible and invisible—is good.

> *Thesis 10: On the other "side," the recalcitrant, reprobate, and irredeemable powers will finally experience (self) destruction, also understood as the other side of the incomprehensible judgment of God.*

Here, I will simply note that Yong wisely used scare quotes around the word "side" which is helpful so long as he does not posit destruction or judgment as a "place" apart from, and equal and opposite to, the full eschatological participation of creation in the triune life.

*Conclusion*

In summation, this section began as a critique of the philosophical and theological grounding of what academic pentecostal theology—namely, Yong—has said regarding the metaphysics that makes sense of a creation open to spirit. Yong follows a modern approach in allegiance to modern scientific empirical reifiability—undergirded by emergence and supervenience—and aims to resource them theologically. I went against this approach arguing that a metaphysics of participation is more philosophically coherent, theologically sound, biblical, and it does not deny the scientific method as a focused *method* made for specific ends but rejects its hegemonic metastasization into a picture of reality itself. "Science" needs to be *situated*, not overcome, or succumbed to. Once freed from Peircean Thirdness, and subsequently, emergence and supervenience, I briefly traced Yong's theses for a pluralistic cosmos and raised some brief questions and critiques via conversation with the creedal and dogmatic Christian metaphysical tradition. I engaged these theses biblically and aimed to be consistent with the metaphysics and ontology that I have already constructed. Therefore, God is the only necessary act of existence and what he creates is good; angels—as we will see more thoroughly in the following section on liturgical renewal—are formal apocalyptic "beings" that "appear" on earth *as* the word of the Lord and manifest eschatological realities; demonic realities are subpersonal *privatio boni* which deceive good creatures, aiming to harm and destroy the goodness of creation; and the church resists such privations aiming to bring goodness to bear in participation with God's purposes. For the Christian, then, the world is indeed enchanted.

## *"This Is My Body"*: How Matter Matters

*Introduction*

To begin this section, I will remind the reader that the overall aim of this monograph is to offer a constructive and critical engagement with pentecostal spirituality and academic pentecostal theology via conversation with the larger historic, dogmatic Christian metaphysical tradition; this effort works toward constructing a pentecostal metaphysics that does justice to what is best in the first-level pentecostal experience while also confronting that which is problematic. In this specific section, there will be explications of the pentecostal experience of divine healing as a first-level practice that affirms the goodness of the material world. This material affirmation theologically coheres with the first and second-level discourses of the historic Christian tradition which confesses the Nicene Creed and thereupon explicates God's nearness to the material world through its Christological formulations. I will put pentecostal practice in conversation with the Christian tradition to display the affirmation of the material world—beginning with a brief sketch of the Christological formulations in the Christian tradition followed by a brief theology of the pentecostal practice of healing.

The conversation between pentecostal practice and the larger Christian tradition will be undergirded by the participatory ontology already constructed in the previous sections. It is a participatory ontology that—unlike Smith when he offers his Reformed caveat—does not hold that the material order needs to be "autonomous" for it to retain its integrity. Creation's utter ontological dependence on God for its existence—per Thomas's existence-essence distinction—is precisely what dignifies it, so that its integrity is divine gift. Indeed,

> physical reality cannot account for its own existence for the simple reason that nature … is that which by definition already exists; existence … lies logically beyond the system of causes that nature comprises … This means not only that at some point nature requires or admits of a supernatural explanation, but also that at no point is anything purely, self-sufficiently natural in the first place.[268]

Therefore, one need not unhinge the material world from its transcendent source in order to affirm its goodness, as its goodness is participatory. Neither does this affirmation flirt with occasionalism (per Smith's concerns), as the ontological underpinning of this work insists that God does not constantly "reach into" material reality in order to "tinker" with it, precisely because God is not a univocal being among beings.

The full gospel, we have said, values created reality as good. The life of Jesus proceeding from the Father by the power of the Holy Spirit displays God's actively personal, intricate, communicative, creative, and enveloping involvement with the created order, which includes physical, mental, and spiritual beings. My eschatological orientation and radical openness sections posited a participatory and narratable ontology which would make a dualistic understanding of the God-world relation impossible. Therefore, this section will be relatively very brief as it will mostly involve the explication of the tacit nondualistic implications of the ontology already proposed.

---

268. Hart, *The Experience of God*, p. 96.

### Likeness in Unlikeness: Christological Paradoxes and the (Im)Possibility of Naming Reality

The incarnation of Jesus is the locus wherein at once, "God enacts the difference between himself and creation ... which realizes for us what God determines himself to be. Taking up creatureliness as his own, assuming humanity to himself, God ensures once and for all that there is a difference between himself and creation—and that difference is perfectly good for us."[269] Precisely through that enforcement of difference, however, we see that "In Jesus, the divine and the human, the Creatorly and the creaturely, are at-one-ed."[270] This at-one-ment is crucial for understanding the creator-creature distinction, and through the confession of the Nicene Creed as done in traditional church settings, that simultaneous enforcement and overcoming of difference is bespoken and enacted.

We now turn our attention to the theological tradition which grappled for centuries with said paradoxes and implications.[271] The content of this tension is that Jesus is revealed *both* as creator *and "within"* creation so that his identity is somehow simultaneously characterized by divine freedom and prayerful dependence. Through the first three centuries of Christological discourse, it became abundantly clear that the unconditional and divine initiative in Jesus could not be compromised lest he conceived as anything less than God; neither could the contingent character of his humanity be violated lest it compromises his assumption for those whose experience he shares. The tradition's first step to resolving the paradox can be found in the discourse resulting in the Nicene doctrine of the *homoousion* which essentially affirms that "When we use the word 'God' for the *source* of all things and for the *eternal response* to that outpouring as it is finally embodied in Jesus, we

---

269. Green, *The End Is Music*, p. 56.
270. Green, *The End Is Music*, p. 56.
271. Origen and Athanasius have earlier been evoked on a similar point as representatives of the tradition and will briefly be recalled again. I must note here that Maximus the Confessor has also done extensive work on the logic of the Incarnation, attending rigorously to the hypostatic union. Maximus follows what is called "Neochalcedonian," or Cyrillian christology (which I utilized in the previous chapter) as a way into engaging the paradox of the two natures of Christ and the relation between God and creatures. Maximus says "The Word of God, very God, wills that the mystery of his Incarnation be actualized always and in all things" (*Amb* 7:22). My work is in alignment with his vision. For an entire thesis dedicated to unpacking this very quote in conversation with the rest of Maximus' corpus, see Jordan Daniel Wood, *That Creation Is Incarnation in Maximus Confessor* (PhD thesis, Boston University, 2018). See also chapter 6 of Hans Urs von Balthasar, *Cosmic Liturgy: The Universe According to Maximus the Confessor* (San Francisco: Ignatius Press, 2003). Finally, as both a Protestant and a Neochalcedonian himself, Robert Jenson has been a powerful contemporary interlocutor of how to work through this paradox by focusing on the one person of Jesus as the metaphysical principle of reality (see *ST* I, ch. 8). The theological metaphysics proposed is one read through the lens of the Neochalcedonian tradition.

mean exactly the same kind of life."[272] This doctrine further allows us to imagine an "analogue of 'createdness' within the divine life—that is, a form of living the divine life in a mode of reception and response, which is no less truly divine (possessed of unconditional freedom) than its source."[273] As such this tension embodied in Jesus overcomes the perceived chasm between God and finite agents.

Let us push this dogmatic point a bit further. Previously, when tracing God's relationship to creation along the lineaments of the triune God, we have argued—following Origen and Athanasius—that the Father's relationship to creation is that of Source, and he acts thus antecedently in his own life. That is, the Father, freed by the Spirit, eternally *generates* the Son, and that act precedes the act of creation. Eternal generation, its relationship to the *homoousion*, and connected to the life of Jesus provide further revelation of the relation of God to creation. That is, just as these paradoxical distinctions (of perfect unity and otherness) cannot be spoken of as different items alongside one another, partnered together, nor added to each other—and neither will the notion of a non-distinct identity do—so it is with God's relationship to creation. If the Father's relation to the Son by the Spirit grounds God's relation to creation, then there is an unthinkably intimate, non-dual existence of one in the other.[274] In the incarnate life of Jesus, then, we may say that

> God is literally and personally acting within the world but does so only in the sense that this particular finite agent acts in such unbroken alignment with the Word's way of being God ... that the effect of this action is completely continuous with the effect of divine action in Israel's history and ultimately with the divine liberty in the act of creation itself.[275]

---

272. Williams, *Christ the Heart of Creation*, p. 220 (emphases mine).

273. Williams, *Christ the Heart of Creation*, p. 220. Christ reveals that reception does not imply an ontological deficit. Norris Clarke puts it this way, "If self-communication is a fundamental aspect of real being, so too must be *receptivity*, the complementary pole of self-communication." Therefore, "Receptivity as such should be looked on not as essentially a sign of imperfection, of poverty, of potentiality in the receiver, as we have tended to look on it, but as in itself a positive aspect or *perfection* of being." He goes on to say that "Without it love, authentic mutual love, would necessarily remain incomplete—and love is of itself a purely positive perfection." See W. Norris Clarke, *Person and Being* (Milwaukee: Marquette University Press, 2004), p. 20.

274. If this is true, then Smith's concerns that the goodness of creation requires its autonomy and his anxieties regarding occasionalism are mistaken. When talking about occasionalism he explicitly uses the language of God's constant tinkering or need to "reach into creation for it to *be* creation" (Smith, *IRO*, p. 204), thus implying a univocity whereby God and creatures are understood as two separate agents set alongside each other.

275. Williams, *Christ the Heart of Creation*, p. 221.

The Spirit joins creation to participate in that life, and the church—who is an eschatological step ahead of creation—does so "more intensely."

Given what has been revealed in Christ about the creator creature distinction: a nondualistic affirmation that affirms the goodness of creation *and* its participatory dependence on God for its existence should follow. I must hasten to add here, that there are historically pentecostal-privileging practices that are of significance when it comes affirming the goodness of creation precisely by relating those embodied practices as participating in transcendence by the Holy Spirit. Namely, the practice of divine healing and the practices that surround it.

*The Means of Grace and the Hope of Glory: Nondualistic Participatory Ontology and Pentecostal Models of Healing*

On account of the first-level practices which are emphasized by pentecostals, our nondualistic affirmation is especially displayed in the pentecostal practice of divine healing, and the theology thereof. Kimberly Alexander's monograph argues that divine healing as practiced by pentecostals is a definitive pushback on the notion that pentecostals are non-sacramental.[276] In fact, as we have argued, the pentecostal experience of Spirit baptism is a realization of the sacramental reality established by the outpouring of the Holy Spirit. When reality is understood sacramentally, "divine healing occupies a participatory character in both worlds, nature and the divine."[277] Therefore, "divine healing is possible because nature is inhabited by the Spirit,"[278] as such, the embodied set of pentecostal practices that accompany divine healing are "efficacious as actions of the Spirit of God."[279]

Included in the central practice and belief of divine healing are material bodies directly acting upon each other, both with and without objects. These acts include (1) the vocalization of faith,[280] (2) the laying on of hands,[281] (3) the anointing with

---

276. It's important to note here that the theology backing the practice is not monolithic. Alexander surveys the distinct and somewhat juxtaposed theological underpinnings of divine healing as expressed by Wesleyan pentecostalism and Finished Work pentecostalism. See Kimberly Ervin Alexander, *Pentecostal Healing: Models in Theology and Practice*, JPTS 2 (Sheffield: Deo, 2006), pp. 195–214. I will be working from the Wesleyan perspective because it is indeed the more sacramental, embodied, and eschatologically oriented with respect to living faithfully in the now-not-yet tension of the two. Finished Work, on the other hand, emphasizes an "attitude of faith" which makes the embodied and material practices unnecessary at best, and superfluous at worst.

277. Vondey, *Pentecostal Theology*, p. 126.

278. Vondey, *Pentecostal Theology*, p. 126.

279. Vondey, *Pentecostal Theology*, p. 126.

280. Prayer is the primary example of this. See Vondey, *Pentecostal Theology*, pp. 109–11.

281. See Kimberly Alexander, "'And the Signs Are Following': Mk. 16:9-20—A Journey into Pentecostal Hermeneutics," co-authored with John Christopher Thomas. *JPT* 11.2 (April 2003), pp. 147–70; Pavel Hejzlar, *Two Paradigms for Divine Healing: Fred F. Bosworth,*

oil,[282] and (4) the use of handkerchiefs and cloths.[283] These acts do not exist as separate rituals adhered to monolithically but are rather interdependent and varied. Moreover, they take place most often through a public community of faith wherein the interactive play between the visible and invisible takes place. These practices correspondingly communicate the nondualistic truths that (1) corporeal mouths speak to or against incorporeal realities to effect or inaugurate the healing of a body; (2) subjects lay hands on the sick *as* physical manifestations of our ascended Christ; (3) visible, tangible, and often scented oil topically covers an infirm body as a multisensory experience demonstrating the Spirit's acting upon said body; and finally, (4) mediating substances (cloths and handkerchiefs) that are prayed for and anointed by a believing community "convey the healing power of the Spirit, but also point beyond the materiality of the sign to the Spirit who heals."[284]

*Conclusion*

In sum, the participatory ontology this thesis is working with fundamentally rejects any kind of dualism and affirms the goodness of the material world. The first and second-level discourse of the Christian tradition by way of the Nicene Confession and the theologizing therefrom insists that God in Christ cannot be known as an item alongside creation; rather, the goodness of the material world is asserted by God freely being at-one-ed with it through the incarnate life of Jesus. Practically, pentecostals affirm this at-one-ment and the goodness of creation through healing. The belief in and practice of divine healing is a way of understanding the material world as Spirit-infused and at-one-d with God. The world with its corporeal bodies and mediating physical substances are ontologically open to God, and thus primed to be at once agents of healing and receivers of it. Just so, pentecostals posit a nondualistic affirmation of embodiment and materiality.

*Kenneth E. Hagin, Agnes Sanford, and Francis MacNutt in Dialogue* (Leiden: Brill, 2010), pp. 41-72; Matthew Marostica, "Learning from the Master: Carlos Annacondia and the Standardization of Pentecostal Practices in and beyond Argentina," in Gunther Brown (ed.), *Global Pentecostal and Charismatic Healing* (Oxford: Oxford University Press, 2011), pp. 207-27.

282. See Walter J. Hollenweger, *The Pentecostals: The Charismatic Movement in the Churches* (Minneapolis: Augsburg, 1972), pp. 353-62; Mark J. Cartledge, "Pentecostal Healing as an Expression of Godly Love: An Empirical Study," *MHRC* 16.5 (2013), pp. 501-22. This act was done in obedience to Jas 5:14-16. For a pentecostal reading of that text, see John Christopher Thomas, *Devil, Disease and Deliverance* (Cleveland: CPT Press, 2011), pp. 5-25.

283. See John Christopher Thomas, "Toward a Pentecostal Theology of Anointed Cloths," in Lee Roy Martin (ed.), *Toward a Pentecostal Theology of Worship* (Cleveland: CPT Press, 2016), pp. 89-112. Kimberly Alexander, "The Pentecostal Healing Community," in John Christopher Thomas (ed.), *Toward a Pentecostal Ecclesiology: The Church and the Five-Fold Gospel* (Cleveland: CPT Press, 2010), pp. 183-206.

284. John Christopher Thomas, "Theology of Anointed Cloths," p. 111.

## "Do This for My Remembrance": Relating (to) the Truth

*Introduction*

We have finally arrived at the last element of a pentecostal worldview in our constructive section, which aims to give an account of how pentecostals claim to know reality and the God who created it.²⁸⁵ The following will do so by giving a personally *holistic* account of knowledge consistent with what my constructive section has thus far posited about God and creatures. God is triune, and just so not a monadic mind to be extrinsically discovered. Moreover, all of created reality *is* by virtue of its participation in an active, communicative, and personally relational God who is Father, Son, and Spirit. We are affective creatures (eschatologically) oriented toward intimacy, with a narrative identity, and just so enveloped in the story of God with us. The church is likewise enveloped, but participates more intensely by the Spirit, as a witness to all of creation for what God intends for it. The proceeding epistemological account aims to be consistent with these convictions. In service of the overall aim of the project—part of which is to construct a pentecostal metaphysics that does justice to what is best in first-level pentecostal experience—what follows will highlight what I take to be a strength of pentecostal spirituality and the fruit it produces: its affective and narrative epistemology.

*Life in the Spirit as Storied Existence*

Narrative has been a recurring theme throughout this work, and it culminates here with an epistemology which privileges it. Pentecostal knowledge—we and other pentecostal theologians have said—is narrative knowledge. It is a kind of knowledge tacit in the first-level practice of testimony, wherein the testifier locates her micronarrative—consisting of personal experiences—in the macronarrative

---

285. A brief note on our primary interlocutors thus far: Yong and Smith's epistemological visions vary mostly with regard to where they locate their sources of theological knowledge and divine experiences. Justified by his foundational pneumatology, Yong's pneumatological imagination posits all of creation as charged by the Spirit so that divine encounters—from which theological knowledge emerges—happen everywhere and can therefore be publicly accessed and located across disciplines. Smith puts more weight on the pentecostal practices and stories that are shared in a Christian communal context. For Smith, then, participation in a community of faith is primarily what yields theological knowledge. Both Yong and Smith move beyond modernistic epistemologies and favor experiential knowledge over against *a priori* knowledge. Metaphysically speaking, both would also affirm that the cosmos is Spirit-infused. But Smith provides a stronger Christological and ecclesial framework wherein pentecostals train their affections, and know reality as charged by the Spirit, by feeling their way through the narratives and experiences within a church community. Given my method and approach thus far, it should come as no surprise that I follow Smith over against Yong here.

which speaks of God with his creatures, as revealed through Scripture. Narrative knowledge functions as "a way of perceiving the world (and God's action in it) that operates on a pre-intellectual register."[286] Therefore, "at issue in an epistemology of narrative knowledge is not so much a 'justified true belief' but rather providing an account of how we understand the world."[287] This kind of epistemology functions as hermeneutics—the filter of which is given through personal stories fitted to the story of Israel, and the life of Jesus, in particular.

Narrative knowledge—as it emerges from not only personal testimonies, but the story that traditional liturgical worship aims to tell and embody—is further characterized by the valuing and engagement of the whole self, and not merely the mind. That is to say, it is attentive to the emotive registers of worshippers so that narrative and affections work connaturally and primally to "create" (world-making) or make sense of our world and our experience in it. This kind of knowledge is pre-rational, beyond propositional, and does not reduce a worshipper to be a mere subjective mind. Drawing on Ian Scott's work, Smith argues that this understanding of knowledge is in alignment with Scripture, specifically in Paul who demonstrates a kind of knowing that is fully attuned to the whole human person, which is typically evoked using the metaphor of "heart." Moreover, in what Smith (following Scott) calls Paul's "Spirit-infused epistemology," "the Spirit effects a narratival relocation, situating the believing community within a story that provides a new context for understanding their experience."[288] Thus, Paul's thoughts on theological matters consist of *actions* and *events* which are "governed by the overarching plot of God's rescue of his creation."[289] As such, Paul invited Jews and Gentiles to embrace "not just a constellation of beliefs, or a collection of doctrines; rather, their salvation depended on actively and imaginatively absorbing a story—and seeing themselves in that story."[290]

In addition to an epistemology that honors the synthesis of narrative and affections, equally beneficial for pentecostals, is Chris Tilling's observation of a *relational* epistemology at work in Paul.[291] In fact, Tilling argues that a relational epistemology is at the heart of Paul's understanding of God as triune. In Paul's Epistles, God is transcendent and unique precisely in that his life is constituted by a "unique-to-God-relation-pattern." As a Jew, Paul is concerned about God's

---

286. James K. A. Smith, "Pentecostalism: Epistemic Fit and Pentecostal Experience," in William J. Abraham and Frederick D. Aquino (eds), *The Oxford Handbook of The Epistemology of Theology* (Oxford: Oxford University Press, 2017), p. 611.

287. Smith, "Pentecostalism," p. 611.

288. Smith, "Pentecostalism," p. 614.

289. Ian Scott, *Paul's Way of Knowing: Story, Experience, and Spirit* (Grand Rapids: Baker Academic, 2006), p. 118; *via* Smith, "Pentecostalism," p. 614

290. Smith, "Pentecostalism," p. 615

291. Chris Tilling, "Paul the Trinitarian," in Lincoln Harvey (ed.), *Essays on the Trinity* (Eugene: Cascade Books, 2018), pp. 36–62.

Godness being affirmed by the transcendent uniqueness of the *One* God. Faithful to Paul's Jewish tradition, he does not understand God to be passively known as static object, rather, God is known as he relates and is related to.

Paul's trinitarian theology, says Tilling, is apparent when one pays attention to the pattern of relational themes. First of all, God is communicative in that he *speaks* and receives speech from others than himself through prayer. Moreover, this unique God is *personally* present, *active,* and *faithful*.[292] In the same way one can locate a God-relation pattern of language in Paul which bespeaks the transcendent uniqueness of God, one can also find a *Christ*-relation pattern of language articulated in the same terms, therefore, "God's Godness is expressed in terms of *both* the Father and the risen Lord."[293] That is, the same relational predicates Paul attributes to God so as to assert this God's uniqueness over against all that is not God, Paul uses to attribute the same to Jesus. Finally, "The Spirit mediates and actualizes both the God and Christ relations; hence the Spirit's activity is that relationality which articulates Paul's way of speaking about the Godness of God."[294] The epistemological point for Tilling is that in Paul's thought, God is known as triune precisely because he relationally reveals himself as such. Tilling goes on to argue that in Paul's letters, God relates to the world—is present and active in it—by the Spirit in his people. "The Spirit, then, is God relating to his people, the activity of the Spirit *is* the 'transcendent uniqueness' of the one God, and so expresses the Godness of God."[295] As such, the biblical witness of Paul's trinitarian theology posits God's oneness by the mutual, relational, communicative, and personal action of Father, Son, and Spirit.[296]

This relational pattern in God opens up for us, so that God is known by us holistically and relationally. Indeed, Cheryl and Jackie Johns point to the biblical idea of *yada* which describes the kind of knowledge that comes by means of experience and intimate encounter. Therefore, a person who knows God "was encountered by one who lived in the midst of history who initiated a covenant and called for a response of the total person."[297] Knowing God, then, is not contingent upon the mind merely possessing information about God, but on a life lived in faithful relationship to him. Cheryl and Jackie Johns also contend that the Paraclete's

---

292. To briefly recall, "talkative," "personal," "active," and "faithful" were all crucial predicates in the section wherein I discussed the being of the one God.

293. Tilling, "Paul," p. 52.

294. Tilling, "Paul," p. 54.

295. Tilling, "Paul," p. 54.

296. While I have excluded them for lack of space, it is important to note here that Tilling offers an exhaustive amount of textual support from the Pauline corpus when naming the predicates in relation to the persons (see Chris Tilling, *Paul's Divine Christology*, pp. 236–9; Tilling, "Paul the Trinitarian," pp. 49–50, 52–3).

297. Cheryl Bridges Johns and Jackie Johns, "Yielding to the Spirit: A Pentecostal Approach to Group Bible Study," *JPT* 1 (1992), p. 112.

didactic function is to communicate the words of Jesus which can be faithfully heard primarily through participation in the community of faith. Knowledge of God in communal context is not so much ascertained as it is journeyed toward. In this *via salutis,* as envisioned by Kenneth Archer, we are continuously nourished by ordinances[298] which "provide worshippers opportunities for the ongoing spiritual formation of being conformed to the image of Christ through encountering the Spirit of Christ through the participatory reenactment of the story of Jesus."[299] And so, we know God as we sojourn communally to live the story of his Son by the power of the Spirit.

*Conclusion: Knowing as Affective Participation in the Truth*

How, then, once more, can God be known by creatures as it relates explicitly to an ontology of participation? We cannot univocally apply how we know other creatures and project it on how we might know God. For that would be the error of positing God as one thing, and creatures another—only to thereafter attempt to discern how creatures given their capabilities, can know God given his characteristics. I want to avoid this mistake as it would be inconsistent with the participatory ontology traced above while erroneously positing a mere causal relation between God and creatures as two extrinsic objects. The consequence of which is that creatures' knowledge of God would be explainable by the influences and effects God and creatures have on each other as separate agents. Again, we must insist that God is not monadic but triune, and that fact makes all the metaphysical and epistemological difference in the world.

Being is radical openness to participation we have said, and that matters profoundly for what it means for creatures to know God. Given that pentecostals intimately know (*yada*) God narratively, affectively, and relationally, we experience God as true, good, and beautiful. Utilizing the corresponding adjectives of these transcendental properties of being, we may say that God is knowable, lovable, and enjoyable. Here is where our openness to participation and the doctrine of the trinity come to bear on us once more: "God is truth and goodness and beauty because and only because knowledge and love and enjoyment in fact occur in the triune life. And God's truth and goodness and beauty are his knowability and lovability and enjoyability because the triune life opens to others than the three who are God."[300] This inclusion, and roominess, we have said does not overcome

---

298. Kenneth Archer links sacrament with ordinance and argues that pentecostal ordinances ought to include: water baptism, footwashing, the Lord's Supper, and tongues—which serve as a prophetic sign. See Kenneth J. Archer, "Nourishment for Our Journey: The Pentecostal *via Salutis* and Sacramental Ordinances," in Chris E. W. Green (ed.), *Pentecostal Ecclesiology: A Reader* (Boston: Brill, 2016), pp. 149-51.

299. Kenneth J. Archer, "Nourishment for Our Journey," p. 149.

300. Jenson, *ST.1*, p. 226.

the difference between God and creature but enforces it. God's act of making room in himself for others than himself to be, is the act of creation.

In light of the above, we may say that to know God is to be given room in his life to participate in God's knowing of himself. In Scripture, we learn that God's knowing of himself is actualized in history, primarily (or more intensely) through the people to whom he has properly introduced himself.[301] By the Spirit, said community has been joined to him to be his body; God is thus at once present *to* and present *in* this community. Just so, we may audaciously, yet in fear and trembling, describe the following as what happens when we assemble:

> When the gospel of Christ's Resurrection is spoken by and heard in the church, it is the very word of the Father to the Son we hear. When the church prays to the Father in the Son's name, she is taken into the obedient response of the Son to what the Father tells him. As the church speaks and hears the gospel and as the church responds to prayer and confession, the church's life is a great conversation, and this conversation is none other than our participation in the converse of the Father and the Son in the Spirit. As the church is enlivened and empowered by this hearing and answer, this inspiration is by none other than the Spirit who is the life between the Father and the Son. *So* do we know God.[302]

## Conclusion

This chapter proceeded from the suggestion that rather than idealizing or assuming that pentecostal spirituality, on its own, can give the best and most mature expression of our faith, pentecostals would be better served to explicate an orthodox and ecumenically promising theological metaphysics that resonates with their self-understanding, and on that basis, critique the forms of pentecostal spirituality and theology that have lost touch with historical Christian teaching. We thus attempted to develop a more thorough and cohesive pentecostal metaphysics informed by Scripture and the Christian dogmatic tradition, as well as pentecostal distinctives via Smith's categories. The following paragraph is a brief summation of what was constructed.

Ontologically, creatures *are* in that the capacious and ecstatically loving triune life has been spilled over toward that which is other than Father, Son, and Holy Spirit. Creatures thus live, move, and have their being in that Life of Love. That life itself *is* God, the infinite wellspring of being. The church *is* in that it participates in that life more intensely by being an eschatological step ahead of the rest of creation—historically manifesting, witnessing to, and foretasting what God

---

301. Exo. 3:14; 20:2; Jn 8:59; Heb. 1. Or recall Tilling's point that in Paul, God relates to and is active in the world by the Spirit in his people.

302. Jenson, *ST.1*, p. 228.

intends for all things. Epistemologically, we know God and what he intends as we participate in the life of the church. The church itself intimately participates in the life of the triune God as it has been ontologically joined to Christ by the Spirit in anticipation of the *totus Christus*. The nondualistic immediacy and intimacy of God's presence that pentecostals have come to expect in an enchanted creation, and in the community of faith, is thus accounted for in the metaphysical vision just posited.

## Chapter 6

## THE WORK OF GOD IN THE WORK OF THE PEOPLE: BEING-IN-THE-SPIRIT AND LITURGICAL RENEWAL

### *Introduction*

The preceding section was an attempt at developing a thorough and cohesive pentecostal metaphysics informed by Scripture, the Christian dogmatic tradition, and pentecostal experience in conversation with what pentecostal scholars have already partially posited on the matter. My constructive metaphysical vision aims to help pentecostal scholars and ministers discern the theological integrity and soundness of contemporary beliefs and practices in various ministerial contexts. The "soundness" is determined by whether or not it bespeaks and reinscribes in our imaginations the God who is Father, Son, and Spirit, and his relationship to creatures in a way that is faithful to what the historical Christian tradition has said. Now that a particular vision of pentecostal spirituality—heretofore assumed by many pentecostal scholars—has been shown to be out of practice in many contemporary pentecostal churches, room for reflection on a pentecostal spirituality that is informed by the first-level discourse of the Christian tradition has been opened. Hence with this monograph, I am offering a constructive and critical engagement of pentecostal spirituality, and academic pentecostal theology via conversation with the larger ecumenical, creedal, and dogmatic Christian metaphysical tradition; this effort is aimed at constructing a metaphysics that simultaneously does justice what is best in the first-level pentecostal experience while confronting that which may be problematic. By "best" in the previous sentence, I mean that in the sense that it is ecumenically promising and does not run counter to what the classical Christian tradition has said about God and creatures; also, "best" as described per my engagement with Smith's "five elements of a pentecostal worldview."

Prior to constructing a pentecostal metaphysics, I argued that contemporary pentecostal scholars have been working with an idealized form of Land's pentecostal spirituality which is not representative of what many contemporary pentecostal churches are practicing today. Furthermore, I showed that once other versions of pentecostal practice are considered, we discover that in various contexts, there is a disconnect between pentecostal theology and ecclesial pentecostal practice and spirituality. Thus, rather than idealizing or assuming a particular form of pentecostal spirituality can, on its own, give the most mature expression of our faith, I argued that pentecostals would be better served to explicate an orthodox and ecumenically promising theological metaphysics that resonates with our self-understanding, and on the basis of this theological metaphysics, critique the forms of pentecostal spirituality and theology that have lost touch with historical Christian teaching. Now that said metaphysics has been constructed above, we have arrived at the final portion of this constructive section whereby I argue that the best way to reform unfaithful beliefs and practices is through liturgical renewal. The discoveries of what actually takes place in some pentecostal ecclesial contexts via the studies of Albrecht, Cartledge, Parker, and Samuel in an earlier section of this work exposed a wide gap between the second-level discourses of pentecostal scholarship, and that of the first-level discourse in churches in North America, and the UK. For the sake of moving toward a theological grounding for pentecostal practice and speech, and closing said gap, in this section I am going to argue for a scripted liturgy which aims to be faithful to the historical Christian tradition (in that it explicitly evokes the triune God and tells the story of Jesus) in light of Pentecost (in that it creates space for spontaneity, and dynamic expression). I will then construct a partially scripted pentecostal liturgy in conversation with the classical pentecostal metaphysics just constructed which aims to be faithful to the same.

## Pentecost and the Spirit of the Liturgy

Theology as defined in this work is the reflective enterprise wholly connected to the practices, and speech acts of church assemblies. As such, all the norms of theological judgment as used in the church service must be utilized to properly do the work of theology. Also, as noted in Chapter 1, the mutually informative character of first and second-level discourse means that theology can also be corrective for practice. Hence my utilizing the theological metaphysical vision developed in Chapter 5 to call for liturgical renewal. Theology so described is practical, speculative, and thus a hermeneutic. As stated above, it functions like a grammar which guides the church's speech first within itself, then *subsequently* to the world.

I have further argued, using the work of Vondey and others, that pentecostal theology—like all Christian theology—is liturgical theology. Given the importance of liturgy for the theological enterprise, Chris Green advised us against inventing our own liturgical forms without regard for the historical Christian tradition, as doing so often fails us theologically. He therefore reminded us that liturgical worship (1) gifts us with a narrative identity in God's story, (2) properly orders our affections, and (3) disciplines our imaginations and ambitions. As important as liturgy is for guiding our speech and practices, we must also remember that it is faithful just insofar as it witnesses to the Spirit who is not self-referential, but self-effacing (Jn 16:13). As such, the liturgy is most formative when it makes no claims about itself, but rather, when it aims at drawing attention to the God who has claimed it. As worshipers of God, then, we ought to be a people who let the liturgy have a kind of authority over our lives, while simultaneously recognizing that the authority the liturgy has is an authority that comes primarily in its own openness to *God's* authority. I mention this here because there are anxieties that face us: primarily, those of the revivalists and postcolonial liberationists. I want to speak to those head-on by saying that when I speak positively about the liturgy, I am not here talking about a divine framework which cannot be in any way modified. Rather, in order to see the liturgy rightly, I suggest that we need to see it as the historically accumulated wisdom of Christian worshipers in their openness to God. Precisely by its transparency to the Spirit, liturgy is both capacious and just so attentive to what "the Spirit is saying to the churches," so that the liturgy cannot be used as a colonial tool of oppression to silence the voiceless, as liberationists might be concerned about. Nor would it—as revivalists might object—restrict the freedom of the Spirit to act on us in new and surprising ways.

I want to expand on Green's third point above by arguing that one of the ways that liturgical worship may discipline our imaginations is by shaping our understanding of what "freedom" means. The notion of "freedom" merits brief discussion considering that the primary reason consistently cited for pentecostal reluctance to participate in traditional worship is the potential quenching of God's—and thereupon the worshipers'—"freedom." In response, I must note here that there is a theological distinction between what it means for God to be free, and what it means for creatures to be free. These distinct notions of freedom are both integrated in the life of Jesus so that Jesus is at once free in the way that God is free, and, he is free in the way that human beings are *meant* to be free. Precisely because Jesus is aligned to the freedom of God, he reveals freedom and obedience to be mutually determining. Or, put differently, Jesus reveals that freedom is the fullness of obedience to the will of God. The liturgy, then, is restrictive only in the sense that it is freeing us to obey. Our humanity is not yet whole, and as such our desires remain conditioned by a multitude of factors which disease it. Precisely because our humanity remains under the influence of things that disease us, there is a need for "restriction" through the liturgy. One such symptom of our humanity's not-yet wholeness is its being subjected to the modern notions of what freedom means in the first place, that is, sheer autonomy through lack of restraint and unconditionedness. Freedom as revealed through the life of Jesus, on the other hand, is perfect conditionedness. That is, true freedom is to be so transparent to God that what I am to do, and who I am is one. The liturgy, then, is Spirit-ed just insofar as it frees us to obey, and does so in a self-effacing, roomy, and hospitable manner. Just so, "the liturgy is simply a way of structuring worship that is faithful to what the Spirit is doing in the church: forming it into the body of Christ."[1]

---

1. Simon Chan, *Liturgical Theology*, p. 126.

As pentecostals, I suggest we welcome practices in our assemblies which we may find immediately disappointing. Leaning into practices such as scripted prayers, repetitive sayings, and gestures may feel unnatural, but perhaps that is a move toward submitting to the fact that liturgy disciplines our imaginations and spiritual ambitions as Green has suggested. Submitting to a process that feels unnatural would serve as a needed reminder to us that "A 'God' who meets us always where our desires demand is not in fact the God of Jesus Christ ... Liturgy in this sense is like a yoke: bearing it rightly, we find ourselves gracefully restricted and redemptively directed."[2]

Green has proposed a helpful six-phase liturgical structure which honors *both* the restrictive liturgical forms received from the historical Christian tradition and the extemporaneous pentecostal spirituality that continues to form us.[3] It includes scripted prayers, assigned public reading of Scripture, and space for spontaneity with personal prayers, testimony, petition, and lament. Furthermore, this proposed liturgy climaxes at the altar (as pentecostals would have it), but this altar places the Lord's Table at its center (as the historical Christian tradition and indeed many Early Pentecostal congregations would have it).[4] Furthermore, pentecostal theologian, Simon Chan, has also written a liturgy which will be taken into consideration in this work, and he has done so around the traditional connatural "parts" of Word and sacrament.[5] These "parts" of the liturgy promote both faithfulness to orthodoxy and faithfulness to the roominess of pentecostal expression. Chan says, "unless our respective orders of service (and there could be many) conform to the basic *ordo*," that is, the *ordo* of Word and sacrament, then

---

2. Chris Green, "Saving Liturgy," p. 112.

3. The six phases proposed by Green are: (1) a scripted call to worship with a scripted response from the congregation, (2) congregational singing (including praise, testimony, petition, lament), (3) intercessory prayer both scripted and spontaneous, corporate and personal), (4) public reading of OT and NT scriptural texts, (5) a homily which climaxes with an altar call, which has the Lord's Table as its center, (6) a closing with a benediction and commissioning to ministry as the scattered people of God. See Green, "Saving Liturgy," p. 115. It is also important to note here that the desire for a scripted pentecostal liturgy is hardly novel. From the very beginning, Classical Pentecostals have longed for some kind of scripted liturgical worship for various reasons. See Aaron Friesen, "Classical Pentecostal Liturgy: Between Formalism and Fanaticism," in Mark J. Cartledge and A. J. Swoboda (eds), *Scripting Pentecost: A Study of Pentecostals, Worship, and Liturgy* (New York: Routledge, 2017), pp. 53–68.

4. Chris Green, *Toward a Pentecostal Theology of the Lord's Supper: Foretasting the Kingdom* (Cleveland: CPT Press, 2012).

5. As Chan reminds us, "There is a general agreement among liturgiologists today that for all the variations in liturgical expressions, there is nonetheless a basic shape or *ordo* underlying these expressions." That *ordo* is Word and sacrament (Chan, *Liturgical Theology*, p. 62). For Simon Chan's written liturgy, see Chan, *Liturgical Theology*, pp. 129–30.

"we are not being shaped into the community we are meant to be."[6] Notice, that there could be many respective orders of service, which opens up the liturgy for pentecostal creativity and spontaneity as long as our extemporaneous expressions are banked by the logic of Word and sacrament.[7] Moreover, the language of Word and sacrament is resonant with the language of Incarnation wherein "the Word became flesh" (Jn 1:14). As the Body of Christ, the church incarnates Christ in the world through her gathering and practices, and the logic of that fact ought to be reflected in our liturgies. It is not only Chris Green and Simon Chan's liturgical proposals which will serve as guides for the liturgy that follows, utilizing the scripted liturgy from the Book of Common Prayer, will also prove fruitful for the purposes of this work.[8]

Finally, it is important to reiterate that I am not claiming to write *the* definitive liturgy for pentecostals. Rather, I am proposing one as a model for what it might look like for pentecostals to participate in a traditional liturgical worship expression *as* pentecostals, with scripted acts and speech-acts. Therefore, there is room for thoughtful exceptions and innovations, in fact, I invite them. As pentecostals, historically there is no clear line of continuity wherein a liturgy is gifted to us; as such, should it be decided that some kind of liturgy is a good way forward, we are going to have to discern *communally* what a faithful liturgy looks like.[9] That said,

---

6. Chan, *Liturgical Theology*, p. 62.

7. Another protestant and ecumenical thinker who has made some helpful proposals around the rite of baptism that are worth considering is Jenson. See Robert Jenson, *Visible Words: The Interpretation and Practice of Christian Sacraments* (Minneapolis: Fortress Press, 2010), pp. 166-73. Indeed, the entire monograph helpfully displays the world-making character of what we practice in our local assemblies and also calls for careful attention to it considering the snares of modernity.

8. I am utilizing the Anglican BCP because, first of all, there is a historical connection between the present pentecostal movement and the Anglican liturgical tradition through Wesleyanism and the Holiness movements. Moreover, to my historical point, the rubric for celebrating the Lord's Supper in the 1911 Constitution and General Rules of the Pentecostal Holiness Church (IPHC) provides a prayer which is an adaptation from the Prayer of Consecration in the 1662 BCP (Green, "Saving Liturgy," pp. 109-11). Second, it is something I am currently practicing *as* a pentecostal, and as these practices are integrated in me personally, I am writing from that place. Third, beyond the personal integrationist concerns and the historical precedent, there is a way in which it is ecumenically promising to engage the Anglican tradition as a way into conversations with Orthodox and Catholic traditions.

9. This includes communally discerning the best means for adjudication. Part of the issue that pentecostals have to contend with is the question of canonicity; that is, given our restorationist and free church history, what are the canons that determine the validity of a liturgical proposal? These are the kinds of questions we must continually return to. I must note here that even in a tradition as dependent upon a magisterium as the Orthodox, the issue of canonicity remains pervasive. Indeed, Schmemann laments what canonicity

positively speaking, the aim of this proposed scripted liturgy is also to move us back—through critical reflection—toward restoring our spirituality to something like a *gestalt* from which pentecostal theologians can work for the sake of speaking both *to* our tradition, and *from* it. However, that aim is in service to a greater one: to compose a liturgy that is ecumenically promising and therefore true to the tradition and thus aimed at a future unity insofar as it is aimed at Christ and his coming kingdom. Perhaps what may be in order for the future of pentecostalism is a willingness to engage liturgical forms for a significant amount of time. As Daniel did to the skeptical guard of the palace master, I invite pentecostal ministers to "put this proposal to the test … then compare."[10] A final reminder to us pentecostals when it comes to our experiences in worship: our experiences derived from our spirituality are important, yet we must remember that "our experiences of God are never ends in themselves but belong to the Spirit's work of revealing Christ to the world as the revelation of the Father. We are bound not only to testify but also to *teach*,"[11] thus making second-level discourse an absolute necessity for discerning "theologically appropriate ways of identifying what happens in God's coming near to us."[12] I thus close this chapter with my liturgical proposal. Included with it will be a brief commentary in some of the footnotes that suggest how this proposed liturgy might work with the grain of my metaphysical construct in the previous chapter.

has become as he discusses the issue of "canonical subordinationism," which he argues has become more concerned with "victories" and "security" than it is with unity and truth—thus ceasing to be in alignment with the whole purpose of canons in the first place. When the focus is on canonical subordination, "the reality of the church is reduced to the formal principle of 'jurisdiction', i.e. subordination to a central ecclesiastical power." As a result, "the Bishop becomes a simple representative of a higher jurisdiction, important not in himself, not as the charismatic bearer and guardian of his Church's *continuity* and *catholicity*, but as a means of this Church's subordination to 'jurisdiction.'" This must not be the case precisely because the "Church cannot be reduced to 'jurisdiction'. She is a living organism and her continuity is precisely that of life … the ministry of power is not *create* the church but is created by God within the Church, which is ontologically prior to all functions, charisms and ministries." What Schmemann laments is exactly what I want to avoid at all costs. See Fr. Alexander Schmemann, "Problems of Orthodoxy in America: The Canonical Problem," *St. Vladimir's Seminary Quarterly* 8.2 (1964), pp. 70-1.

10. See Daniel 1:8-17. This "test" of adhering to a partially scripted liturgy of some kind, of course, would have to be for a significant amount of time, perhaps at least a generation so that we might communally discern whether or not we see signs of bearing positive fruit. Perhaps in the now—what seems to be—post "church growth movement" era, we would be open to renewing our assemblies with the aim of traditional faithfulness and openness to the Spirit for the sake of our future.

11. Chris Green, "'In Your Presence is Fullness of Joy': Experiencing God as Trinity," in Lee Roy Martin (ed.), *Toward a Pentecostal Theology of Worship* (Cleveland: CPT Press, 2020), p. 189 (emphasis original).

12. Green, "In Your Presence," p. 189.

## 6. The Work of God in the Work of the People

### A Proposed Liturgy for Ordinary Time[13]

*A liturgy for Ordinary Time*

*The Word of God (The Liturgy of the Word)*

Prelude[14]
*Often, when there is music accompanying the service, the musician will begin with an instrumental piece of music.*

Processional Song
*An anthem is sung*

THE ACCLAMATION[15]

*The People standing, the Celebrant says this or a seasonal greeting*

| | |
|---|---|
| *Celebrant* | Blessed be God: The Father, the Son, and Holy Spirit |
| *People* | And blessed be his kingdom, now and forever. Amen. |

THE GLORIA (omit during penitential or fasting seasons)[16]

---

13. Parts one through five fit under the heading of "Word." It is the portion of the liturgy wherein we are confronted by God and his people, and thereby prepare ourselves to meet God in the sacrament (part six). Finally, we are commissioned back into the world.

14. Prelude to the Gloria constitute "phase one" which is "A call to worship" in Green's liturgical proposal.

15. This liturgy begins by identifying the God in whom we worship, and toward whom we are sojourning (*via salutis*). This God is none other than the triune God of the gospel, Father, Son, and Holy Spirit. This is important as I have noted in Chapter 4, that the trinity functions like a syntax in how Christians talk about and identify God. Given this importance, I argued in a lengthy footnote in a section of that same chapter that this name must be explicitly spoken in our worship. The empirical and ethnographic work of Cartledge and Parker both demonstrate that we cannot assume in pentecostal worship that God is automatically named and worshiped as triune. Given that the triune God is essential to the orthodox understanding of the Christian God, I constructed a metaphysics from that vantage. Naming and conceiving God trinitarianly, then, is essential to first- and second-level discourse.

16. In this Gloria, God is once again explicitly named, conceived of, and addressed, trinitarianly—as is my theological metaphysical vision. Indeed, the title of "Lord" is applied initially to God (the Father), then coequally to Jesus, the Son of the Father. Furthermore, the Father and Jesus Christ are identified as the Holy One *with* the Holy Spirit. Thus, Father, Son, and Spirit in this first-level discourse are coequally one as I argued in my second-level

*Celebrant and the people:*

Glory to God in the highest, and peace to his people on earth.
Lord God, heavenly King, almighty God and Father, we worship you, we give you thanks, we praise you for your glory. Lord Jesus Christ, only Son of the Father, Lord God, Lamb of God, you take away the sin of the world: have mercy on us; you are seated at the right hand of the Father: receive our prayer. For you alone are the Holy One, you alone are the Lord, you alone are the Most High, Jesus Christ, with the Holy Spirit, in glory of God the Father. Amen.

CONGREGATIONAL SINGING[17]

*Praise and Worship songs selected by the song leader.*

INTERCESSORY PRAYERS OF THE PEOPLE[18]

*While the following typically consists of short and scripted prayers, space may also be given for spontaneous testimony, lament, and prayer.*

*Prayer is offered with intercession for*
  *The Universal Church, its members, and its mission*
  *The Nation and all in authority*
  *The welfare of the world*
  *The concerns of the local community*
  *Those who suffer and those in any trouble*
  *The departed*

*The Celebrant concludes with this or some other appropriate Collect.*

discourse in the previous chapter (especially, "'For from Him and through Him and to Him Are All Things': The Triune Determination(s) of Creation" and all of "I Am That You Are: The Radical Openness of God"). Moreover, this prayer is resonant with the God-relation and Christ-relation pattern also mentioned above (Ch. 5, "Life in the Spirit as Storied Existence"), wherein I demonstrated that the same relational predicates the Apostle Paul uses to assert God's uniqueness above all that is not God (e.g., "King," "Lord"), he also uses to ascribe the same to Jesus with the Spirit. God's oneness both in my work and in this prayer is posited by the mutual, relational, communicative, and tri-personal action of Father, Son, and Spirit. All subsequent prayers and confessions in the scripted portion of the liturgy are likewise construed.

  17. "Phase two" of Green's liturgical proposal.
  18. "Phase three" of Green's liturgical proposal.

"Heavenly Father, grant these our prayers for the sake of Jesus Christ, our only Mediator and Advocate, who lives and reigns with you in the unity of the Holy Spirit, one God, now and forever. Amen."[19]

PUBLIC READING OF BIBLICAL TEXTS[20]

*A reader is selected to read aloud selected texts from Old Testament and New Testament before the congregation*[21]

OT reading
Psalm

*End reading of the Psalm with Gloria:*

*Celebrant and the people*
"Glory be to the Father, Son, and Holy Spirit, as it was in the beginning, is now, and ever shall be, world without end."[22]

---

19. In this prayer, we understand the preceding intercessory prayers of the people as having been done petitioning the Father (for Jesus' sake), in the Son (as Mediator) by the Holy Spirit who at once unifies Father and Son, as well as us to the Father through the "Mediating Son." As the Son mediates the Father by the Spirit, the church intercedes and mediates God to the world *as* the body of Christ in intercessory prayer. Hence the "foundational ecclesiological pneumatology" (Chapter 5, "A Foundational Ecclesiological Pneumatology") and concomitant "participatory ontology" ("'The Lord, Your God': Being-in-the-World as Ontological Participation") laid out in the previous chapter.

20. "Phase four" of Green's liturgical proposal.

21. Following the Lectionary is highly recommended as these texts are selected according to the church calendar which tells and retells the story of Jesus, thus forming worshipers to embody Jn 5:39.

22. I'm thankful to my priest, Fr. Howard Giles of Jesus the Good Shepherd Anglican Church for his insight on why this *Gloria* is stated after the reading of the Psalm. He pointed out in a conversation we had on February 10, 2019, that the Psalms are the centerpiece of the Daily Office. As such, this Gloria is also placed at the center of the public liturgy as a reminder to the community as they are gathered, of the centrality of the triune God by naming him trinitarianly, in connection with the poles of time. Time has a triadic and narratable structure of past, present, and future because God is Father, Son, and Spirit (as I argued in "'For from Him and through Him and to Him Are All Things': The Triune Determination(s) of Creation" and developed in the subsections under it). This Gloria, then, explicitly embodies that which I argued in greater detail above: that the Father is the Source of creation ("as it was in the beginning"), the Spirit draws creation toward its eschatological future ("ever shall be, world without end"), and the Son is the mediatory present ("is now"), reconciling past and future in himself.

NT reading (Acts, Epistle, Apocalypse)
Gospel reading.

*After the Gospel, the Reader says*
  The Gospel of the Lord.

*People* Praise to you, Lord Christ.

THE SERMON[23]

CONFESSION OF THE NICENE CREED[24]

*Celebrant* Let us confess our faith in the words of the Nicene Creed:

*Celebrant and People*

We believe in one God, the father, the Almighty, maker of heaven and earth, of all this is, visible and invisible.

We believe in one Lord, Jesus Christ, the only-begotten Son of God, eternally begotten of the Father, God from God, Light from Light, true God from true God, begotten, not made, of one Being with the Father; through him all things were made. For us and for our salvation he came down from heaven, was incarnate from the Holy Spirit and the Virgin Mary, and was made man. For our sake he was crucified under Pontius Pilate; he suffered death and was buried. On the third day he rose again in accordance with the Scriptures; he ascended into heaven and is seated at the right hand of the Father. He will come again in glory to judge the living and the dead, and his kingdom will have no end.

We believe in the Holy Spirit, the Lord, the giver of life, who proceeds from the Father (and the Son), who with the Father and the Son is worshiped and

---

23. "Phase five" of Green's liturgical proposal is the sermon, and he is insistent that the sermon must climax at the altar which has as its center, the Table of the Lord. This is resonant with where the liturgy of the BCP climaxes.

24. Once again, Fr. Giles was crucial in showing me that the sermon ought to be placed between the reading of the word and the confession of the creed. Should he err, or even unwittingly preach heresy, Fr. Giles trusts that the preceding Scriptures and the proceeding creed, by the power of the Spirit, do the work of reorienting the parishioners back into Christian orthodoxy. Moreover, the first-level confession of the Nicene Creed imposes upon the church a second-level task of reflection on what it might mean for the triune God to *be*, considering we confess that "We believe in God, *the* ..." and that Jesus is "of *one being* with the Father ..." Therefore, the entirety of "I Am That You Are: The Radical Openness of God", was, in part, my attempt at just this sort of reflection. I did so while considering centuries of Christian thought that this very creed inspired throughout Chapter 5.

glorified, who has spoken through the prophets. We believe in one holy catholic and apostolic Church. We acknowledge one Baptism for the forgiveness of sins. We look for the resurrection of the dead, and the life of the world to come. Amen.

*Sacrament: The Liturgy of the Table*

THE SURSUM CORDA[25]

| | |
|---|---|
| *Celebrant* | The Lord be with you. |
| *People* | And with your spirit. |
| *Celebrant* | Lift up your hearts. |
| *People* | We lift them up to the Lord |
| *Celebrant* | Let us give thanks to the Lord our God |
| *People* | It is right to give him thanks and praise |

*The Celebrant*
It is right, our duty and our joy, always and everywhere to give thanks to you, Father Almighty, Creator of heaven and earth. Therefore, we praise you, joining our voices with Angels and Archangels and with all the company of heaven, who forever sing this hymn to proclaim the glory of your Name:

---

25. This marks the beginning of the Sacramental portion of the liturgy, in which after being lovingly confronted and addressed by God through the Word portion, we are invited to "lift our hearts" in anticipation of celebrating the Eucharist. In the scripted *Sanctus*, when God is praised as thrice holy, the bells ring three times to indicate the sound of angels singing with us. The song is in reference to Isa. 6:1-3, which contains an acclamation wherein the Seraphim who stand immediately before the throne of God in heaven sing: "Holy, Holy, Holy, is the Lord Almighty; the whole earth is full of your glory." Worshipers in the church join that song thus bringing us before the throne in heaven so that the overlap of heaven and earth which occurs as the church gathers, is actualized. We ought not be surprised that our meek and humble gatherings can be understood as such. For in the latter part of the *Sanctus* itself, we are reminded that this enthroned, highly exalted, and glorious one who has majestic creatures singing his praises is also the meek and humble one, riding into Jerusalem on a donkey with Hebrew children singing his praises, "Hosanna in the highest." Therefore, it is embodied and bespoken in Christian worship, that humanity and angels have intimate interaction (see the section of the previous chapter entitled: "Deep Calls out to Deep: Re-Enchanting Nature and Rediscovering Creation") in the overlapping realities of heaven and earth. The section in which I work out a "foundational ecclesiological pneumatology," and the participatory ontology that follows it, make this very point: that the assembled people of God simultaneously inhabit this material world whilst intensely participating in the life of God. Indeed, heaven and earth are full of God's glory, hence the pentecostal enchanted theology of creation, and nondualistic affirmation of the material world.

## THE SANCTUS

*Celebrant and People*
Holy, Holy, Holy, Lord God of power and might, heaven and earth are full of your glory. Hosanna in the highest. Blessed is he who comes in the Name of the Lord. Hosanna in the highest.

## THE PRAYER OF CONSECRATION[26]

*Celebrant*
Now, O merciful Father, in your great goodness, we ask you to bless and sanctify, with your Holy Spirit, these gifts of bread and wine, that we, receiving them according to your Son our Savior Jesus Christ's holy institution, in remembrance of his death and passion, may be partakers of his most blessed Body and Blood.

*At the following words concerning the bread, the Celebrant is to hold it, or to lay a hand upon it, and here may break the bread; and at the words concerning the cup, to hold or place a hand upon the cup and any other vessel containing the wine to be consecrated.*

For on the night that he was betrayed, our Lord Jesus Christ took bread; and when he had given thanks, he broke it (break bread here), and gave it to his disciples saying, "Take, eat; this is my Body, which is given for you: Do this in remembrance of me."

Likewise, after supper, Jesus took the cup, and when he had given thanks, he gave it to them, saying "Drink this, all of you; for this is my Blood of the New Covenant, which is shed for you, and for many, for the forgiveness of sins: Whenever you drink it, do this in remembrance of me."

Therefore, O Lord and heavenly Father, according to the institution of your dearly beloved Son our Savior Jesus Christ, we your humble servants celebrate and make here before your divine Majesty, with these holy gifts, the memorial your Son commanded us to make; remembering his blessed passion and precious death, his mighty resurrection and glorious ascension, and his promise to come again. And we earnestly desire your fatherly goodness mercifully to accept this,

---

26. The pentecostal nondualistic affirmation of the material world is once again explicitly affirmed as the triune God is bespoken, and ordinary material particulars are consecrated to be the very intendable presence of God himself, by the Spirit. As mentioned in the previous chapter, pentecostals believe in the goodness of the material world and participate in practices in which physical materials can mediate the presence of God (e.g., anointing oil, handkerchiefs, and cloths). Moreover, in the reading of this text, and in the acts of the pastor as she or he breaks the bread and blesses the wine, the narrative character of pentecostal existence is embodied as we participate in the story of Jesus with his disciples, so that we may be partakers of his body and blood.

our sacrifice of praise and thanksgiving; asking you to grant that, by the merits and death of your Son Jesus Christ, and through faith in his Blood, we and your whole Church may obtain forgiveness of our sins, and all other benefits of his passion. And here we offer and present to you, O Lord, ourselves, our souls and bodies, to be a reasonable, holy, and living sacrifice. We humbly pray that all who partake of this Holy Communion may worthily receive the most precious Body and Blood of your Son Jesus Christ, be filled with your grace and heavenly benediction, and be made one body with him, that he may dwell in us, and we in him. And although we are unworthy, because of our many sins, to offer you any sacrifice, yet we ask you to accept this duty and service we owe, not weighing our merits, but pardoning our offenses, through Jesus Christ our Lord. By him, and with him, and in him, in the unity of the Holy Spirit, all honor and glory is yours, Almighty Father, now and forever. Amen.

THE OUR FATHER[27]

*The Celebrant continues*
And now, as our Savior Christ has taught us, we are bold to pray,

*People and celebrant*
Our Father, who art in heaven, hallowed be thy Name, thy kingdom come, thy will be done on earth as it is in heaven. Give us this day our daily bread, and forgive us our trespasses, as we forgive those who trespass against us. And lead us not into temptation, but deliver us from evil. For thine is the kingdom, and the power, and the glory, forever and ever. Amen

THE MINISTRATION OF COMMUNION[28]

*Facing the people, the Celebrant may say the following invitation*
The gifts of God for the people of God.

---

27. This prayer is a crucial first-level practice that coheres with many important aspects of my metaphysical construct. In the previous chapter, I argued that because God is triune and thus not a being among beings, prayer does not constitute God's people praying to an external monadic agent (see specifically, "The Spirit of Jesus is the Spontaneity of Natural Process" section). It is this prayer that demonstrates—notably, right before we celebrate the Eucharist—that we not only pray to God, we pray *in* God, and with God. Jesus brings the church into his filial address and invites us not merely to pray to his Father, but to *our* Father. As such, the church is indeed the body of Christ in that he grants us access to address God in and with him right before we partake of the Eucharist.

28. This is the invitation to the Table of the Lord. This follows from the "our Father" prayer which—as I suggested in the previous footnote—is Jesus' invitation for the church to pray *in* and *with* him right before we celebrate the Eucharist. It is this Eucharistic supper wherein right after Jesus has invited us to be in him, he invites himself to materially indwell

*Or this*

Behold the lamb of God, behold him who takes away the sins of the world. Blessed are those who are invited to the marriage supper of the Lamb.

*After eating and drinking, there can be space made for spontaneous "altar time." In Anglican liturgies, the space after partaking of the eucharist is often accompanied by music and a time of reflection as parishioners continue to make their way to the Table. Worshippers may stay at the altar to pray, receive prayer, prophetic words, etc.*

THE POST COMMUNION PRAYER

*After Communion and altar time, the celebrant says*
Let us pray.

*Celebrant and People together say the following,*
Almighty and everliving God, we thank you for feeding us, in these holy mysteries, with the spiritual food of the most precious Body and Blood of your Son our Savior Jesus Christ; and for assuring us, through this Sacrament, of your favor and goodness towards us: that we are true members of the mystical body of your Son, the blessed company of all faithful people; and are also heirs, through hope, of your everlasting kingdom. And we humbly ask you, heavenly Father, to assist us with your grace, that we may continue in that holy fellowship, and do all the good works that you have prepared for us to walk in; through Jesus Christ our Lord, to whom, with you and the Holy Spirit, be all honor and glory, now and forever. Amen.

DISMISSAL (Benediction and Commissioning)[29]

---

us by the power of the Holy Spirit. We thus "foretaste the kingdom," as Green suggests, where Christ will be unstintingly in us and we in him. It is fitting for pentecostals that the service climaxes with such a profound encounter with Jesus at the altar. It is a climax we have narratively journeyed toward. This *via salutis* in which we sojourn communally to live the story of Jesus, in Jesus, by the power of the Spirit, can be argued to work with the grain of the metaphysical vision previously posited. That is, this partially scripted liturgy works with the grain of worshiping the triune God, and with the grain of being formed as a people who are eschatologically oriented, radically open to God, enchanted by creation, nondualistic, and come to know reality affectively and narratively. I must also note here that such an encounter, and such a formation, grants space at the altar for practices that are recognized as distinctly pentecostal.

29. "Phase six" of Green's liturgical proposal. This is the blessing and sending forth to ministry as the scattered people of God.

*The Priest gives this or an alternate blessing*[30]
The peace of God, which passes all understanding, keep your hearts and minds in the knowledge and love of God, and of his Son Jesus Christ our Lord; and the blessing of God Almighty, the Father, the Son, and the Holy Spirit, be among you, and remain with you always. Amen.

*Or an unscripted prayer of dismissal*

## Conclusion

Once again, the preceding was a liturgical proposal aimed at honoring both the liturgical forms received from the historical Christian tradition and the extemporaneous pentecostal spirituality that has formed and continues to form us. I did so in conversation with the proposals of other pentecostal theologians, namely, Green and Chan, along with the Book of Common Prayer, demonstrating that script and Spirit are not at odds, but can be mutually informing. This hopefully moves pentecostal spirituality toward an explicitly trinitarian expression: shaped by the life of Jesus, willed by God the Father in the freedom of the Holy Spirit. Thus, the possibility of our first and second-level discourses joining toward faithfully thinking, bespeaking, and enacting the God of the gospel and his relation to creation is opened up.

---

30. Once more, the triune God is named as we are dismissed. As such, the service embodies a kind of *inclusio* in that it begins (is centered by) and ends with the naming of God as Father, Son, and Spirit. This fact, along with my previous commentary in the footnotes above, suggests that this partially scripted liturgy works with the grain of my metaphysical construct. Of course, that is not to say that mine is the only metaphysics that can be constructed from it; however, I believe this suggested liturgy opens the possibility for our spirituality to have historical and material grounds for ecumenically faithful, and mutually informing, discourse and debate.

# CONCLUSION

## *Contributions of This Work and Suggestions for Further Study*

This study produced a number of contributions to academic pentecostal theology. It is the first of its kind in that there has not been an exhaustive attempt to discern what pentecostals have said regarding a cohesive metaphysical vision of the whole; moreover, it is the first of its kind in that it has also attempted to construct a metaphysical vision that is resonant with pentecostal spirituality. This monograph carefully traced the relevant work of a number of pentecostal theologians, including, in particular, James K. A. Smith and Amos Yong, exploring both their explicit and implicit metaphysical assumptions. It was also demonstrated that it has been customary among academic pentecostals to think of pentecostal spirituality as the *gestalt* of pentecostalism(s), thus overlooking the need to turn a critical eye toward it as the pentecostal movement has perdured. That may have sufficed in the past, however, considering the multiple and various local expressions—along with the internationally influential ones—that claim to be pentecostal, it is now impossible to assert that there is one version of pentecostal spirituality from which we are all theologizing.

Precisely because my aim was to construct a vision of the whole in light of the internal logic of pentecostal spirituality and the historical Christian theological and liturgical tradition, first of all, what my work has pointed to is the need of paying close attention to our worship and speech. Second, it has aimed at providing a cohesive metaphysics that could possibly function as a way to move toward a kind of measuring stick or lens from which to observe our spirituality. In the effort to develop a coherently pentecostal and ecumenical metaphysical vision, what this work has further contributed is a method for discerning the theological faithfulness of worship practices. Researchers and pastors might take it as a model for discerning what is practiced at their churches. This is certainly worth the effort as Paul warns us that we are not commended simply because we gather in worship, but it deeply matters *how* we gather (1 Cor. 11). Indeed, as Christians, when assembled we are compelled to speak and enact the gospel—the same message that Christians have gathered around for millennia—along with its metaphysical import, albeit in ways that are appropriate to missional contexts. Moreover, the message itself—that the Father has raised his Son Jesus from the dead by the power of the Holy Spirit—and the world it creates for those who gather around it, must be shared by pentecostals.

Obviously, one cannot claim to have the last word on pentecostal metaphysics. To the point of suggestions for further research, then, there can be many ways to improve sections and indeed even all of what I have laid out here. The same could be said about my proposed partially scripted liturgy. I fully expect it to be improved upon and even changed by other pentecostal thinkers. Yet, the simple act of putting much weight and focus on the formative power of our worship, hermeneutics, and speech to determine whether or not we are thinking and living faithfully in light of the glorious gospel is what I most hope to contribute to pentecostal first and second-level discourse. I hope it inspires pentecostal ministers and theologians by giving them a helpful model to do the same.

# BIBLIOGRAPHY

Albrecht, D. E., "Pentecostal Spirituality: Looking through the Lens of Ritual," *Pneuma* 14.2 (1996), pp. 107–25.

Albrecht, D. E., *Rites in the Spirit: A Ritual Approach to Pentecostal/Charismatic Spirituality* (JPTSup 17; Sheffield: Sheffield Academic Press, 1999).

Alexander, K. E., and John Christopher Thomas, "'And the Signs Are Following': Mark 16.9-20—A Journey into Pentecostal Hermeneutics," *JPT* 11.2 (April 2003), pp. 147–70.

Alexander, K. E., and John Christopher Thomas, "The Pentecostal Healing Community," in John Christopher Thomas (ed.), *Toward a Pentecostal Ecclesiology: The Church and the Five-fold Gospel* (Cleveland: CPT Press, 2010), pp. 183–206.

Alexander, K. E., and John Christopher Thomas, *Pentecostal Healing: Models in Theology and Practice*, JPTS 2 (Sheffield: Deo, 2006).

Althouse, P., "Ascension—Pentecost—Eschaton: A Theological Framework for Pentecostal Ecclesiology," in John Christopher Thomas (ed.), *Toward a Pentecostal Ecclesiology: The Church and the Fivefold Gospel* (Cleveland: CPT Press, 2010), pp. 225–47.

Althouse, P., "Pentecostal Eschatology in Context: The Eschatological Orientation of the Full Gospel," in Peter Althouse and Robby Waddell (eds), *Perspectives in Pentecostal Eschatologies: World Without End* (Eugene: Pickwick Publications, 2010), pp. 205–31.

Althouse, P., "The Landscape of Pentecostal and Charismatic Eschatology," in Peter Althouse and Robby Waddell (eds), *Perspectives in Pentecostal Eschatologies* (Eugene: Wipf and Stock, 2010), pp. 1–21.

Althouse, P., *Spirit of the Last Days: Pentecostal Eschatology in Conversation with Jürgen Moltmann* (New York: Bloomsbury Academic, 2003).

Althouse, P., "Towards a Pentecostal Ecclesiology: Participation in the Missional Life of the Triune God," in Chris E. W. Green (ed.), *Pentecostal Ecclesiology: A Reader* (Boston: Brill Academic Pub, 2016), pp. 88–103.

Anderson, A., *An Introduction to Pentecostalism: Global Charismatic Christianity* (Cambridge: Cambridge University Press, 2004).

Archer, K. J., *The Gospel Revisited* (Eugene, OR: Pickwick Publishing, 2011).

Archer, K. J., "Nourishment for Our Journey: The Pentecostal via Salutis and Sacramental Ordinances," in Chris E. W. Green (ed.), *Pentecostal Ecclesiology: A Reader* (Boston: Brill, 2016), pp. 144–60.

Archer, K. J., "Pentecostal Story: The Hermeneutical Filter for the Making of Meaning," in Ken Archer (ed.), *The Gospel Revisited: Towards a Pentecostal Theology of Worship and Witness* (Eugene: Pickwick Pub., 2011), pp. 18–42.

Armstrong, J. J., "Introduction," in Maximus the Confessor, *On the Ecclesiastical Mystagogy: A Theological Vision of the Liturgy* (Yonkers: SVS Press, 2019), pp. 13–45.

Astley, J., *Ordinary Theology: Looking, Listening and Learning in Theology* (Aldershot: Ashgate, 2002).

Athanasius, "On the Incarnation," in John Behr (ed.), *Popular Patristics Series 44b* (Yonkers: SVS Press, 2011).

Augustine, *De Trinitate* (Hyde Park: New City Press, 1991).
Augustine, D., "Creation as Perichoretic Trinitarian Conversation," in Stephen John Wright and Chris E. W. Green (eds), *The Promise of Robert Jenson's Theology: Constructive Engagements* (Minneapolis: Fortress Press, 2017), pp. 99–113.
Ayers, L., "Athanasius' Initial Defense of the Term ὁμοούσιος; re-reading the De Decretis," *JECS* 12 (2004b), pp. 337–59.
Baker, C. D., "Created Spirit Beings: Angels," in Stanley Horton (ed.), *Systematic Theology* (Springfield, MO: Logion Press, 1994), pp. 179–94.
Balthasar, H. U. V., *Cosmic Liturgy: The Universe According to Maximus the Confessor* (San Francisco: Ignatius Press, 2003).
Barrett, D. B., and T. M. Johnson, "Global Statistics," in S. M. Burgess and E. M. van der Mass (eds), *NIDPCM* (Grand Rapids: Zondervan, 2002), pp. 284–302.
Basil the Great, "Letter to Count Terentius," in Philip Schaff and Henry Wace (eds), *NPNF*, vol. 8 (Peabody: Hendrickson, 1994).
Behr, J., *Formation of Christian Theology Volume 2: The Nicene Faith Part 1* (Crestwood: SVS Press, 2004), pp. 117–22, 163–259.
Boersma, H., *Heavenly Participation: The Weaving of a Sacramental Tapestry* (Grand Rapids: Eerdmans, 2011).
Boersma, H., *Nouvelle Theologie & Sacramental Ontology: A Return to Mystery* (Oxford: OUP, 2009).
Bonhoeffer, D., *Dietrich Bonhoeffer Works*. Vol. 6, *Ethics* (Minneapolis: Fortress Press, 2005).
Boyd, G. A., *God at War: The Bible and Spiritual Conflict* (Downers Grove: IVP Academic, 1997).
Boyd, G. A., *Satan and the Problem of Evil: Constructing a Trinitarian Warfare Theodicy* (Downers Grove: IVP Academic, 2001).
Bradnick, D., *Evil, Spirits, and Possession: An Emergentist Theology of the Demonic* (Leiden: Brill, 2017).
Bradnick, D., and B. McCall, "Making Sense of Emergence: A Critical Engagement with Leidenhag, Leidenhag, and Yong," *Zygon* 53.1 (2018), pp. 240–57.
Bunge, M. A., *Causality: The Place of the Causal Principle in Modern Science* (Cambridge: Harvard University Press, 1959).
Burgess, S. M., "Introduction," in S. M Burgess and E. M. van der Maas (eds), *NIDPCM* (Grand Rapids: Zondervan, 2002), pp. xvii–xxiii.
Burtt, E. A., *The Metaphysical Foundations of Modern Science* (Kettering: Angelico Press, 2016).
Cartledge, M., "Pentecostal Healing as an Expression of Godly Love: An Empirical Study," *MHRC* 16.5 (2013), pp. 501–22.
Cartledge, M., *Practical Theology: Charismatic and Empirical Theology* (London: Paternoster, 2003).
Cartledge, M., *Testimony in the Spirit: Rescripting Ordinary Theology* (New York: Routledge, 2016).
Castelo, D., *Pneumatology: A Guide for the Perplexed* (London: Bloomsbury T&T Clark, 2015).
Castelo, D., *Revisioning Pentecostal Ethics—The Epicletic Community* (Cleveland: CPT Press, 2012).
Chan, S., *Liturgical Theology: The Church as Worshipping Community* (Downers Grove: IVP Academic, 2006).

Chan, S., *Pentecostal Theology and the Christian Spiritual Tradition* (JPTSup 21; Sheffield: Sheffield Academic Press, 2000).
Chan, S., *Spiritual Theology: A Systematic Study of the Christian Life* (Downers Grove: IVP Academic, 1994).
Clark, C. J., R. Lints, and J. K. A. Smith (eds), *101 Key Terms in Philosophy and Their Importance for Theology* (Louisville: WJK, 2004), pp. 51–2.
Clarke, W. N., "Causality and Time," in W. Norris Clarke (ed.), *The Creative Retrieval of St. Thomas Aquinas: Essays in Thomistic Philosophy, New and Old* (New York: Fordham University Press, 2009), pp. 27–38.
Clarke, W. N., "Fifty Years of Metaphysical Reflection: The Universe as Journey," in S. J. Gerald A. McCool (ed.), *The Universe as Journey: Conversations with W. Norris Clarke, S.J.* (New York: Fordham University Press, 1988), pp. 49–91.
Clarke, W. N., "The Limitation of Act by Potency in St. Thomas: Aristotelianism or Neoplatonism?," in W. Norris Clarke (ed.), *Explorations in Metaphysics* (Notre Dame: University of Notre Dame Press, 1994), pp. 65–88.
Clarke, W. N., "The Meaning of Participation in St. Thomas," in W. Norris Clarke (ed.), *Explorations in Metaphysics: Being-God-Person* (Notre Dame: University of Notre Dame Press, 1995), pp. 89–101.
Clarke, W. N., *The One and the Many: A Contemporary Thomistic Metaphysics* (Notre Dame: University of Notre Dame Press, 2001).
Clarke, W. N., *Person and Being* (Milwaukee: Marquette University Press, 2004).
Clayton, P., *Adventures in the Spirit: God, World, Divine Action* (Minneapolis: Fortress, 2008).
Clayton, P., "The Emergence of Spirit," *CTNS Bulletin* 20.4 (2000), pp. 3–20.
Clayton, P., *In Quest of Freedom: The Emergence of Spirit in the Natural World*, Religion Theologie and Naturwissenschaft/Religion Theology and Natural Science 13 (Gottingen: Vandenhoeck & Ruprecht, 2009).
Clayton, P., *Mind and Emergence: From Quantum to Consciousness* (Oxford: Oxford University Press, 2004).
Clayton, P., and P. Davies (eds), *The Re-emergence of Emergence: The Emergentist Hypothesis from Science to Religion* (Oxford: Oxford University Press, 2006).
Coakley, S., "Living into the Mystery of the Holy Trinity: Trinity, Prayer, and Sexuality," *ATR* 80 (1998), pp. 223–32.
Congar, Y., "The Reasons for the Unbelief of Our Time: A Theological Conclusion," Part I, *Integr* 2 (December 1938), pp. 13–21.
Dayton, D. W., *Theological Roots of Pentecostalism* (Grand Rapids: Baker Academic, 2011, 1987).
Del Colle, R., *Christ and the Spirit: Spirit-Christology in Trinitarian Perspective* (New York: Oxford University Press, 1994).
Diemer, J., *Nature and Miracle* (Toronto, Canada: Wedge Pub. Foundation, 1977).
Dionysius the Areopagite, "The Complete Works," in John Farina (ed.), *The Classics of Western Spirituality* (Mahwah: Paulist Press, 1987).
Dupre, L., *Passage to Modernity: An Essay in the Hermeneutics of Nature and Culture* (New Haven: Yale University Press, 1993).
Ellington, S. A., "'Can I Get a Witness?' The Myth of Pentecostal Orality and the Process of Traditioning in the Psalms," *JPT* 20 (2011), pp. 1–14.
Ellington, S. A., "The Reciprocal Reshaping of History and Experience in the Psalms: Interactions with Pentecostal Testimony," *JPT* 16.1 (October 2007), pp. 18–31.

Faupel, D. W., *The Everlasting Gospel: The Significance of Eschatology in the Development of Pentecostal Thought* (Sheffield: Sheffield Academic Press, 1996).
Feser, E., *Aquinas: A Beginner's Guide*. Oneworld Beginner's Guides (Oxford: Oneworld, 2009).
Feser, E., *Aristotle's Revenge: The Metaphysical Foundations of Physical and Biological Science* (Neunkirchen-Seelscheid: Editiones Scholasticae, 2019).
Frei, H., *The Eclipse of Biblical Narrative* (New Haven: Yale University Press, 1980).
Frestadius, S., "In Search of A 'Pentecostal' Epistemology: Comparing the Contributions of Amos Yong and James K.A. Smith," *Pneuma* 38 (2016), pp. 93–114.
Frestadius, S., *Pentecostal Rationality: Epistemology and Theological Hermeneutics in the Foursquare Tradition* (New York: T&T Clark, 2019).
Friesen, A., "Classical Pentecostal Liturgy: Between Formalism and Fanaticism," in Mark J. Cartledge and A. J. Swoboda (eds), *Scripting Pentecost: A Study of Pentecostals, Worship and Liturgy* (New York: Routledge, 2017), pp. 53–68.
Gabriel, A. K., "The Intensity of the Spirit in a Spirit-Filled World: Spirit Baptism, Subsequence, and the Spirit of Creation," *Pneuma* 34 (2012), pp. 365–82.
Gelpi, D. L., *The Gracing of Human Experience: Rethinking the Relationship between Nature and Grace* (Collegeville: Liturgical Press, 2001).
Gelpi, D. L., *The Turn to Experience in Contemporary Theology* (New York: Paulist, 1994).
Gelpi, D. L., *The Varieties of Transcendental Experience: A Study in Constructive Postmodernism* (Collegeville: Liturgical Press, 2000).
Gilson, É., *Being and Some Philosophers* (Toronto: PIMS, 1952).
Gilson, É., *The Christian Philosophy of St. Thomas Aquinas* (Notre Dame: Notre Dame Press, 1956).
Gilson, É., *History of Christian Philosophy in the Middle Ages* (Washington, DC: CUA Press, reprinted 2019).
Gilson, É., *Spirit of Medieval Philosophy* (New York: C. Scribner and Son, 1936).
Goff, J. R., *Fields White unto Harvest: Charles F. Parham and the Missionary Origins of Pentecostalism* (Fayetteville, AK: University of Arkansas Press, 1988).
Goodman, F. D., *How about Demons? Possession and Exorcism in the Modern World* (Bloomington: Indiana University Press, 1988).
Green, C. E. W., https://macrinamagazine.com/sermon/guest/2021/03/28/transfiguring-being/
Green, C. E. W., https://macrinamagazine.com/sermon/guest/2021/03/07/transfiguring-death/
Green, C. E. W., *All Things Beautiful: An Aesthetic Christology* (Waco: Baylor University Press, 2022).
Green, C. E. W., "The Altar and the Table: A Proposal for Wesleyan and Pentecostal Eucharistic Theologies," *Wesleyan Theological Journal* 53.2 (2018), pp. 54–61.
Green, C. E. W., "Breathing Underwater: Re-forming the Wesleyan Theology of Evil," forthcoming in *Wesley and Methodist Studies* 13.2 (2021).
Green, C. E. W., "From His Fullness We Have All Received: Reflections on Divine Agency, Time, and the Experience(s) of Salvation," in Lincoln Harvey (ed.), *Essays on the Trinity* (Eugene: Cascade Books, 2018), pp. 125–39.
Green, C. E. W., *The End Is Music: A Companion to Robert W. Jenson's Theology* (Eugene: Cascade Books, 2018).
Green, C. E. W., "'In His Presence Is Fullness of Joy' Experiencing God as Trinity," in Lee Roy Martin (ed.), *Toward a Pentecostal Theology of Worship* (Cleveland: CPT Press, 2020), pp. 237–49.

Green, C. E. W., "'In My Flesh I Shall See God': (Re)Imagining Parousia, Last Judgment, and Visio Dei," *JEPTA* 33.2 (2013), pp. 176–95.

Green, C. E. W., "Saving Liturgy: (Re)imagining Pentecostal Liturgical Theology and Practice," in Mark J. Cartledge and A. J. Swoboda (eds), *Scripting Pentecost: A Study of Pentecostals, Worship and Liturgy* (New York: Routledge, 2017), p. 109.

Green, C. E. W., *Surprised by God: How and Why What We Think about the Divine Matters* (Eugene: Cascade Books, 2018).

Green, C. E. W., "'Then Their Eyes Were Opened' Pentecostal Reflections on the Church's Scripture and the Lord's Supper," in Chris Green (ed.), *Pentecostal Ecclesiology: A Reader* (Leiden: Brill, 2016), pp. 196–210.

Green, C. E. W., *Toward a Pentecostal Theology of the Lord's Supper: Foretasting the Kingdom* (Cleveland: CPT Press, 2012).

Gregory of Nazianzus, *Oration* 34 in Philip Schaff and Henry Wace (eds), *NPNF* vol. 7 (Peabody: Hendrickson, 1994).

Gregory of Nyssa, "Against Eunomius," in Philip Schaff and Henry Wace (eds), *NPNF*, vol. 5 (Peabody: Hendrickson, 1994).

Gregory of Nyssa, "On 'Not Three Gods' to Ablabius," in Philip Schaff and Henry Wace (eds), *NPNF*, vol. 5 (Peabody: Hendrickson, 1994).

Guthrie, S. L., *Gods of This World: A Philosophical Discussion and Defense of Christian Demonology* (Eugene: Pickwick, 2018).

Gwynn, D. M., *The Eusebians: The Polemic of Athanasius of Alexandria and the Construction of the "Arian Controversy"* (Oxford: Oxford University Press, 2007).

Harrison, J. E., *Prolegomena to the Study of Greek Religion* (Cambridge: Cambridge University Press, 1903).

Hart, D. B., *The Beauty of the Infinite: The Aesthetics of Christian Truth* (Grand Rapids: Eerdmans, 2003).

Hart, D. B., *The Experience of God: Being, Consciousness, Bliss* (New Haven: Yale University Press, 2013).

Hart, D. B., "Providence and Causality: On Divine Innocence," in Francesca Aran Murphy and Philip G. Ziegler (eds), *The Providence of God* (London: T&T Clark, 2009), pp. 34–56.

Hart, D. B., "Remarks Made to Jean-Luc Marion Regarding Revelation and Givenness," in David Bentley Hart (ed.), *Theological Territories: A David Bentley Hart Digest* (Notre Dame: University of Notre Dame Press, 2020), pp. 26–44.

Hart, D. B., "Science and Theology: Where the Consonance Really Lies," *Renovatio* 2.1 (2018), pp. 13–24.

Hart, D. B., *That All Shall Be Saved: Heaven, Hell, and Universal Salvation* (New Haven: Yale University Press, 2019).

Harvey, L., "Introduction," in Lincoln Harvey (ed.), *Essays on the Trinity* (Eugene: Cascade Books, 2018), pp. 1–13.

Hauerwas, S., *Hannah's Child: A Theologian's Memoir* (Cambridge: Eerdmans, 2010).

Hauerwas, S., *The Peaceable Kingdom* (Notre Dame: University of Notre Dame Press, 1983).

Hauerwas, S., and W. H. Willimon, "Embarrassed by God's Presence," *The Christian Century* 102.4 (January 30, 1985), pp. 98–100.

Hauerwas, S., and W. H. Willimon, *The Holy Spirit* (Nashville: Abingdon Press, 2015).

Hector, K., *Theology without Metaphysics: God, Language, and the Spirit of Recognition* (Current Issues in Theology; New York: Cambridge University Press, 2011).

Hejzlar, P., *Two Paradigms for Divine Healing: Fred F. Bosworth, Kenneth E. Hagin, Agnes Sanford, and Francis MacNutt in Dialogue* (Leiden: Brill, 2010).
Heidegger, M., *Identity and Difference*, trans. Joan Stambaugh (Chicago: University of Chicago Press, 2002).
Heidegger, M., *Introduction to Metaphysics*, 2nd ed., trans. Gregory Fried and Richard F. H. Polt (New Haven: Yale University Press, 2014).
Hodgson, L., *The Doctrine of the Trinity* (New York: Scribner's, 1944).
Hollenweger, W. J., *The Pentecostals* (Peabody: Hendrickson, 1988).
Hollenweger, W. J., *The Pentecostals: The Charismatic Movement in the Churches* (Minneapolis: Augsburg, 1972).
Hume, D., *An Enquiry Concerning Human Understanding*, ed. Eric Steinberg (Cambridge: Hackett Publishing Company, 1977).
Hume, D., *Treatise of Human Nature*, ed. David Fate Norton and Mary J. Norton (Oxford: Oxford University Press, 2000).
Irenaeus, "Against Heresies," in Alexander Roberts and James Donaldson (eds), *ANF*, vol. 1 (Peabody: Hendrickson, 1994).
Irenaeus, "On the Apostolic Preaching," in John Behr (ed.), Popular Patristic Series 17, trans, John Behr (Yonkers: SVS Press, 1997).
Jacobsen, D. G., *Thinking in the Spirit: Theologies of the Early Pentecostal Movement* (Bloomington: Indiana University Press, 2003).
Jaeger, W., *The Theology of Early Greek Philosophers* (Oxford: Clarendon Press, 1947).
Jenson, R. W., "Cosmic Spirit," in Carl E. Braaten and Robert W. Jenson (eds), *Christian Dogmatics: Volume Two* (Minneapolis: Fortress Press, 2011), pp. 165–78.
Jenson, R. W., "Creation as a Triune Act," *Word & World* 2.1 (1982), pp. 34–42.
Jenson, R. W., "The Nicene-Constantinopolitan Dogma," in Carl Braaten and Robert W. Jenson (eds), *Christian Dogmatics: Volume One* (Minneapolis: Fortress Press, 2011), pp. 115–35.
Jenson, R. W., "A Reply," in S. J. Wright (ed.), *Theology as Revisionary Metaphysics: Essays on God and Creation* (Eugene: Cascade Books, 2014), p. 3.
Jenson, R. W., *Systematic Theology*, 2 vols (New York: Oxford University Press, 1997–9).
Jenson, R. W., *The Triune Identity: God According to the Gospel* (Philadelphia: Fortress Press, 1982).
Jenson, R. W., *Visible Words: The Interpretation and Practice of Christian Sacraments* (Minneapolis: Fortress Press, 2010).
Jenson, R. W., "What if It Were True," in Stephen John Wright (ed.), *Theology as Revisionary Metaphysics: Essays on God and Creation* (Eugene: Cascade Books, 2014), pp. 23–37.
John of Damascus, "Expositio Fidei," in Philip Schaff and Henry Wace (eds), *NPNF*, vol. 9 (Peabody: Hendrickson, 1994).
Johns, C. B., *Pentecostal Formation: A Pedagogy among the Oppressed* (Sheffield, UK: Sheffield Academic Press, 1993).
Johns, C. B., and J. Johns, "Yielding to the Spirit: A Pentecostal Approach to Group Bible Study," *JPT* 1 (1992), pp. 109–34.
Jordan, M. D., *The Alleged Aristotelianism of Thomas Aquinas* (Toronto: PIMS, 1992).
Kant, I., *Critique of Pure Reason*, 2nd ed., trans. Norman Kemp Smith (London: Macmillan,1929).
Kant, I., *Lectures on Philosophical Theology*, trans. Allen W. Wood and Gertrude M. Clark (Ithaca: Cornell University Press, 1986).
Kärkkäinen, V. M., "Epistemology, Ethos and Environment: In Search of a Theology of Pentecostal Education," *Pneuma* 34.2 (2012), pp. 248–50.

Kärkkäinen, V. M., "Spirit(s) in Contemporary Christian Theology: An Interim Report of the Unbinding of Pneumatology," in Veli-Matti Kärkkäinen, Kirsteen Kim and Amos Yong (eds), *Interdisciplinary and Religio-cultural Discourses on a Spirit-Filled World: Loosing the Spirits* (New York: Palgrave Macmillan US, 2013), pp. 29–40.

Kärkkäinen, V. M., Kirsteen Kim, and Amos Yong (eds), *Interdisciplinary and Religio-cultural Discourses on a Spirit-Filled World* (New York: Palgrave Macmillan US, 2013).

Kay, W. K., *Pentecostalism: A Very Short Introduction* (Oxford: Oxford University Press, 2011).

Kelly, J. N. D., *Early Christian Creeds*, 3rd ed. (London: Continuum, 2006).

Kerr, F., *After Aquinas: Versions of Thomism* (Oxford: Blackwell, 2002).

Klaus, B., "The Holy Spirit and Mission Is Eschatological Perspective: A Pentecostal Viewpoint," *Pneuma* 27.2 (2005), pp. 322–42.

Keener, C. S., *Miracles: The Credibility of the New Testament Accounts*, 2 vols (Grand Rapids: Baker Academic, 2011).

Kraft, C., "Spiritual Warfare: A Neocharismatic Perspective," in Stanley M. Burgess and Eduard M. van der Mass (eds), *The New International Dictionary of Pentecostal Charismatic Movements* (Grand Rapids: Zondervan, 2002), pp. 1091–6.

Kreeft, P. J., *Angels and Demons: What Do We Really Know about Them?* (San Francisco: Ignatius Press, 1995).

Kreeft, P. J., *Socrates' Children: The 100 Greatest Philosophers*, vol. 1, *Ancient Philosophers* (South Bend: St. Augustine's Press, 2019).

Kuzmic, K., "To the Ground of Being and Beyond: Toward a Pentecostal Engagement with Ontology," in Nimi Wariboko and Amos Yong (eds), *Paul Tillich and Pentecostal Theology* (Bloomington: Indiana University Press, 2015), pp. 45–57.

Land, S. J., *Pentecostal Spirituality: A Passion for the Kingdom* (Cleveland: CPT Press, 2010).

Levering, M., *Proofs of God: Classical Arguments from Tertullian to Barth* (Grand Rapids: Baker Academic, 2016).

Levering, M., *Scripture and Metaphysics: Aquinas and the Renewal of Trinitarian Theology* (Malden: Blackwell Publishing, 2004).

Lewis, C. S., *The Discarded Image* (Cambridge: Cambridge University Press, 2013).

Lewis, P. W., "Towards a Pentecostal Epistemology," *The Spirit & Church* 2.1 (May 2000), pp. 95–125.

Lindbeck, G. A., *The Nature of Doctrine: Religion and Theology in a Postliberal Age* (Philadelphia: Westminster Press, 1984).

Lindhardt, M. (ed.), *Pentecostalism in Africa: Presence and Impact of Pneumatic Christianity in Postcolonial Societies* (Leiden: Brill, 2014).

Lonergan, B., *Grace and Freedom: Operative Grace in the Thought of St. Thomas Aquinas* (Toronto: University of Toronto Press, 2000).

Lossky, V., *The Mystical Theology of the Eastern Church* (Crestwood: SVS Press, 1976).

Ma, J., "Eschatology and Mission: Living in the 'Last Days' Today," *Transformation* 26.3 (2009), pp. 186–98.

MacIntyre, A., "Ontology," in Paul Edwards (ed.), *The Encyclopedia of Philosophy: Volumes 5 and 6* (New York: Macmillan Publishing), pp. 542–3.

Macchia, F. D., *Baptized in the Spirit: A Global Pentecostal Theology* (Grand Rapids: Zondervan, 2006).

Marion, J., *God without Being: Hors-texte*, 2nd ed., trans. Thomas A. Carlson and David Tracy. Religion and Postmodernism (Chicago: The University of Chicago Press, 2012).

Marostica, M., "Learning from the Master: Carlos Annacondia and the Standardization of Pentecostal Practices in and beyond Argentina," in Gunther Brown (ed.), *Global Pentecostal and Charismatic Healing* (Oxford: Oxford University Press, 2011), pp. 207–27.

Martin, L. R., *The Spirit of the Psalms: Rhetorical Analysis, Affectivity, and Pentecostal Spirituality* (Cleveland: CPT Press, 2018).

Martin, L. R., *The Unheard Voice of God: A Pentecostal Hearing of the Book of Judges* (JPTSup 32; Blandford Forum: Deo Publishing, 2008).

Mascall, E. L., *Existence and Analogy* (London: Longmans, 1949).

Maximus the Confessor, *Ambigua: On Difficulties in the Church Fathers*, ed. and trans. Nicholas Constas, Dumbarton Oaks Medieval Library (Cambridge: Harvard University Press, 2014).

Maximus the Confessor, *Questiones ad Thalassium* in C. Laga and C. Steel. CCG 7 Q.1–55 (1990).

Maximus the Confessor, *On the Ecclesiastical Mystagogy: A Theological Vision of the Liturgy*, in John Behr (ed.), Popular Patristic Series 59, trans. Jonathan J. Armstrong (Yonkers: SVS Press, 2019).

May, J. D., *Global Witnesses to Pentecost: The Testimony of "Other Tongues"* (Cleveland: CPT Press, 2013).

Mays, J. L., *Interpretation: A Bible Commentary for Teaching Preaching, Psalms* (Louisville: Westminster John Knox Press, 1994).

McClymond, M. J., "Charismatic Renewal and Neo-Pentecostalism: From North American Origins to Global Permutations," in Cecil M. Robeck Jr. and Amos Yong (eds), *The Cambridge Companion to Pentecostalism* (New York: Cambridge University Press, 2014), pp. 31–51.

McFarland, I. A., *The Word Made Flesh: A Theology of the Incarnation* (Louisville: Westminster John Knox Press, 2019).

McInerny, R., "Saint Thomas on De Hebdomadibus," in Scott MacDonald (ed.), *Being and Goodness: The Concept of the Good in Metaphysics and Philosophical Theology* (Ithaca and London: Cornell University Press, 2001), pp. 74–97.

McQueen, L., *Toward a Pentecostal Eschatology: Discerning the Way Forward* (Sheffield: Deo Publishing, 2012).

Menzies, R. P., *Speaking in Tongues: Jesus and the Apostolic Church as Models for the Church Today* (Cleveland: CPT Press, 2016).

Milbank, J., "The Programme of Radical Orthodoxy," in Laurence Paul Hemming (ed.), *Radical Orthodoxy?: A Catholic Enquiry* (New York: Routledge, 2017), pp. 33–45.

Milbank, J., *Theology and Social Theory: Beyond Secular Reason* (Oxford: Blackwell Pub., 2006).

Milbank, J., *The World Made Strange: Theology, Language, Culture* (Oxford: Blackwell, 1997).

Milbank, J., G. Ward, and C. Pickstock, "Suspending the Material: The Turn of Radical Orthodoxy," in John Milbank, Graham Ward, and Catherine Pickstock (eds), *Radical Orthodoxy: A New Theology* (London: Routledge, 1999), pp. 1–20.

Moore, R. D., *The Spirit of the Old Testament* (JPTSup 35; Blandford Forum: Deo, 2011).

Moore, R. D., J. C. Thomas, and S. J. Land, "Editorial," *JPT* 1 (1992), pp. 1–18.

Murphy, N., *Anglo-American Postmodernity: Philosophical Perspectives on Science, Religion, and Ethics* (Boulder: Westview Press, 1997).

Murphy, N., "Nonreductive Physicalism: Philosophical Issues," in Warren S. Brown, Nancey Murphey, and H. Newton Malony (eds), *Whatever Happened to the Soul?*

*Scientific and Theological Portraits of Human Nature* (Minneapolis: Fortress, 1998), pp. 127-48.

Murphy, N., "Supervenience and the Nonreduciblity of Ethics to Biology," in Robert John Russell, William R. Stoeger, S.J., and Francisco J. Ayala (eds), *Evolutionary and Molecular Biology: Scientific Perspectives on Divine Action* (Vatican City State: Vatican Observatory Publications; Berkeley: Center for Theology and the Natural Sciences, 1998), pp. 463-89.

Murphy, N., and George F. R. Ellis, *On the Moral Nature of the Universe: Theology, Cosmology, and Ethics* (Minneapolis: Fortress, 1996).

Newbigin, L., *The Open Secret: An Introduction to the Theology of Mission* (Grand Rapids: Eerdmans, 1995).

Nichols, D. R., "The Search for Pentecostal Structure in Systematic Theology," *Pneuma* 6.2 (Fall 1984), pp. 57-76.

Nilsson, M. P., *A History of Greek Religion*, trans, F. J. Fielden (Oxford: Clarendon Press, 1925).

Noll, S., *Angels of Light, Powers of Darkness: Thinking Biblically about Angels, Satan, and Principalities* (Downers Grove: Wipf & Stock Pub, 2003).

Origen, "On First Principles," 2 vols, in John Behr (ed.), *Oxford Early Christian Texts* (Oxford: OUP, 2017).

Owens, J., *An Elementary Christian Metaphysics* (Notre Dame: University of Notre Dame Press, 1963).

Owens, J., *The Doctrine of Being in Aristotelian Metaphysics: A Study in the Greek Background of Mediaeval Thought* (Toronto: PIMS, 1951).

Owens, J., "The Relation of God to the World in the Metaphysics," in Pierre Aubenque (ed.), *Études sur la Metaphysique d'Aristote* (Paris: J. Vrin, 1979), pp. 208-28.

Pabst, A., *Metaphysics: The Creation of Hierarchy* (Grand Rapids: W.B. Eerdmans Publishing Company, 2012).

Padgett, A., *God, Eternity, and the Nature of Time* (Eugene: Wipf and Stick, 2000), pp. 38-54.

Parker, S., *Led by the Spirit* (Sheffield: Sheffield Academic Press, 1996).

Parry, R., *Worshipping Trinity: Coming Back to the Heart of Worship* (Milton Keynes: Paternoster, 2007).

Pelikan, J., *The Christian Tradition: A History of the Development of Doctrine*, vol. 1 (Chicago: University of Chicago Press, 1971).

Pickstock, C., *After Writing: On the Liturgical Consummation of Philosophy* (Malden: Blackwell Publishers, 1998).

Pickstock, C., *Aspects of Truth: A New Religious Metaphysics* (Cambridge: Cambridge University Press, 2020).

Pickstock, C., "Duns Scotus: His Historical and Contemporary Significance," in John Milbank and Simon Oliver (eds), *The Radical Orthodoxy Reader* (New York: Routledge, 2009), pp. 116-48.

Polkinghorne, J., *Science and the Trinity: The Christian Encounter with Reality* (New Haven: Yale University Press, 2002).

Przywara, E., *Analogia Entis: Metaphysics* (Grand Rapids: W.B. Eerdmans Publishing Company, 2014).

Purdy, V. L., "Divine Healing," in Stanley Horton (ed.), *Systematic Theology* (Springfield: Logion Press, 1995), pp. 489-523.

Rahner, K., *Foundations of Christian Faith: An Introduction to the Idea of Christianity* (New York: The Seabury Press, 1978).

Rahner, K., *The Trinity* (New York: The Crossroad Publishing Company, 1997).
Robeck, C. M. Jr., "The Origins of Modern Pentecostalism," in Cecil M. Robeck Jr. and Amos Yong (eds), *The Cambridge Companion to Pentecostalism* (New York: Cambridge University Press, 2014), pp. 18–23.
Robeck, C. M. Jr., and A. Yong (eds), *The Cambridge Companion to Pentecostalism* (New York: Cambridge University Press, 2014).
Rogers, E. F., *After the Spirit: A Constructive Pneumatology from Resources Outside the Modern West* (Grand Rapids: Eerdmans, 2005).
Samuel, J. P. S., *The Holy Spirit in Worship Music, Preaching, and the Altar* (Cleveland: CPT Press, 2018).
Soulen, R. K., *The God of Israel and Christian Theology* (Minneapolis: Augsburg Fortress Press, 1996).
Schafroth, V., "An Exegetical Exploration of 'Spirit' References in Ezekiel 36 and 37," *JEPTA* 29.2 (2009), p. 71.
Schloss, J., "Hovering over Waters: Spirit and the Ordering of Creation," in Michael Welker (ed.), *The Spirit in Creation and New Creation: Science and Theology in Western Orthodox Realms* (Grand Rapids: Eerdmans, 2012), pp. 26–49.
Schmemann, A., "Problems of Orthodoxy in America: The Canonical Problem," *St. Vladimir's Seminary Quarterly* 8.2 (1964), pp. 67–85.
Scott, I., *Paul's Way of Knowing: Story, Experience, and Spirit* (Grand Rapids: Baker Academic, 2006).
Smith, J. K. A., *Awaiting the King: Reforming Public Theology* (Grand Rapids: Baker Academic, 2017).
Smith, J. K. A., *Desiring the Kingdom: Worship, Worldview, and Cultural Formation* (Grand Rapids: Baker Academic, 2009).
Smith, J. K. A., *Imagining the Kingdom: How Worship Works Cultural Liturgies* (Grand Rapids: Baker Academic, 2013).
Smith, J. K. A., *Introducing Radical Orthodoxy: Mapping a Post-Secular Theology* (Grand Rapids: Baker Academic, 2004).
Smith, J. K. A., "Is There Room for Surprise in the Natural World?," in James K. A. Smith and Amos Yong (eds), *Science and the Spirit: A Pentecostal Engagement with the Sciences* (Bloomington: Indiana University Press, 2010), pp. 34–49.
Smith, J. K. A., "Pentecostalism: Epistemic Fit and Pentecostal Experience," in William J. Abraham and Frederick D. Aquino (eds), *The Oxford Handbook of The Epistemology of Theology* (Oxford: Oxford University Press, 2017), pp. 606–18.
Smith, J. K. A., *Radical Orthodoxy and the Reformed Tradition* (Grand Rapids: Baker Academic, 2005).
Smith, J. K. A., "The Spirit, Religions, and the World as Sacrament: A Response to Amos Yong's Pneumatological Assist," *JPT* 15 (2007), pp. 251–61.
Smith, J. K. A., *Thinking in Tongues: Pentecostal Contributions to Christian Philosophy* (Grand Rapids: Eerdmans, 2010).
Smith, J. K. A., "What Hath Cambridge to Do with Azusa Street? Radical Orthodoxy and Pentecostal Theology in Conversation," *Pneuma* 25.1 (Spring 2003), pp. 97–114.
Smith, J. K. A., "What's Right with the Prosperity Gospel," *Calvin Theological Seminary Forum* 13.3 (Fall 2009).
Smith, J. K. A., *Who's Afraid of Postmodernism? Taking Derrida, Lyotard, and Foucault to Church* (Grand Rapids: Baker Academic, 2006).

Smith, J. K. A., *Who's Afraid of Relativism? Community, Contingency, and Creaturehood* (Grand Rapids: Baker Academic, 2014).

Smith, J. K. A., "Will the Real Plato Please Stand Up: Participation versus Incarnation," in James K. A. Smith and James H. Olthius (eds), *Radical Orthodoxy and the Reformed Tradition* (Grand Rapids: Baker Academic, 2005), pp. 61–72.

Smith, J. K. A., and A. Yong (eds), *Science and the Spirit: A Pentecostal Engagement with the Sciences* (Bloomington: Indiana University Press, 2010).

Soulen, R. K., *The God of Israel and Christian Theology* (Minneapolis: Augsburg Fortress Press, 1996).

Stephenson, C. A., "Reality, Knowledge, and Life in Community: Metaphysics, Epistemology, and Hermeneutics in the Work of Amos Yong," in Wolfgang Vondey and Martin William Mittelstadt (eds), *The Theology of Amos Yong And the New Face of Pentecostal Scholarship* (Leiden: Brill, 2013), pp. 63–81.

Stronstad, R., *The Prophethood of All Believers: A Study in Luke's Charismatic Theology* (Cleveland: CPT, 2010).

Synan, V., *Aspects of Pentecostal-Charismatic Origins* (Plainfield: Logos International, 1975).

Thomas, Aquinas, *Commentary on the Gospel of John*, in The Aquinas Institute (eds), trans. Fr. Fabian R. Larcher, O.P. (Lander: The Aquinas Institute for the Study of Sacred Doctrine, 2013).

Thomas, Aquinas, "On Being and Essence," in Ralph McInerny (ed.), *Thomas Aquinas: Selected Writings* (New York: Penguin Books, 1998).

Thomas, Aquinas, "Sententia de Caelo et mundo," in Fabian R. Larcher and Pierre H. Conway (eds), *Exposition of Aristotle's Treatise on the Heavens*, 2 vols (Columbus: College of St. Mary of the Springs, 1964).

Thomas, Aquinas, "Summa Theologiae," in the Fathers of the English Dominican Province (eds), *The Summa Theologica*, 5 vols (Notre Dame, IN: Christian Classics, 1981).

Thomas, J. C., *Devil, Disease, and Deliverance: Origins of Illness in New Testament Thought* (Cleveland: CPT Press, 2011).

Thomas, J. C., *He Loved Them until the End: The Farewell Materials in the Gospel According to John* (Cleveland: CPT Press, 2015), p. 35.

Thomas, J. C., "Pentecostal Theology in the Twenty-First Century," *Pneuma* 20.1 (1998), pp. 3–19.

Thomas, J. C., *The Apocalypse: A Literary and Theological Commentary* (Cleveland: CPT Press, 2012).

Thomas, J. C., "Toward a Pentecostal Theology of Anointed Cloths," in Lee Roy Martin (ed.), *Toward a Pentecostal Theology of Worship* (Cleveland: CPT Press, 2016), pp. 89–112.

Thomas, J. C., and F. D. Macchia, *Revelation: The Two Horizons New Testament Commentary* (Grand Rapids: Eerdmans, 2016).

Thompson, M. K., *Kingdom Come: Revisioning Pentecostal Eschatology* (Blandford Forum: Deo, 2010).

Tilling, C., "Paul the Trinitarian," in Lincoln Harvey (ed.), *Essays on the Trinity* (Eugene: Cascade Books, 2018), pp. 36–62.

Tilling, C., *Paul's Divine Christology* (Grand Rapids: Eerdmans, 2012).

Triffett, B. P., "*Processio* and the Place of Ontic Being: John Milbank and James K. A. Smith on Participation," *The Heythrop Journal* 57 (2016), pp. 900–16.

Velde, R. A., *Participation and Substantiality in Thomas Aquinas* (Leiden: Brill, 1995).

Volf, M., *After Our Likeness: The Church in the Image of the Trinity* (Grand Rapids: Eerdmans, 1998).
Vondey, W., "A Passion for the Spirit: Amos Yong and the Theology and Science Dialogue," In Wolfgang Vondey and Martin William Mittelstadt (eds), *The Theology of Amos Yong and the New Face of Pentecostal Scholarship: Passion for the Spirit* (Leiden: Brill, 2013), pp. 179–97.
Vondey, W., *Beyond Pentecostalism: The Crisis of Global Christianity and the Renewal of the Theological Agenda* (Grand Rapids: William B. Eerdmans Publishing Company, 2010).
Vondey, W., *Pentecostalism: A Guide for the Perplexed* (London: T&T Clark, 2012).
Vondey, W., "Pentecostalism and the Possibility of Global Theology: Implications of the Theology of Amos Yong," *Pneuma* 28.2 (2006), pp. 297–8.
Vondey, W., *Pentecostal Theology: Living the Full Gospel* (London: Bloomsbury T&T Clark, 2017).
Vondey, W., "Religion at Play," *Pneuma* 40 (2018), pp. 17–36.
Vondey, W., "The Theology of the Altar and Pentecostal Sacramentality," in Mark J. Cartledge and A. J. Swoboda (eds), *Scripting Pentecost: A Study of Pentecostals, Worship and Liturgy* (Aldershot, UK: Ashgate, 2016), pp. 94–107.
Vondey, W., and M. W Mittelstadt, "Introduction," in Wolfgang Vondey and Martin Mittelstadt (eds), *The Theology of Amos Yong and the New Face of Pentecostal Scholarship: Passion for the Spirit* (Leiden: Brill, 2013), pp. 1–24.
Wagner, C. P., "New Apostolic Reformation," in S. M. Burgess and E. M. van der Mass (eds), *NIDPCM* (Grand Rapids: Zondervan, 2002), pp. 928–30.
Wariboko, N., *The Pentecostal Principle: Ethical Methodology in New Spirit* (Grand Rapids: Eerdmans, 2012).
Wariboko, N., *The Split God: Pentecostalism and Critical Theory* (Albany: SUNY Press, 2018).
Weiss, P., *Modes of Being* (Carbondale: Southern Illinois University Press, 1958).
Weiss, P., *Nature and Man* (Charleston: Nabu Press, 2011).
Widdicombe, P., *The Fatherhood of God from Origen to Athanasius* (Oxford: Oxford University Press, 1994).
Wilkie, J. S., "The Problem of the Temporal Relation of Cause and Effect," *British Journal for the Philosophy of Science* I (1950), pp. 211–29.
Williams, R., "The Authority of the Church," *Modern Believing* 46.1 (2005), pp. 16–28.
Williams, R., *Christ the Heart of Creation* (London: Bloomsbury, 2018).
Williams, R., "The Deflections of Desire: Negative Theology in Trinitarian Closure," in Oliver Davies and Denys Turner (eds), *Silence and the Word: Negative Theology and Incarnation* (Cambridge: Cambridge University Press, 2002), pp. 115–35.
Williams, R., *The Edge of Words: God and the Habits of Language* (London: Bloomsbury Press, 2014).
Wink, W., *Engaging the Powers: Discernment and Resistance in a World of Domination* (Minneapolis: Fortress, 1992).
Wink, W., *Naming the Powers: The Language of Powers in the New Testament* (Philadelphia: Fortress, 1984).
Wink, W., *Unmasking the Powers: The Invisible Forces That Determine Human Existence* (Philadelphia: Fortress, 1986).
Wippel, J. F., *The Metaphysical Thought of Thomas Aquinas: From Finite Being to Uncreated Being* (Washington: CUA Press, 2000).
Wright, N. T., *Colossians and Philemon* (Downers Grove: IVP Academic, 1986).
Wright, N. T., *Evil and the Justice of God* (Downers Grove: IVP, 2006).

Wright, N. T., *Surprised by Hope: Rethinking Heaven, the Resurrection, and the Mission of the Church* (New York: Harper One, 2008).
Wright, S. J., *Dogmatic Aesthetics: A Theology of Beauty in Dialogue with Robert W. Jenson* (Minneapolis: Fortress Press, 2014).
Wright, S. J., "Introduction," in Stephen John Wright (ed.), *Theology as Revisionary Metaphysics: Essays on God and Creation* (Eugene: Wipf and Stock Publishers, 2014), pp. ix–xiii.
Wood, J. D., *That Creation Is Incarnation in Maximus Confessor* (PhD thesis, Boston University, 2018).
Work, T., "Charismatic and Pentecostal Worship", in Geoffrey Wainwright and Karen B. Westerfield (eds), *The Oxford History of Christian Worship* (Oxford: Oxford University Press, 2006), pp. 574–85.
Yong, A., *Beyond the Impasse: Toward a Pneumatological Theology of Religions* (Eugene: Wipf & Stock, 2014).
Yong, A., *Discerning the Spirit(s): A Pentecostal-Charismatic Contribution to Christian Theology of Religions* (Sheffield: Sheffield Academic Press, 2000).
Yong, A., "The Demise of Foundationalism and the Retention of Truth: What Evangelicals Can Learn from C.S. Peirce," *Christian Scholar's Review* 29.4 (2000), pp. 563–88.
Yong, A., "Going Where the Spirit Goes: Engaging the Spirit(s) in J.C. Ma's Pneumatological Missiology," *JPT* 10.2 (2002), pp. 110–28.
Yong, A., *Hospitality and the Other: Pentecost, Christian Practices, and the Neighbor* (Maryknoll: Orbis Books, 2008).
Yong, A., "How Does God Do What God Does? Pentecostal-Charismatic Perspectives on Divine Action in Dialogue with Modern Science," in J. K. A. Smith and Amos Yong (eds), *Science and the Spirit: A Pentecostal Engagement with the Sciences* (Bloomington: Indiana University Press, 2010), pp. 50–74.
Yong, A., "In Search of Foundations: The Oeuvre of Donald L. Gelpi, SJ, and Its Significance for Pentecostal Theology and Philosophy," *JPT* 11.1 (2002), pp. 3–26.
Yong, A., "Natural Laws and Divine Intervention: What Difference Does Being Pentecostal or Charismatic Make?" *Zygon* 43.4 (December 2008), pp. 974–81.
Yong, A., "On Divine Presence and Divine Agency: Toward a Foundational Pneumatology," *AJPS* 3.2 (2000), pp. 167–88.
Yong, A., "Oneness and Trinity: The Theological and Ecumenical Implication of Creation Ex Nihilo for an Intra-Pentecostal Dispute," *Pneuma* 19.1 (1997), pp. 81–107.
Yong, A., *Pneumatology and the Christian-Buddhist Dialogue: Does the Spirit Blow through the Middle Way?* (Leiden: Brill, 2012).
Yong, A., "Radically Orthodox, Reformed, and Pentecostal: Rethinking the Intersection of Post/modernity and the Religions in Conversation with James K.A. Smith," *JPT* 15 (2007), pp. 233–50.
Yong, A., *Renewing Christian Theology: Systematics for a Global Christianity* (Waco: Baylor University Press, 2014).
Yong, A., "Ruach, the Primordial Waters, and the Breath of Life: Emergence Theory and the Creation Narratives in Pneumatological Perspective," in Michael Welker (ed.), *The Work of the Spirit: Pneumatology and Pentecostalism* (Grand Rapids: Eerdmans, 2006), pp. 183–204.
Yong, A., *Spirit-word-community: Theological Hermeneutics in Trinitarian Perspective* (Eugene, OR: Wipf & Stock, 2002).
Yong, A., *The Cosmic Breath: Spirit and Nature in the Christianity-buddhism-science Trialogue* (Leiden: Brill, 2012).

Yong, A., *The Spirit of Creation: Modern Science and Divine Action in the Pentecostal Imagination* (Grand Rapids: Eerdmans, 2011).

Yong, A., *The Spirit Poured Out on All Flesh: Pentecostalism and the Possibility of Global Theology* (Grand Rapids: Baker Academic, 2005).

Yong, A., "The Spirit, Vocation, and the Life of the Mind: A Pentecostal Testimony," in Steven M. Fettke and Robby Waddell (eds), *Pentecostals in the Academy: Testimonies of Call* (Cleveland: CPT Press, 2012), pp. 203–20.

Yong, A. (ed.), *The Spirit Renews the Face of the Earth: Pentecostal Forays in Science and Theology of Creation* (Eugene: Pickwick Publications, 2009).

Young, F. M., *From Nicaea to Chalcedon: A Guide to the Literature and Its Background*, 2nd ed. (Grand Rapids: Baker Academic, 2010).

# INDEX

act and potency 29, 101, 127 n.168, 128, 134 n.191, 137 n.204, 141
affections 6, 14, 19–21, 33, 58, 62, 148, 166–9, 174, 186 n.28
Albrecht, Daniel 3, 61 n.7, 62–7, 70, 74 n.2, 76 n.5, 174
altar 21, 64 n.12, 64–7, 76 n.5, 77, 78 n.7, 79, 80 n.14, 81 n.19, 82, 118, 176, 182, 186
angels, *see* personhood, angelic
anointing 65, 97, 126, 164–5, 184 n.26
Aquinas, Thomas 8 n.15, 14 n.3, 88, 95 n.62, 112, 115–17, 119, 120, 123 n.155, 127–31, 134–9, 161
Archer, Kenneth 19 n.22, 20 n.26, 61, 70, 76–8, 169
Aristotle 24, 113–15, 127–8, 133–40
Ascension 83 n.24, 95, 99–100, 165, 182, 184
Athanasius 88 n.37, 93 n.51, 119, 162–3
Augustine 23 n.38, 39 n.9, 48, 95 n.62

baptism 98, 169 n.298, 177 n.7, 183
    Spirit baptism 9 n.20, 16, 66 n.20, 98, 124, 164
being
    being among beings 8, 154, 161, 185 n.27
    beyond 8, 94 n.54, 116, 137, 153–4
    equivocity of 8, 66, 129 n.173
    finite 116, 123 n.155, 128–9, 142 n. 217, 154, 163
    of the church 105–10, 126, 130, 164, 170
    of God 8, 112–21, 129–30, 154, 170
    univocity of 8, 88 n.39, 122 n.151, 129 n.173, 135, 138, 141–2, 161, 163 n.274, 169
Boersma, Hans 8 n.14, 122 n.151, 124 n.158, 126 n.164, 135 n.194, 140 n.211, 142, 151 n.251

Cappadocians 95, 112, 119–20, 130
Cartesian dualism 20, 151 n.253

Cartledge, Mark 3, 19 n.23, 62–4, 66–70, 74 n.2, 79–81, 165 n.282, 174, 176, 179 n.15
cause(s)
    efficient 8, 24, 114 n.124, 133, 136–43
    final 25, 27, 29, 75, 82, 93, 97, 114 n.124, 132, 134 n.191, 135–7, 142–8, 150–2
    first/primary 114, 139–41
    formal 114 n.124, 123, 127–8, 135–7, 143, 150–2, 155, 160
    higher 135, 137, 151–2
    material 24, 114 n.125, 115, 133, 136–8, 143, 155, 161
    ontological 138, 141
    secondary 138–9, 141
Chan, Simon 8 n.15, 10 n.22, 63, 66, 93, 105–10, 111 n.120, 175–7
Clarke, Norris 8–9, 82 n.22, 115 n.127, 121, 123 n.155, 127–9, 134 n.191, 135, 137, 141, 163 n.273
Clayton, Philip 27–8, 147, 150–2
community 1, 10, 15, 19–20, 23, 25, 38, 47, 48 n.50, 54–5, 57, 59, 61, 63–5, 76–8, 86, 88, 95, 97–101, 103, 108–9, 125–6, 133, 145 n.231, 158, 165–71, 177, 180–1
consummation 25, 39 n.10, 77 n.6, 82, 87, 100, 105–10, 126, 131, 148–9
cosmic soteriology 77–82, 90
cosmic pneumatology 28–30 *see also* creation, salvation of
creation 8–10, 14, 16–17, 22–33, 40–6, 48, 50–8, 59, 66, 68, 70, 75–9, 81–3, 85–95, 97–8, 100–7, 109–12, 122–6, 129–33, 141–67, 170–1, 180 n.16, 181 n.22, 183 n.25, 186 n.28, 187
    *ex nihilo* 29, 31 n.84, 49–50, 85, 89, 94, 152–4

enchanted theology of 17–18, 26, 31–3
Genesis narrative of 29, 31–2, 92
history as 87–104
nature and character of 8–10, 40–1, 43–6, 50–8, 82–3, 89–90, 92–104
new 25, 78, 82–7, 92, 94
salvation of 22 n.34, 75 n.4, 77–82, 92–4 *see also* cosmic soteriology
creed 2, 87, 89, 112, 118, 119 n.137, 138, 160–2, 177, 182
Cyril of Alexandria 148 n.242, 162 n.271

Dionysius the Areopagite 94 n.54
divine action 24–5, 27, 28, 31, 48, 117, 131–3, 138–46, 148–9, 153–5, 163–4

ecclesiology 20, 53–4, 60–3, 66, 68, 74, 76, 82–3, 86, 100, 105–10
emergence, theory of 23, 27–31, 38, 48, 52, 124 n.157, 132, 134, 143–4, 147–52, 154–6, 160
enchanted creation 7, 14, 17–18, 28, 44–5, 131–2, 147, 152, 160, 171, 183 n.25, 186 n.28
epistemology 6 n.6, 14, 19–21, 33–5, 47–9, 54, 57 n. 93, 76 n.5, 135 n.194, 166–71
eschatological orientation 14–17, 34, 75–82, 104, 110–11, 126, 132, 153 n.257, 161
essence 29, 52, 94 n.54, 110 n.118, 115–16, 128–34, 137, 141
eternal generation 31, 88, 163
evil 19, 29 n.74, 31 n.81, 140, 147, 149, 153, 156–8, 185
existence
existence-essence 115 n.27, 137 n.202, 161
infinite act of 8, 115–17, 160
experience 2, 5–7, 17, 19–20, 22, 25, 32–4, 39, 46, 48–9, 54, 56–7, 61–6, 75–7, 80–1, 84–91, 97, 110 n.118, 112–13, 117–18, 132, 149, 156, 158–62, 164–71, 173–5, 177–8

Father, God the 14, 23 n.38, 48–9, 69, 80 n.14, 83 n.24, 87–90, 92–5, 100, 102–4, 109, 111, 116 n.129, 118–20, 130–2, 148, 157, 159, 161, 163, 168, 170, 178–87, 189–90
five elements of a Pentecostal worldview 2, 13–14, 21, 22, 35, 37–9, 73, 76 n.5, 110–11
foundational ecclesiological pneumatology 105–10, 181 n.19
foundational pneumatology 21–5, 33–4, 48, 51, 57, 109, 133, 153, 166
freedom 28 n.64, 61–2, 89 n.44, 98, 139–41, 162–63, 175, 187
of natural process 103–4, 147 n.239
of universal history 101–3
full gospel 6, 15 n.6, 16–19, 69, 77–83, 90, 92, 161

Gelpi, Donald 32, 49, 54
Green, Chris E. W. 17 n.11, 20 n.26, 60–2, 76, 82–91, 107 n.112, 110 n.118, 117–21, 145, 149, 156, 162, 169, 174–78, 187
Gregory of Nazianzus 120 n.140, 120 n.141
Gregory of Nyssa 14 n.3, 120 n.141

Hart, David Bentley 8 n.14, 14 n.3, 82 n.23, 89 n.42, 116, 129 n.175, 136–7, 141, 148, 151–2, 161 n.268
Hauerwas, Stanley 60 n.1, 81, 83, 101 n.89
healing 9 n.20, 18, 98, 160–1, 164–5
Holy Spirit 1, 5, 16, 22, 27, 34, 41, 45, 61, 65, 66, 69, 75, 76, 78–81, 86, 88, 90, 95, 100–4, 107–9, 117–21, 123, 126, 129–30, 132, 148, 154, 157, 159, 161, 164, 170, 179–80, 182–7, 190

impassibility 113
incarnation 40–1, 49, 92–3, 100, 106, 115, 120 n.141, 145–6, 148–9, 154, 159, 162, 177
intensity of the Spirit 124–5
Irenaeus 23 n.38, 48, 93 n.51

Jenson, Robert W. 6 n.7, 9 n.1, 14 n.3, 61 n.3, 84 n.27, 88-9, 95, 101-4, 108-9, 114, 121, 158, 162 n.271, 169-70, 177 n.7
John of Damascus 14 n.3, 88 n.37, 155
Johns, Cheryl Bridges 19, 60, 168

Kingdom of God 6, 9, 15, 20, 25, 27, 39, 60, 83, 100, 110, 131, 144, 146, 153, 178, 179, 182, 185, 186

Land, Steven Jack 6, 15 n.5, 16 n.7, 19 n.22, 38, 61 n.5, 70, 74, 173
laying on of hands 164-5
liturgy 4, 25, 38, 61-3, 65 n.16, 76 n.5, 79, 81, 104 n.102, 118 n.132, 126 n.163, 145-6, 162 n.271, 173-87
Lossky, Vladimir 131

Macchia, Frank 15-16, 21 n.33, 38
Martin, Lee Roy 68 n.26, 96 n.64, 165 n.283
materiality 14, 18-19, 29, 31, 33, 38-46, 51-2, 54, 85, 89, 114-15, 122-4, 128, 130, 132-8, 143, 146, 155, 159, 161, 164-5, 183-5, 187
materialism 148, 150-1
    material monism 151
    nonreductive materialism 28 n.65, 40, 150, 156 n. 233
Maximus the Confessor 61 n.4, 93-4, 162 n.271
modernity 8-9, 20, 38-41, 44, 59, 103, 135, 151, 177 n.7
Moore, Rickie 20 n.27, 38, 96
Murphey, Nancey 28, 147

narrative 5-6, 10, 14, 17, 19-21, 24, 29, 31-2, 50, 54, 57, 62, 76-98, 105-7, 110, 113-14, 121, 147, 149, 152, 154, 166-7, 169, 174, 184, 186
naturalism 31, 39, 44-5, 53, 135, 146 n.233, 150
    methodological naturalism 146, 150
    pneumatological naturalism 26, 101-4
Neoplatonism 40 n.10, 127-8, 137

nominalism 52-3, 122 n.151, 135
nondualism 14, 18-19, 31-3, 76, 161, 164-71, 183 n.25, 184 n.26, 186 n.28

Ockham, William of 122 n.151, 135, 151
ontology/metaphysics 3, 6-8, 14 n.3, 27, 33-4, 37, 39-48, 51, 53-5, 106, 110-12, 116, 122-30, 134, 140-2, 151, 160-5, 169, 181, 183 n.25
    ontotheology 8-9
Origen 87-8, 162-3
Owens, Joseph 9 n.19, 113-14, 129 n.173

participatory ontology/metaphysics of participation 7-8, 27, 40-1, 44-6, 54-7, 96 n.63, 105, 110-31, 135, 137-8, 140-2
Peirce, Charles Sanders 23, 27-9, 32, 48-9, 54, 132-3, 136, 142-7, 150-3, 160
pentecostal spirituality 1-3, 6-11, 18-20, 25, 34-5, 45, 59-65, 68-71, 73-80, 87, 103-5, 111, 122, 148, 155, 160, 166, 170, 173-4, 176, 178, 187, 189
pentecostal theology 1-3, 5-11, 16-23, 32, 39, 47, 61-4, 68-71, 73-80, 87, 90, 105-6, 108, 111-12, 131, 138, 160, 165, 170, 173-4, 189
personhood
    angelic 18, 29-31, 91-2, 115, 128, 155-6, 158, 160, 183
    demonic 18, 29-31, 132-3, 156-60
    divine 48, 75, 87-9, 91, 92, 95, 103-5, 109, 117, 119-21, 130, 147 n.239, 148 n. 242, 158, 161, 162 n.271, 163, 166, 168, 180 n.16
    human 19-20, 29, 55, 59, 65, 77, 91, 92, 97, 124, 137, 156, 166-8
Plato 39-44, 115, 122-4, 127-8
Plotinus 115, 127-8
pneumatological imagination 19, 24, 30-1, 34, 49
praxis 60, 70, 74, 138
prayer 6, 63, 65, 69, 73, 76, 103-4, 117-18, 138, 140, 147 n.239, 162, 164 n.280, 168, 170, 176-7, 180-1, 184-7

process metaphysics 23–4, 51–3, 57 n.57
prophecy 65, 67, 96–100, 125

Radical Orthodoxy (RO) 7–8, 27, 38–41, 57, 142
rationality 20, 23, 33, 48–51, 106, 133, 137, 148, 152, 167
realism 32–4, 49, 135
　critical realism 33
relationality 23, 48, 141, 168

sacramentality 8 n.13, 20, 38, 45, 54, 76 n.5, 79 n.14, 122, 124, 135, 140, 142, 164, 183
science 22, 24–8, 33 n.94, 44–7, 59, 78–9, 82, 84–5, 132, 134–8, 142, 144–50, 152–3, 160
Scotus, Duns 8, 122, 135, 151
Scripture 3, 20, 31–2, 50, 64–5, 67–8, 75, 78, 84–95, 101, 106, 111, 116, 118, 121, 125–6, 138, 140, 155–8, 167, 170, 173, 176, 182
Smith, James K. A. 2–4, 6–8, 13–22, 26–7, 34–5, 37–46, 53–60, 62, 70, 73–6, 103, 110–11, 122–6, 130, 132, 136, 142, 146, 148, 150, 161, 163, 166–7, 170, 173, 189
Son, of the Father 1, 14, 23, 48, 80, 83, 85, 86–95, 104, 109, 111, 118–20, 129–31, 148, 152, 154, 158–9, 163, 166, 168–70, 173, 179–82, 184–7, 190
　Chalcedonianism 149 n.244, 162 n.271
　Jesus of Nazareth 14, 49 n.56, 87, 112, 148

supervenience 28–9, 124, 147, 150–5, 160

teleology 16, 24–6, 29, 31, 41, 79, 113, 132, 143–8, 150, 152–3
Thomas, John Christopher 6 n.4, 20, 38, 98–100, 165
*totus Christus* 90, 108, 110, 126, 171
transfiguration of history 83–6
Trinity, doctrine of the 48, 50, 69–70, 81, 88 n.39, 91, 104, 109, 117–19, 130, 167, 169 *see also* personhood, divine; Father, God the; Holy Spirit; Son, of the Father;
　hypostasis 94, 118–20
　inseparable operations 88 n.37, 95
　*ousia* 119–20

vocation 10, 97 n.72, 131
Vondey, Wolfgang 5–7, 9–10, 16, 21–2, 31, 33, 47, 61, 76–82, 85, 90, 100, 124–5, 164, 174

Whitehead, Alfred North 24, 51–4, 57, 142
Williams, Rowan 8 n.14, 10 n.24, 14 n.3, 94, 130 n.178, 163
Wink, Walter 29–30, 51–3

Yong, Amos 2–3, 10, 13, 15, 17, 18, 21–35, 37–9, 45–58, 59–60, 62, 70, 73–6, 78–80, 85, 89, 105, 109, 111, 123–6, 130, 131–60, 166 n.285, 189

www.ingramcontent.com/pod-product-compliance
Lightning Source LLC
Chambersburg PA
CBHW051522230426
43668CB00012B/1708